The Internet For Macs For Dummies Starter Kit

Cheat Sheet

FOR Dummies™
COMPUTER BOOK SERIES FROM IDG

Your Internet Mini-Phonebook

Enter the numbers here so you won't lose them.

Service	Local Connect Number	Help Line Number
1.		
2.		
3.		
4.		

Note: Write your password for each service in the index of your favorite cookbook.

Electronic mail

If you have a command-oriented mail reader on your service, fill in the commands here.

For This	Type This
Read New messages	
Reply to message	
Save message	
Delete message	
Browse messages	
Scan messages	

Sample Addressess via On-line Sevices

To Send To	With This Address	Use This Address
AOL	Bob Wilson	bobwilson@aol.com
CompuServe	70340,701	70340.701@compuserve.com
Delphi	bwilson	bwilson@delphi.com
eWorld	Bob Wilson	bobwilson@eworld.com
GEnie	WILSON318	WILSON318@genie.geis.com
Prodigy	HBNM07A	HBNM07A.prodigy.com

FTP

There are two choices: Either your service has its own FTP menu or you FTP directly.

For direct FTP, type	Find what you need with	For file type, remember to specify
`ftp <sitename>` or else	`dir or ls` **and change directories with**	`binary` or
`ftp` `open <sitename>`	`cd`	`ASCII`

The Internet For Macs For Dummies Starter Kit

Cheat Sheet

Five FTP sites

Three rules for you:

1. Don't access these sites during their working hours.

2. Get games and so forth from an on-line service instead.

3. Try to get in and out quickly.

Location	Number	Directory
ftp.dartmouth.edu (Dartmouth)	129.170.16.54	/pub/mac
boombox.micro.umn.edu	128.101.95.95	/pub (gopher, more)
ftp.rrzn.uni-hannover.de	130.75.2.2	/ftp1/mac [sumex]
ftp.ucs.ubc.ca	137.82.27.62	/pub/mac/info-mac
shark.mel.dit.csiro.au	144.110.16.11	/info-mac [sumex]

Internet by Mail

Archie

Send an e-mail message just like this:

```
To:
INTERNET:archie@archie.sura.net
Subject:
prog <file you want>
```

You get the results by e-mail. You may need to use an alternate (less busy) Archie server.

FTP

To get coolfile.txt from the ftp.helpful.com site, send the following e-mail message:

```
TO:INTERNET:ftp.helpful.com
Subject:coolfile.txt

reply <your own Internet address>
connect ftp.helpful.com
chunksize 24000
get coolfile.txt
quit
```

For chunksize, use a number that is 1000 less than the maximum mail message size your service allows.

Internet Search Programs

Archie searches for files by name. It's the lowest-level search, and the other searches usually give you better results. A good shareware Mac version called **Anarchie** is available from all the on-line services.

List two Archie sites:

1.

2.

Gopher can look through Archie sites and uses a simple menu. It's often preferable to Archie. There's a Mac version called **TurboGopher** available from boombox.micro.umn.edu.

List two gopher sites:

1.

2.

Veronica can search over many Gophers. If you see Veronica listed on a menu, start your search here!

WAIS can search for file contents, not just filenames. If you find a Gopher that has WAIS on the menu, give it some content keywords.

WWW does hypertext searches in document databases. The best Mac program for WWW use is **Mosaic**, available from uiui.ncsa.edu.

. . . For Dummies: #1 Computer Book Series for Beginners

THE
INTERNET
FOR MACS FOR
DUMMIES™
STARTER
KIT

THE INTERNET FOR MACS FOR DUMMIES™ STARTER KIT

by Charles Seiter

Foreword by David Pogue
Macworld Contributing Editor, and author of *Macs For Dummies*

IDG Books Worldwide, Inc.
An International Data Group Company

Foster City, CA ♦ Chicago, IL ♦ Indianapolis, IN ♦ Braintree, MA ♦ Dallas, TX

The Internet For Macs For Dummies Starter Kit

Published by
IDG Books Worldwide, Inc.
An International Data Group Company
919 E. Hillside Blvd.
Suite 400
Foster City, CA 94404

Library of Congress Catalog Card No.: 94-79831

ISBN: 1-56884-244-9

Printed in the United States of America

10 9 8 7 6 5 4 3 2 1

1D/RS/QX/ZU

Distributed in the United States by IDG Books Worldwide, Inc.

Distributed in Canada by Macmillan of Canada, a Division of Canada Publishing Corporation; by Computer and Technical Books in Miami, Florida, for South America and the Caribbean; by Longman Singapore in Singapore, Malaysia, Thailand, and Korea; by Toppan Co. Ltd. in Japan; by Asia Computerworld in Hong Kong; by Woodslane Pty. Ltd. in Australia and New Zealand; and by Transworld Publishers Ltd. in the U.K. and Ireland.

For general information on IDG Books in the U.S., including information on discounts and premiums, contact IDG Books 800-434-3422 or 415-312-0650.

For information on where to purchase IDG Books outside the U.S., contact Christina Turner at 415-312-0650.

For information on translations, contact Marc Jeffrey Mikulich, Director Foreign & Subsidiary Rights, at IDG Books Worldwide; 415-312-0650.

For sales inquiries and special prices for bulk quantities, write to the address above or call IDG Books Worldwide at 415-312-0650.

For information on using IDG Books in the classroom, or ordering examination copies, contact Jim Kelly at 800-434-2086.

is a registered trademark of
IDG Books Worldwide, Inc.

About the Author

Charles Seiter wrote his first computer programs on ancient IBM iron in the 1960s and, at one point, had a college summer job writing FORTRAN code for Atlas missile guidance simulation. That's right, he *is* a rocket scientist.

Well, not really. He got a Ph.D. in chemistry from Caltech and then worked as a chemistry professor for years. His academic career was derailed by winning a pile of money on a television game show, at which point he freed himself from the job of flunking a certain percentage of premed students in freshman chemistry every year and moved away to a redwood forest in northern California.

He began consulting on the design of DNA sequencing equipment and other biochemistry hardware for firms in the Bay Area and, by chance, just happened to be hanging around when Macworld was founded. Over the course of ten years, he has probably reviewed more Mac technical software than anyone in history.

ABOUT IDG BOOKS WORLDWIDE

Welcome to the world of IDG Books Worldwide.

IDG Books Worldwide, Inc. is a subsidiary of International Data Group, the world's largest publisher of computer-related information and the leading global provider of information services on information technology. IDG was founded more than 25 years ago and now employs more than 7,000 people worldwide. IDG publishes more than 220 computer publications in 65 countries (see listing below). More than fifty million people read one or more IDG publications each month.

Launched in 1990, IDG Books Worldwide is today the #1 publisher of best-selling computer books in the United States. We are proud to have received 3 awards from the Computer Press Association in recognition of editorial excellence, and our best-selling ...For Dummies™ series has more than 12 million copies in print with translations in 25 languages. IDG Books, through a recent joint venture with IDG's Hi-Tech Beijing, became the first U.S. publisher to publish a computer book in the People's Republic of China. In record time, IDG Books has become the first choice for millions of readers around the world who want to learn how to better manage their businesses.

Our mission is simple: Every IDG book is designed to bring extra value and skill-building instructions to the reader. Our books are written by experts who understand and care about our readers. The knowledge base of our editorial staff comes from years of experience in publishing, education, and journalism — experience which we use to produce books for the '90s. In short, we care about books, so we attract the best people. We devote special attention to details such as audience, interior design, use of icons, and illustrations. And because we use an efficient process of authoring, editing, and desktop publishing our books electronically, we can spend more time ensuring superior content and spend less time on the technicalities of making books.

You can count on our commitment to deliver high-quality books at competitive prices on topics consumers want to read about. At IDG, we value quality, and we have been delivering quality for more than 25 years. You'll find no better book on a subject than an IDG book.

John J. Kilcullen

John Kilcullen
President and CEO
IDG Books Worldwide, Inc.

WINNER
*Eighth Annual
Computer Press
Awards 1992*

WINNER
*Ninth Annual
Computer Press
Awards 1993*

IDG Books Worldwide, Inc. is a subsidiary of International Data Group, the world's largest publisher of computer-related information and the leading global provider of information services on information technology. International Data Group publishes over 220 computer publications in 65 countries. More than fifty million people read one or more International Data Group publications each month. The officers are Patrick J. McGovern, Founder and Board Chairman; Kelly Conlin, President; Jim Casella, Chief Operating Officer. International Data Group's publications include: **ARGENTINA'S** Computerworld Argentina, Infoworld Argentina; **AUSTRALIA'S** Computerworld Australia, Computer Living, Australian PC World, Australian Macworld, Network World, Mobile Business Australia, Publish!, Reseller, IDG Sources; **AUSTRIA'S** Computerwelt Oesterreich, PC Test; **BELGIUM'S** Data News (CW); **BOLIVIA'S** Computerworld; **BRAZIL'S** Computerworld, Connections, Game Power, Mundo Unix, PC World, Publish, Super Game; **BULGARIA'S** Computerworld Bulgaria, PC & Mac World Bulgaria, Network World Bulgaria; **CANADA'S** CIO Canada, Computerworld Canada, InfoCanada, Network World Canada, Reseller; **CHILE'S** Computerworld Chile, Informatica; **COLOMBIA'S** Computerworld Colombia, PC World; **COSTA RICA'S** PC World; **CZECH REPUBLIC'S** Computerworld, Elektronika, PC World; **DENMARK'S** Communications World, Computerworld Danmark, Computerworld Focus, Macintosh Produktkatalog, Macworld Danmark, PC World Danmark, PC Produktguide, Tech World, Windows World; **ECUADOR'S** PC World Ecuador; **EGYPT'S** Computerworld (CW) Middle East, PC World Middle East; **FINLAND'S** MikroPC, Tietoviikko, Tietoverkko; **FRANCE'S** Distributique, GOLDEN MAC, InfoPC, Le Guide du Monde Informatique, Le Monde Informatique, Telecoms & Reseaux; **GERMANY'S** Computerwoche, Computerwoche Focus, Computerwoche Extra, Electronic Entertainment, Gamepro, Information Management, Macwelt, Netzwelt, PC Welt, Publish, Publish; **GREECE'S** Publish & Macworld; **HONG KONG'S** Computerworld Hong Kong, PC World Hong Kong; **HUNGARY'S** Computerworld SZT, PC World; **INDIA'S** Computers & Communications; **INDONESIA'S** Info Komputer; **IRELAND'S** ComputerScope; **ISRAEL'S** Beyond Windows, Computerworld Israel, Multimedia, PC World Israel; **ITALY'S** Computerworld Italia, Lotus Magazine, Macworld Italia, Networking Italia, PC Shopping Italy, PC World Italia; **JAPAN'S** Computerworld Today, Information Systems World, Macworld Japan, Nikkei Personal Computing, SunWorld Japan, Windows World; **KENYA'S** East African Computer News; **KOREA'S** Computerworld Korea, Macworld Korea, PC World Korea; **LATIN AMERICA'S** GamePro; **MALAYSIA'S** Computerworld Malaysia, PC World Malaysia; **MEXICO'S** Compu Edicion, Compu Manufactura, Computacion/Punto de Venta, Computerworld Mexico, MacWorld, Mundo Unix, PC World, Windows; **THE NETHERLANDS'** Computer! Totaal, Computable (CW), LAN Magazine, Lotus Magazine, MacWorld; **NEW ZEALAND'S** Computer Buyer, Computerworld New Zealand, Network World, New Zealand PC World; **NIGERIA'S** PC World Africa; **NORWAY'S** Computerworld Norge, Lotusworld Norge, Macworld Norge, Maxi Data, Networld, PC World Ekspress, PC World Nettverk, PC World Norge, PC World's Produktguide, Publish& Multimedia World, Student Data, Unix World, Windowsworld; **PAKISTAN'S** PC World Pakistan; **PANAMA'S** PC World Panama; **PERU'S** Computerworld Peru, PC World; **PEOPLE'S REPUBLIC OF CHINA'S** China Computerworld, China Infoworld, China PC Info Magazine, Computer Fan, PC World China, Electronics International, Electronics Today/Multimedia World, Electronic Product World, China Network World, Software World Magazine, Telecom Product World, **PHILIPPINES'** Computerworld Philippines, PC Digest (PCW); **POLAND'S** Computerworld Poland, Computerworld Special Report, Networld, PC World/Komputer, Sunworld; **PORTUGAL'S** Cerebro/PC World, Correio Informatico/Computerworld, MacIn; **ROMANIA'S** Computerworld, PC World, Telecom Romania; **RUSSIA'S** Computerworld-Moscow, Mir - PK (PCW), Sety (Networks); **SINGAPORE'S** Computerworld Southeast Asia, PC World Singapore; **SLOVENIA'S** Monitor Magazine; **SOUTH AFRICA'S** Computer Mail (CIO),Computing S.A.,Network World S.A., Software World; **SPAIN'S** Advanced Systems, Amiga World, Computerworld Espana, Communicacions World, Macworld Espana, NeXTWORLD, Super Juegos Magazine (GamePro), PC World Espana, Publish; **SWEDEN'S** Attack, ComputerSweden, Corporate Computing, Macworld, Mikrodatorn, Natverk & Kommunikation, PC World, CAP & Design, Datalngenjoren, Maxi Data,Windows World; **SWITZERLAND'S** Computerworld Schweiz, Macworld Schweiz, PC Tip; **TAIWAN'S** Computerworld Taiwan, PC World Taiwan; **THAILAND'S** Thai Computerworld; **TURKEY'S** Computerworld Monitor, Macworld Turkiye, PC World Turkiye; **UKRAINE'S** Computerworld, Computers+Software Magazine; **UNITED KINGDOM'S** Computing / Computerworld, Connexion/Network World, Lotus Magazine, Macworld, Open Computing/Sunworld; **URAGUAY'S** PC World Uraguay; **UNITED STATES'** Advanced Systems, AmigaWorld, Cable in the Classroom, CD Review, CIO, Computerworld, Computerworld Client/Server Journal, Digital Video, DOS World, Electronic Entertainment Magazine (E2), Federal Computer Week, Game Hits, GamePro, IDG Books, Infoworld, Laser Event, Macworld, Maximize, Multimedia World, Network World, PC Letter, PC World, Publish, SWATPro, Video Event; **VENEZUELA'S** Computerworld Venezuela, PC World; **VIETNAM'S** PC World Vietnam.   11/16/94

Acknowledgments

The author would like to thank Janna Custer at IDG Books for approaching me about this project, and Jim Heid and Maryellen Kelly for talking me into it. Thanks also to Nancy Dunn for getting me into this racket in the first place. The staff at Macworld, particularly Carol Person and Galen Gruman, have shown great forbearance about my frequent and unseemly disappearances into cyberspace.

I would like to thank Laurie Smith, my project editor at IDG's Indianapolis office, for floating some deadlines so that we could include late-breaking developments. She worked straight through Memorial Day weekend in *Indianapolis*. That's dedication. I would also like to thank those members of the editorial and production staff who gave of their time and talents to make this book a success: Shawn MacLaren, Jim Grey, Valery Bourke, Chris Collins, Tyler Connor, Angela Hunckler, Mark Owens, Tricia Reynolds, and Kathie Schnorr.

Thanks also to Suzanne Stefanac and Matthew Hawn for tech editing and for last-minute help with the project; to K. Calderwood for discussions on TCP/IP, gateways, and other matters; and to David Pogue for the hilarious Foreword.

Loretta Toth, rather than seeing an acknowledgment about my wife "putting up with long hours blah, blah, blah," realized at once that she should just do her own book project at the same time. Brilliant! I hope this sparks a domestic-tranquillity revolution in publishing, in which contracts are issued in pairs.

Finally, I would like to thank the pioneers of the Internet, some famous and some unsung, who put together this remarkable system. Bit by bit they made an entity with its own living intelligence and its own strange dreams.

(The publisher would like to give special thanks to Patrick J. McGovern, without whom this book would not have been possible.)

Credits

**Executive Vice President,
Strategic Product Planning
and Reasearch**
David Solomon

Editorial Director
Diane Graves Steele

Acquisitions Editors
Megg Bonar

Brand Manager
Judith A. Taylor

Editorial Managers
Tracy L. Barr
Sandra Blackthorn
Mary C. Corder

Production Director
Beth Jenkins

**Associate Project
Coordinator**
Valery Bourke

Aquisitions Assistant
Suki Gear

Editorial Assistant
Tamara S. Castleman

Associate Production Pre-Press
Tony Augsburger

Project Editor
Laurie Ann Smith

Editors
Jim Grey
Shawn MacLaren

Technical Reviewer
Matthew Hawn
Suzanne Stefanac

Production Staff
Paul Belcastro
Chris Collins
J. Tyler Connor
Mark Owens
Carla Radzikinas
Dwight Ramsey
Patricia R. Reynolds
Kathie Schnorr
Gina Scott

Cover Design
Kavish + Kavish

Proofreader
Jennifer Kaufeld

Indexer
Steve Rath

Book Design
University Graphics

Contents at a Glance

Cartoons at a Glance

By Rich Tennant

Table of Contents

Foreword

by David Pogue
Macworld **Contributing Editor, and author of *Macs For Dummies***

Some topics don't make good *Dummies* books. I doubt the phrase "flying off the bookstore shelves" would ever apply to *Escalators For Dummies, Flossing For Dummies,* or, for that matter, *Neurosurgery For Dummies.*

The Internet, however, begs — pleads — *screams* to be a *Dummies* book.

You must understand that the Internet is our solar system's largest information network, accessible only by computer modem. It's a tangled, seething mass of cobbled-together wiring and computers, designed by a bunch of tangled, seething scientists and government bureaucrats 30 years ago. When I *picture* the Internet, I usually envision something like a set design out of *Alien* or *Brazil.* Abandon hope, ye who enter.

Those Internet designers had in mind a secret network, a huge underground maze of circuitry, so cruelly cryptic that invading Russians would throw up their hands and march right back to their submarines in disgust. The Internet requires its own silly language, in which things like

```
sumex-aim.ncsa.uiuc.edu@ftp(*)
```

means "Yo." The Internet was designed to run on huge humming mainframe computers that dwarfed Manhattan warehouses and had 4K of memory. The Internet is so complex that even complete reclusive computer nerds with few social opportunities had to write utilities like SLIP and WAIS and WWW to manage the Internet's utilities.

And during every step of the tangled, seething construction of the Internet, there's one thing nobody ever stopped to consider.

You.

Nobody intended for the typical, well-meaning American of above-average intelligence and a decent education to be able to make any sense of the Internet. Until *Time* and *Newsweek* and *The New York Times* began hailing the Internet as the biggest news story since Baby Jessica, it was the sole domain of scientists and hackers (the Internet, not the baby).

You haven't a prayer for making your way through the snarled, tangled techno-mass of the Internet without Charles Seiter. He was born with some kind of double-recessive gene, a freak rarity, that lets him make technical topics as accessible as the fridge. Good grief, sometimes I even catch myself reading his *Macworld* articles on things like statistical analysis and quantum physics, just because they're funny and interesting.

In this book, Charles offers two ways for you to get onto the Internet without losing unduly large hair tufts. First — the Great *Internet For Macs For Dummies* Dirty Little Secret — you can avoid the crumbling, archaic dirt roads of the military/university computers entirely. Instead, you can drive on the new, smoothly paved freeways provided by friendly services like America Online.

Second — if clicking a few colorful icons is too sissified for you — Charles also shows you how to get onto the Internet the *regular* way (huge humming mainframes, and so on). And he tells you what few silly Internet-language codes you really need to negotiate the hostile electronic waters — but friendly fellow cybernauts — of the Internet.

Either way, you're likely to be blown away and probably consumed for hours a day by the awesomeness and depth of the information and people you'll find there. Billions of Mac programs. Trillions of facts. 100 messages a day about *Seinfeld*.

And 30 million people.

Correction: 30 million and one.

Welcome to the Internet.

David Pogue

New York City

Introduction

- -

*W*elcome to *The Internet For Macs For Dummies Starter Kit*! When I started taking my Mac onto the Internet, I found there was a lot to learn, mainly because the Internet was not built with the Mac in mind. I'm going to save you plenty of Internet time and trouble because

- ✔ I've already chewed my way through all the hassles.
- ✔ You were kind enough to buy this book.

I assume that since you're a Mac user, you don't want to learn a bunch of mysterious three-letter commands from a different computer operating system just to send an e-mail letter to someone. In the Mac world, the people who sell you the software are supposed make things easier. I'm going to show you ways around the complicated old style of Internet access every chance I get.

Lately, there's been some good news for you and me. Most Internet services providers have been working hard on their Macintosh interfaces during the last year. As recently as January 1994, you still had to learn bits of the notoriously complex Unix operating system to get anything like "real" Internet access. Now you don't.

The Internet is a gold mine of information, but most of the programs you use to access Internet services were based on the state-of-the-art in programmming from the early 1980s, before the Macintosh was even invented. The Internet is a large part of what people mean by the *Information Superhighway*, but I've got to tell you that the pavement on this superhighway has plenty of potholes.

Recently, there have been plenty of changes, all of them making the Internet easier to use. This book may be the first "non-obsolete" Internet book for the Macintosh because it was written *after* the interface revolution.

About This Book

I wrote this book to get you onto the Internet and point you toward its many interesting features. All the material here has been tested on ordinary users. By *users,* I don't mean the people who hang around at users' groups comparing shareware — I mean people who call me with questions about using the spell checker in MacWrite.

This book will be easier to follow than, say, a *Macworld* article. Because I check out the costs and benefits of many different approaches, look through most of this book before you pick out a way to sign on the Internet

Here are some key points explained in the book:

- ✔ What the Internet is (and isn't)
- ✔ How you get connected
- ✔ What you'll find on the Net
- ✔ How to get free software
- ✔ How to make friends on the Internet
- ✔ How to access a whole universe of computers

Using This Book

This is a reference book, but that doesn't mean that it's a computer-systems manual. It's a guide to launch you onto the Net, combined with instructions for navigating the system once you're out there. If you just want to get on and get out there — and you're not interested in studying the history of the Internet — this is the right book for you.

I have a strong prejudice in favor of real Macintosh, point-and-click software. Nonetheless, some of the services that I describe still use the plain old text interface. When you have to type something, I'll indicate it like so:

```
upload goodies.txt
```

In general, it will make a difference whether you type the command in lowercase or in capital letters, so do it exactly as shown.

Not Just a Job, It's an Adventure

Learning about the Internet is not just another computer chore, like learning PageMaker shortcuts. When you sign on to the Internet, you are participating in one of the most exciting intellectual adventures in history. A big chunk of all the information accumulated by the human race since the dawn of time, from satellite photos to Shakespeare, is out there on the Net. Many of the coolest people on the planet are out there, too.

Nobody knows where all this is headed, how big it's going to get, or how the system will evolve. You get to find out, along with everyone else, what happens when tens of millions of intelligent people can communicate all over the planet (or *off* the planet, according to some Internet UFO discussion groups). The next few chapters of this story have yet to be written, but since you have this book, you're going to be part of them!

Being a Newbie

Newbie is a term for newcomers to the Internet. Presumably, that means you.

Sometimes it's used in a neutral context, as in "Newbies are asked to review the FAQ (frequently asked questions) file after joining the conference." This means that before you ask people a bunch of questions on-line that have been asked and answered a hundred times already, the old-timers want you to scan the top twenty or so, set aside in a special file for beginners.

At other times, the term *newbie* is actually intended to be insulting, and it's not rare to find a Net old-timer *flaming* a newbie, meaning that the old-timer answers an innocent question with a string of nasty remarks. Back when the Internet was a sort of exclusive club, there was a bit more patience with beginners, to tell you the truth. Also, when you have 30 million people communicating with each other, the law of averages predicts that some of them will be classic grouches.

In this book, I offer tips for

- ✔ Being an impeccably-mannered newbie
- ✔ Dodging flames
- ✔ Finding a style of your own

What's in This Book

This book is divided into six parts; each has a different function.

Part I: Mac Internet Basics

In this part, I explain the world of the Internet — what's in it, how it came to be, and who's there. You can read this section just to get yourself some Internet background to impress your friends and associates or use it to plan real adventures.

Part II: Internet via Pipeline and Mosaic

The disks included with this book contain the most modern, most efficient, and most entertaining ways to use the Internet. This section tells you how to get connected.

Part III: Internet via National On-Line Services

The easiest Internet access is through the big on-line services. Not only do these people want your business, but they are also furiously upgrading their Internet capabilities on a month-by-month basis, just to make you feel welcome.

Part IV: Do-it-Yourself Internet

If you want to play in the big leagues, I'll tell you what you need. Sometimes it makes sense to be your own Internet site, and sometimes it doesn't, so I'll cover the options.

Part V: The Part of Tens

These are "Top Ten" lists on Internet topics, some serious and some just for fun.

Part VI: Appendixes

In the appendixes, I reveal some extra hints and tips. I also offer you some useful lists that are too long to put in a chapter in the middle of the book.

Icons Used in This Book

As you read this book, you'll see the following icons, which appear in the margins and draw your attention to interesting and useful information.

Technical Stuff

Believe me, the Internet's got plenty of technical aspects. You can skip these sections if you like or read them if you're curious.

Tip

A Tip is a recommended way to accomplish some Internet task with your Mac. Often, a Tip is a shortcut.

Remember

This icon flags background information that you should keep in mind. "Eat your dinner first and then eat the salad" would be a Remember for traveling in Italy.

Warning

"Drive on the left," on the other hand, would be a Warning for travel in Britain.

Navigate

This kind of icon shows you that I'm going to tell you how to get from one service or place on the Internet. Hey, on the highway, do it my way.

Mac Psychology

Every time I can turn the Internet into a Mac-friendly environment, I signal it with this icon. Here you'll find some of the distinctively Mac stuff in the book.

What's Next?

Now it's time to take the plunge. But first I'd like to offer a few words of encouragement: Some parts of the Internet world are fairly confusing. If you find them confusing, it's not a reflection on you. Some aspects are hard—the way English-language spelling is hard—because the Internet, like English, evolved through a series of historic accidents.

I've been the editor in charge of stuff-that's-too-hard-for-English-majors at *Macworld* for nine years. And I found some aspects of Internet use to be as hard as, say, advanced topics in Microsoft Excel. So if you are puzzled by the Internet from time to time, it's not your fault.

IDG is paying me to make this easy for you. Having said that, I think the good old *...For Dummies* series will make Internet access almost as easy as word processing for you — and considerably more fun.

Tell Us What You Think

Please send me your comments at

> IDG Books Worldwide
> 7260 Shadeland Station, Suite 100
> Indianapolis, IN 46256

I'd give you my Internet e-mail address, but it's already so jammed with stuff, I'm more likely to find your comments on paper!

Part I
MacInternetBasics

The 5th Wave   By Rich Tennant

"EXCUSE ME- IS ANYONE HERE _NOT_ TALKING ABOUT THE INTERNET?"

In this part...

The Internet is the wild and woolly frontier of electronic communication. A huge part of all the information ever accumulated is out there somewhere on the Internet. It's just a matter of finding a way to navigate this digital ocean with your Macintosh.

That's why I'm here. This is the first second-generation Internet book. It assumes that you want to use the Internet the same way you use a Macintosh, with icons, menus, and lots of the little details smoothed over.

In this part, you'll travel the Internet, seeing what it has to offer and how you get it for yourself. I hope you enjoy the journey!

Chapter 1

Welcome to the Net — Internet Basics

· ·

In This Chapter

▶ What is the Internet?

▶ Who set all this up, anyway?

▶ How are the Internet and electronic mail linked?

▶ How do you get on the Internet?

· ·

What Is the Internet?

At one time, people thought that the Internet was the natural habitat of rocket scientists. But lately, every newsmagazine in America has told us that the Internet is The Next Big Thing. Newspapers talk about *netsurfing*, a peculiar sport played by people who rarely get wet. And commercials about the so-called information superhighway promise that you'll soon have data coming out of your ears and that a portable fax machine strapped to your wrist will be proper fashion for a beach vacation.

Whew.

Well, when you get into the Internet, you'll find out two things:

✔ It really is pretty amazing.

✔ You don't have to be a rocket scientist anymore to use it. And it won't follow you on vacation, unless you insist.

Caught in the Net

Most computers in offices or universities can talk to each other over *networks*, or sets of wiring and software that let computers communicate with each other.

The Internet is a way for these computer networks to connect to other computer networks. In fact, you can contact people all over the world from your computer through the Internet.

You see, the Internet lets you send files from one computer to another over a big, high-speed system of computer network connections, which the U.S. government paid for and installed. Because all these computers all over the planet can transfer files anywhere, anyone (even you) can access any information that someone wants to place in the *public domain*, meaning that it's available to everyone with no restrictions.

That's right, people develop programs and other valuable stuff and give them away. And a lot of the programs are really good! The next time someone cuts you off in traffic, tell yourself it's probably someone hurrying home to post a free file.

Combining all this information with *electronic mail* (or e-mail) means the following:

- ✔ You can send messages to anyone across the Internet, and they get the messages in a few minutes, usually.
- ✔ You can find thousands of useful files and free (!) programs.
- ✔ You can *chat* on-line with people anywhere (computer chatting is like talking via CB radio).
- ✔ You can get all sorts of instant, up-to-date news.

Macintosh, the easy network machine

Even if you're just sitting at your own Mac and aren't wired to anyone else, you have network capability anyway. The Mac's survival originally hinged on its success in the graphics/printing market, so Apple had to provide a way for several Macs to hook up to one (expensive) laser printer. (Three Macs and a printer is your basic example of a small network.) AppleTalk, a piece of software that lets Macs talk to each other and to a printer, became an essential part of the Macintosh system.

AppleTalk is too slow for larger networks, so vendors produced Mac-compatible hardware for Ethernet, a much faster networking connection. Fortunately, Ethernet is simple enough that lazy Mac users like you and I can use it without daily access to a network guru.

If you're having trouble visualizing the Internet as a network of networks, check out the schematic known as Figure 1-1. Still confused? Read on. (Sure, sure: I know that a picture is worth a thousand words. But, hey, give me a break: I get paid to write, not draw.)

That's you, at your own Macintosh, in the lower left of Figure 1-1. Using a modem, you dial into a computer *bulletin board*, or a central computer that many users can connect to. The bulletin board computer has a direct connection to the Internet, so it can dial up a computer at a university across the country. And that computer can look for files, at your request, on the big, federal computer located just outside Washington, D.C. To summarize: After you make an Internet connection, you can reach tons of files on any Internet computer. This process isn't *hacking*, or gaining illegal access to files; it's legitimately accessing files that people on other networks *want* you to see.

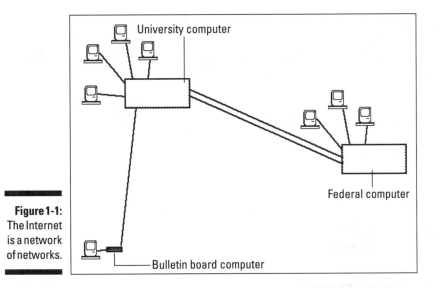

University computer

Federal computer

Figure 1-1:
The Internet is a network of networks.

Bulletin board computer

Mail: Snail versus electronic

Snail mail is computerese for letters delivered by the U.S. Post Office. *E-mail* is computer messages (which can now include sound and pictures) that get sent over a network. When you send a piece of e-mail, it gets there almost immediately. (The only catch is that the person receiving the mail has to connect to the network to receive it.) As a result, the Internet is evolving into an international instant Post Office because it can pick up e-mail on one network and deliver it to another.

Internet Archaeology

How did all this Internet stuff happen? In the 1970s, the Defense Department decided that research efforts would speed up if investigators with funding from the Advanced Research Projects Agency (ARPA) could communicate from one network to another. Usually, these networks were at big national labs like Los Alamos or universities like MIT.

ARPANET, as the new networking setup was called, originally linked about 30 sites, most of which used computers that are now ancient (Burroughs, Honeywell, ancient DEC hardware). Some of the first ARPANET designers were hired for another project that would let ARPANET connect to radio- and satellite-based computer communications. This effort defined the communications hardware and software that make an Internet connection.

In the 1980s, the old ARPA sites converted to the new Internet connections. Then the National Science Foundation (NSF) put together a high-speed network for Internet sites. Companies selling gateway hardware and software (a *gateway* is the actual connection from one network to another) for connecting to the NSFNET began to appear. Commercial Internet service networks were born.

Letting all existing networks connect to the single big Internet produced the well-documented explosion of Internet connections; now every techno-hipster business card has an @ address. At the heart of the system is the nationwide, high-speed NSFNET, which has been funded for the next five years as a sort of government experiment in communications infrastructure.

The number of people connected to the Internet has simply exploded in the last three years (see Figure 1-2). Some authorities are guessing that the system can handle 100 million users without too much trouble. After that, the Internet may need to handle e-mail addresses differently — just as phone companies have had to adjust over the years to the increase in telephone use.

Figure 1-2:
Internet
users (in
millions).

Number of Internet users

Year	Users
1991	1.1
1992	2.4
1993	5
1994	12
mid-1995 (est)	30

This amazing growth is one of the reasons that Internet access is still "under construction," at least in terms of a decent interface for Mac users. In January 1993, the typical Internet user had a research job and was used to dealing with a clunky interface (for example, see the archaic Internet commands listed in Figure 1-3). Very few people involved in designing the Internet foresaw that you and I would be pounding on the gate(way)s by 1994, demanding a user-friendly Mac interface to Internet services.

```
& help
cd [directory]              chdir to directory or home if none given
d [message list]            delete messages
e [message list]            edit messages
f [message list]            show from lines of messages
h                           print out active message headers
m [user list]               mail to specific users
n                           goto and type next message
p [message list]            print messages
pre [message list]          make messages go back to system
mailbox
q                           quit, saving unresolved messages in mbox
r [message list]            reply to sender (only) of messages
s [message list] file       append messages to file
t [message list]            type messages (same as print)
top [message list]          show top lines of messages
u [message list]            undelete messages
v [message list]            edit messages with display editor
x                           quit, do not change system mailbox
z [-]                       display next [previous] page of headers
!                           shell escape
```

Figure 1-3: Internet commands circa 1992.

E-Mail, the Internet, and @

If you glance at a business card for someone who works in a high-tech business or large company, it's likely that a line on the card will list an e-mail address (look for the @). (And to think, six years ago most cards didn't even list a fax number.) For example, an Apple employee named Kermit T. Frog could have the following e-mail address:

```
kermitf@apple.com
```

The @ is the tip-off that this code is actually an Internet-valid e-mail address; the notation .com (the Internet *zone designation*) means that the address is a business. When you read this address, you say "kermit-eff at apple dot com" (the @ is pronounced "at" and the . [period] is pronounced "dot").

Here's why addresses are important: If you have an @ address, you can communicate with anyone else on the planet with an @ address — that includes everyone who's anyone in the computer business and many of the powerful people at most organizations. To be taken seriously as a computer user or businessperson in the next few years, you're going to need your own @ address.

For example, today you can send a message to

    vicepresident@whitehouse.gov

and help educate Al Gore on environmental issues ("Sir, I'd like to volunteer several distant states as nuclear waste dumps").

By the way, the zone designation .gov means that the e-mail address is at a government site. Professors at universities usually have addresses that end in .edu (for education). Sometimes, an address will be a location instead of a job category. For example, I have an address at well.sf.ca.us, which means that you can reach me at a bulletin board site called the WELL near San Francisco, California, in the good old United States. See Table 1-1 and/or Appendix A for more examples.

When you get your own @ address, I promise that you'll feel very official. I know I did.

Table 1-1	Ten Internet Address Types
Address	**Interpretation**
@post.queensu.ca	Queen's University in Canada (.ca by itself means Canada, whereas .ca.us means California)
@coombs.anu.edu.au	Australian National University
@netcom.com	A commercial Internet service provider
@aol.com	America Online, another commercial Internet service provider
@nic.ddn.mil	A military site
@whales.org	A (mythical) nonprofit organization
@nsf.net	The National Science Foundation network
@unicef.int	An international organization
@informatik.uni-hamburg.de	A computer science department in Germany (.de means Deutschland)
@leprechaun.ie	A fantastic address in Ireland

Electronic Libraries on the Net

To recap: As an Internet user, you can exchange messages with other Internet users, from Brazil to Baltimore. By itself, that capability makes the Internet extremely useful. But, wonder of wonders, you also can use the Internet to access incredible files of information stored all over the world.

The Library of Congress, for example, contains copies of all the books (and nearly all the magazines and newspapers) published in the United States. (Of course, only 20,000 or so of the most useful books have been prepared for you to access through the Internet, but several library groups are working to get the whole collection ready for the Internet.) The U.S. Patent Office has files on all the patents it has ever issued. And university libraries across the country (Harvard, Yale, and Illinois are the largest) house all sorts of foreign research material not found in the Library of Congress. Heck, you can find comic books and campaign fliers and recipes and jokes and back issues of *TV Guide* on the Internet.

All this stuff is being merrily scanned into a text-file format that your Macintosh can read. All you must do is retrieve the file from the Internet.

Now, on-screen reading isn't great for novels — try scrolling through an 800-page paperback at the beach. It's ideal, though, if you're looking for specific pieces of information because you can search the files for key words.

Looking for books?

Here's an example: The library in the small town where I live recently got its own Internet connection. (Your library will get a connection soon because Internet access is *the* hot topic at librarians' meetings in the '90s. Come to think of it, it's about time the poor old librarians had a hot topic.) Last week, from my house, I checked the local university library for holdings on a particular topic. I didn't find what I wanted, so I clicked into libraries at the University of California at Berkeley and at the University of Illinois, Champaign-Urbana. I could have tapped into libraries at Oxford, for that matter. Finally, I came back to my own library and made an interlibrary loan request for a book at Berkeley. Not bad for ten minutes work at my own Mac!

In other words, even if you're sitting in front of your Macintosh, you can browse the stacks of most of the world's libraries. Although you may not always be able to get individual books transferred to a library near you, the information in these books is, as I write, steadily being converted to on-line files that you can download.

A connected world

The Internet isn't all serious. Sure, it has resources on programming languages and mathematical physics. But the Internet also is the planet's chief pipeline to news and plain, old, silly gossip.

For example, I regularly check comments made by fans of the strange TV program "Mystery Science Theater 3000." This program has thousands of avid fans who chatter away on-line every day in a huge open bulletin board, called a *newsgroup*. Because "MST 3K" specializes in obscure, funny references, any given line from the show is capable of generating an endless stream of linked messages from fans, explaining various perspectives on the wisecrack.

Inevitably, the Internet reflects what's on people's minds: Just as Egyptians filled their tombs with pornographic graffiti, and just as the first artsy pictures of naked ladies appeared within a year of the invention of photography, many private computer bulletin boards specialize in adult material. And many of those boards are connected to the Net. In fact, it's a matter of record that two of the newsgroups most frequently accessed are `alt.sex` and `rec.arts.erotica`.

Actually, if you want on-line access to dating service communications, bulletin boards are hotter than the Internet.

Looking for love?

The Internet has a service called Internet Relay Chat (IRC), a sort of global conference call. But the chat lines on bulletin boards and big on-line services, such as GEnie, are actually better for this stuff than the Internet. There's no point clogging up the poor old Net if you can have more fun anyway with a specialized connection.

Who Needs the Internet?

Well, the Internet is not just for universities anymore. Millions of people — cyberpunks, grandmothers, business people — have a legitimate need for Internet access. And plenty of Internet users advocate the idea that nearly everyone should be connected.

On a drizzly, spring morning in San Francisco, I decided to find out what sorts of people were willing to take a beginning Internet class. The class was organized by the WELL (415-332-4335), a San Francisco-area computer bulletin board that's probably the finest service of its kind in the country — the East Coast equivalent is ECHO (212-255-3839). The crowd, amazingly enough, consisted of equal parts of:

✔ Generation X-ers, complete with the occasional nose ring and I'm-an-artist-don't-bother-me-OK? fashion

✔ Retired high-school teachers

This pattern has held through several rounds of classes (by the way, you can add entrepreneurs to the mix — to them, the Internet represents a new business opportunity). Of course, I don't quite know what this means. Lately, I've been asked to give Internet talks to every community group north of the Golden Gate Bridge, so my guess is that the sociological profile of Internet users is probably going to look just like the general population within a year or so.

Greek to me

Just about everything ever written in Latin or ancient Greek is available on-line as part of a huge project involving Classics departments all over the world. It's nice when you can read *finished* documents — I don't think that these authors will be writing new editions any time soon.

Your Mac Experience

Mac users buy a Mac for straightforward point-and-click access to serious computer power. Naturally, you and I both want Internet access that uses a traditional Mac interface. If you have free Internet access (for example, you're a university student or your employer has given you an account), you should check out the special considerations in Chapters 14 and 15. The aim of most of this book, however, is to explain Internet access to people who don't have large organizations with systems administrators supporting them.

There is no way, just now, to get full Internet access easily in a single software or service package, so I'm going to recommend an ease-into-it approach. I think that you start with partial access and graduate to full access later. In other words, go ahead and goof off for a few months and let teams of drones do all the grunt labor for you!

There are two reasons for this phased-in, lazy approach:

✔ **The Internet is big.** You can probably get comfortable with Internet e-mail in just a few days, but the amount of other material available is so vast that you can spend weeks just surveying the so-called cyberspace landscape. If you start with an easy-to-use but limited service, you can later step up to full Internet access when you have a better estimate of what you need.

> ✔ **The Internet is changing.** For example, the folks at the National Center for Supercomputing Applications (NCSA) who wrote Mosaic (a very nice Macintosh front-end to the Internet) as a free program have moved to California to produce a commercial version. Either they will sell an easy-to-use version of their own product, or parts of Mosaic will be incorporated into the interface for national on-line services.

One way or another, full Internet access for Macs will happen in the course of the next year. So learning that

```
!sx -a myfile.txt
```

is the command for downloading a file in some systems is a ghastly waste of time.

Using the Internet shouldn't be any harder than using, say, FileMaker Pro — this isn't true right now, but it will be soon. So I say, get on the Net immediately and don't bother with Internet tricks that will be obsolete by Christmas.

The available Internet services are wildly different. Delphi has real Internet, but it uses a text-based menu for navigation. America Online (AOL) has a real Mac interface, but some parts of real Internet are still missing. All other services provide either worse interfaces than AOL or fewer features than Delphi, but they offer some other features as a compromise.

Besides direct Internet access, I'm going to discuss the pros and cons of Internet access with

✔ America Online

✔ CompuServe

✔ Prodigy

✔ Delphi

✔ GEnie

✔ eWorld

In Part II, I detail these services so that you can see what you'll get before you pay to join. I promise, I'm going to make this Internet stuff easy. Hey, and *they* are going to make it cheap: you can find some free-trial coupons from many Internet services at the very end of the book.

Think about it. If there's a research topic that you've always wanted to pursue, you can command the resources of most of the world's universities with your fingers. If you're an Australian frustrated by America's utter lack of interest in cricket, you can get yesterday's scores by making a local call. If you just want to find a large group of people who share your obsessions, you no longer have to leave your home.

And, in most cases, as long as you observe a few basic rules of decorum, you'll find that you are welcomed into these new electronic communities. It's not just the future — it's already happened!

Check these topics

To motivate you, to give you some idea of what's out there, I list here some of the kinds of information on the Internet. You also can take it for granted that there are gigabytes of hard-core techie stuff, too.

- **Urban legends:** Folklorist Jan Harold Brunvand, author of *The Choking Doberman* and *The Mexican Pet*, maintains files on urban myths in a newsgroup called alt.folklore.urban. You can check here to convince yourself that all known poodle-in-a-microwave stories are fiction.

- **QuarkXPress at Indiana University:** Authors of books on Quark have downloaded files to this huge archive of tips and information on using QuarkXPress. Now you can look at this week's tips instead of last year's.

- **GUTNBERG:** Project Gutenberg is the name of an initiative to put almost everything important that was ever printed into on-line form. Time for a bigger hard drive, huh?

- **Hong Kong Polytechnic:** The address @library.hpk.hk takes you into the library of this college in Hong Kong (the country code is hk, naturally). I mention this address because most of the other places on the planet that have computers are as connected as the United States. The curious exception is Japan; the Japanese government telecommunications office hasn't quite decided what to make of all this Internet stuff.

- **Internet Business Journal:** This on-line journal, which exists electronically only, discusses business opportunities on the Internet. (If you send a note to 441495@acadvm1.uottawa.ca, the editor will cheerfully sign you up for a paid subscription.) Advertising businesses is a very controversial topic, and it will be interesting to see how some kinds of business revenues are brought in to support services.

- **Is funny, nyet?** There's an Internet service that reports jokes from the former Soviet Union. These days they can use all the humor they can get.

- **Agriculture:** On a huge range of university-maintained databases, every bit of agricultural research ever assembled is indexed and available. If you're a farmer, there's no need any more to wait for the agent from the ag school to get around to your county.

Chapter 2
Many, Many Nets

The Internet Is a Collection of Nets

At the same time that the Defense Department began sponsoring a communications protocol for connecting research networks, computer use by ordinary people exploded. In the early 1980s, as the old ARPA system gave way to the Internet, Apple II sales soared into the millions and the IBM PC essentially became a new industry. Meanwhile, cheap, fast modems appeared, making computer bulletin boards and assorted on-line services practical for the first time.

Who Are All These Networks Anyway?

When you start exploring the Internet, you'll find all sorts of information, opinion, and outright bafflement. Not only are there nearly 30 million Internet users, but there are comparable numbers of people connected to other nets that pass information to the Internet. Some of these other nets are just tiny private bulletin boards that service five people a day. Some of them are government networks that span the whole globe and connect thousands of solid citizens in white shirts and ties.

Although thousands of nets can exchange messages and data with the Internet, only a few are really important. Four big sources (Usenet, BITNET, university special-interest groups, and government labs and organizations) contribute most of the stuff that you find on the Net, so in this chapter I'm going to give you a quick rundown on them.

The cloudy crystal ball

When you read predictions about where the Internet is going, think about the following:

• How Steve Wozniak started Apple because he couldn't convince his bosses at Hewlett-Packard that a market for small computers existed.

• How Steve Jobs managed to "borrow" much of the Mac interface from Xerox because Xerox thought of work from its Palo Alto Research Center (PARC) as a research lab curiosity.

If you keep old computer magazines for more than a few years, you can laugh yourself silly reading the pundits' columns. Hey, in the early 1950s, Univac figured that the United States could absorb *12 computers* over the years. Wanna bet that the experts are all smarter now?

So by the time you read three chapters of this book, you can consider yourself an Internet guru qualified to make predictions.

If That's the Internet, What's This Usenet Business?

When people think of the Internet, they often think of cool characters swapping sophisticated messages on every topic under the sun. Actually, most of that action takes place on another network, called Usenet. But plenty of Internet sites also are Usenet sites, so the information tends to slosh across the two systems. On the Internet, you can talk to Usenet people, and they can talk to you.

Usenet newsgroups are the source of the most entertaining material accessible on the Internet. For example, the newsgroup `rec.humor.funny` is the most-accessed topic on the Internet; `rec.humor.funny` includes jokes selected diligently from the material found in the larger selection `rec.humor`. That's right, someone screens out the unfunny jokes for you! Is this a great service or what?

Short-sited?

After you make an Internet connection, through an on-line service or bulletin board, you can ask the system operator to add your name to the subscription lists for different newsgroups.

If your connections site does not carry a particular newsgroup, ask your system operators to add it; they almost always are willing to do so.

Usenet also is the source of serious stuff. If you want to study mathematical chaos, for example, you can join a newsgroup called `sci.non-linear`.

Getting network news

More than two million users participate in a scheme referred to collectively as network news; Usenet is the set of newsgroups at the core of the collection. Essentially it's just a set of conferences (organized discussion groups) that allow network discussions of different topics, together with an organized system for passing the discussions along to different nets.

An amazing amount of Usenet material is contributed by graduate students from various distinguished institutions of higher learning. (Considering the many afternoons I whiled away at dear old Caltech playing billiards when I should have been taking magnetic resonance spectra, I find that I envy today's students, whose every wisecrack is recorded for posterity. Now get back to work, folks.) At least they make for lively reading.

Conference calls

Table 2-1 lists a tiny sample of the conferences on Usenet that you can join from an Internet site. In the chapters where I tell you how to sign on, I tell you how to get a current list — many changes occur every few months.

Usenet sites, as a rule, use the operating system UNIX. One of my goals in writing this book is to insulate you from UNIX; I don't want you to have to learn a lot of UNIX commands just to get Internet access.

The reason UNIX appears all over the Internet is that UNIX is a real industrial-strength, bulletproof network operating system. It's also very efficient with computer resources, and both computer memory and computer time used to be more expensive. It's nerd heaven, too. If you feel the urge to learn more, just check out IDG's *UNIX For Dummies* or the UNIX command sections in *The Internet For Dummies*.

Table 2-1	Welcome, Stranger!
Newsgroup	*Topic*
comp.ai	Artificial intelligence
soc.culture.thai	The latest from Bangkok and elsewhere
sci.med.aids	Current AIDS information
alt.hotrod	Souped-up vehicles, natch
alt.rush-limbaugh	Please note the hyphen
alt.sports.baseball.chicago-cubs	Seminar on congenital optimism
talk.abortion	Abortion controversies of all kinds
rec.arts.poems	Write a poem, put it here
misc.answers	About Usenet itself
comp.sys.mac.wanted	Macs for sale

Drinking from a fire hose

The relatively specialized newsgroup for magnetic resonance lists about a hundred messages a day. But face it, even though magnetic resonance has elbowed its way into hospitals, it remains a pretty obscure subject. My point: Newsgroups for popular topics (in other words, where practically anyone may have an opinion) really run some high volume. Figure it out: If magnetic resonance is worth a hundred postings on a good day, how much traffic do you think shows up in alt.fan.howard-stern?

If you join lots of newsgroups indiscriminately, I promise that you won't be able to find the time to read most of the stuff.

So That's Usenet, Now What's BITNET?

BITNET, another system of computer conferences on a big assortment of topics, is a network of nearly 4,000 large computer systems. BITNET, which grew from a single funky operation in North Carolina in the early 1980s, got its name from an old IBM ad that featured the line "Because It's Time." (It's kind of an ironic slogan: at the time, IBM missed every boat leaving the harbor.)

What you have here is your basic collection of IBM mainframe computers with a special program that forwards discussions from one computer to the next on the network. It's as simple as that.

And because many of these BITNET sites are also Internet sites, there's no reason you can't join BITNET discussions from your Internet service. I give you the gory details when you need them. (FYI: The exact mechanism is the LISTSERV mailing list manager; LISTSERV (and another program called MAILSERV) puts you on a computer mailing list, just as you can be on a mailing list of community volunteers.) For now, check Table 2-2 to see some of the topics. Generally, there are more computer-oriented and serious topics on BIT than Use.

Table 2-2	Bits of BIT
Newsgroup	*Content*
bit.listserv.frac-a	Cool stuff about fractals
bit.listserv.lstsrv-1	Uncool stuff about LISTSERV mechanics
bit.mailserv.word-mac	Mac word processors
bit.listserv.games-1	Computer games
bit.listserv.gaynet	Gay discussion groups
bit.listserv.catholic	Catholic topics

Too Cool for School?

Plenty of independent commercial on-line systems offer many of the services that people expect from the Internet. You can find all sorts of shareware to download, for example. You can find special-interest groups with an unlimited (and, I dare say, unhealthy) interest in the details of old Partridge Family shows. You can track the entire universe of day-to-day data (stock quotes, sports scores, weather). The really unique feature of the Internet, aside from its unmatchable vast connectivity, is the contribution made by university networks: If you want to look up biographical details on Marilyn Monroe, you can do so in a library. If you want to keep up with developments in molecular biology, you need the Internet. Internet access means access to most of the important areas of modern scholarship.

In fact, special initiatives now exist on the Internet for a sort of virtual reality international conference for biologists, in which scientists compare data and analysis on-line — including journal figures and photos. In a more pedestrian Internet mode, Internet files are increasingly the standard repository for fast-moving information.

The Internet someday may help level the research-competitive playing fields between richer and poorer institutions. Already, Internet access has enabled people in some fields, most notably mathematics, to enjoy a level of contact that's a vast improvement on the traditional once-a-year-let's-all-meet-in-D.C. style of interaction.

Classes at Electronic U

Universities are using the Internet not just to exchange research results but to offer courses. Think for a moment about the quality of student/teacher interaction in a freshman physics course: it's not uncommon at large universities to stuff 400 students in a lecture hall (and those sitting at the back have to watch the lecture on TV monitors). Doesn't a private on-line tutor sound more desirable? The window in Figure 2-1 is an example of an early version of Internet courseware.

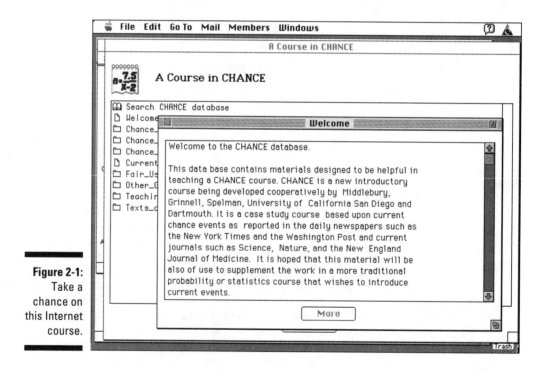

Figure 2-1: Take a chance on this Internet course.

One big argument in favor of on-line courses is the appallingly short shelf life of course material. For example, there's not much you could have learned in a digital-design course in electrical engineering ten years ago that would look very compelling in your personnel file today. In most engineering professions, it's taken for granted that the whole stock of information needs to be overhauled every five years. The need for fluid information flow keeps many schools interested in on-line education despite the hassles involved in designing a new instructional format.

If it's hot, it's here

Lots of the academic journals on the shelves of a university library now have a *one-year* lead time. That time lapse may be OK for medieval historians — the last time I looked, Charlemagne was still dead — but it's not fast enough for biotechnology or AIDS research or dozens of other hot topics. On the Internet, you can encounter not just newsgroups discussing current research but also databases that are updated almost daily by diligent university types.

Caution: People at work

Right now, there is open access to huge areas on university-maintained networks that maintain Internet connections. Stanford University and the University of Minnesota, just to name two, do heroic public interest work. Stanford, in particular, has enough Macintosh stuff to keep you happy for years.

Of course, if millions of people start logging onto these university networks in the middle of the day, users will complain. And when it becomes clear that the university network is jammed with users downloading Snoopy screen-savers, the powers that be are going to change the open-access rules.

Your Tax Dollars at Work

Universities around the world contribute a great deal to the information base of the Internet, but the U.S. government pays lots of the bills. Come to think of it, that means *you* pay a lot of the bills. Umm . . . hey, thanks!

It's pretty clear that almost no one in the government had any idea (what else is new?) what was being created when the funding for the high-speed NSFNET and another net called NASA Science Internet was approved. Actually, I'm talking about a trivial amount of money by Defense Department standards — remember, we live in a world where new fighter-plane designs cost tens of billions of dollars. It would have taken Nostradamus to realize that the world could be stood on its ear by a few hundred million doled out over a few decades to scientists.

Good guys and bad guys?

Although many Internet old-timers are convinced that the U.S. government in total is too dumb to impose any sort of regulation on the Net, lots of advanced thinkers working for the government have become quite agitated about the prospect of a high-speed, nearly anonymous, nonwiretappable international communications network.

As a result, topics of net access and security are controversial. Most traditional Internet people favor unrestricted use, and a minority favor some way of guaranteeing law-enforcement access to suspicious activities. It's probably naive to disregard the possibility that some Internet users will find a way to use the Net to foster criminal activities (send opinions to psuarez@medellin.cartel.com?), but it's also naive to suppose that there's an unobtrusive way to check a significant fraction of messages. Expect plenty of debate in these areas in the years to come.

Dear Congressman (from a concerned citizen who can afford a computer)

You can find lots of old-time government data on the Internet (I tell you where in the access chapters). Some of it is the kind of info the government's printing office still ships from Boulder, Colorado, with a hundred fun recipes for powdered milk, or pamphlets on *The Soybean, Our Versatile Friend*, or travel tips on avoiding exotic diseases.

Another way to use the Internet is to make yourself heard in the corridors of power. Because newspapers have many staffers in the forefront of the on-line revolution, you're likely to find Internet e-mail addresses for everyone with the slightest pretensions to authority, including state legislators, congressional representatives, governors, senators, and cabinet members. Usually these @ addresses are listed on the editorial page of the paper (sometimes printed as a shameless way to fill space).

The handful of people I know who have worked this contact channel (some old hands at PeaceNet and EcoNet, for example, pioneering public-interest network groups) claim to have obtained better results electronically than with traditional paper and pen.

Despite the millions of Net residents now on-line, the whole scheme is probably new enough to politicians that an Internet message still has a certain mystique. And if you send an Internet message to a politician, you're more likely to be taken seriously. The U.S. Senate, by the way, now has an anonymous FTP site with files of current Senate information. (Curiously, Teddy Kennedy was essentially the senator who sponsored this initiative. *I* was surprised, but I'm a Democrat and so thought that old Ted's mind was on other things.)

How Did All This Stuff Get Here?

Before most day-to-day Mac users heard of the Internet, people were pumping out information and discussions from Usenet, BITNET, university special-interest groups, and government labs and organizations. They were doing it in the United States, and they were doing it everywhere else, too.

Finland, for example, jumped on the Internet early. Finland is snowed-in five months of the year (they're the world champs at icebreaker-ship technology), so on-line communication makes plenty of sense compared to frozen snail mail. A big Internet presence keeps Finnish researchers in contact with the rest of the planet.

As you head out into cyberspace, I have good news and bad news. The bad news: The landscape is even more crowded. You're visiting a 30-million-user Internet, not a 2-million-user Internet. The good news: The landscape is more crowded and therefore richer.

To get your hardware set up to cruise this strange new world, turn to the next chapter.

The 5th Wave

Larry's newsgroup friends pay an in-person visit.

Chapter 3
Modem Mania

• •

In This Chapter

▶ Understanding what modems do

▶ Selecting the right modem for use with the Internet

▶ Finding out why faster is better, up to a point

▶ Choosing software for signing on

• •

You Gotta Have a Modem to Get on the Net

All the wonderful files of information on the Internet are out there on other computers. Your Macintosh is sitting on your desk. If you want to join the Internet, a cable has to connect your Mac to the rest of the world.

That cable plugs into the little port with a picture of a telephone on the back of your Mac. The other end of the cable goes to a modem, which plugs into your phone line. That's all there is to it.

That is, assuming that you're an individual Mac user. If someone has handed you a network-connected Mac at a university or business, you're a separate case. You can skip this chapter, unless you also want to get on-line at home.

A modem is one of the more mysterious computer accessories. In the Mac world, for example, a printer is fairly self-explanatory. That's because the Macintosh was *designed* to be the first computer that worked easily with printers.

A modem, in contrast, is distinctly *not* self-explanatory. The bulk of the modem business is still in the hands of people who don't see why DOS on IBM-PC compatibles is an objectionable interface. Nearly all modems respond to a command code developed in the 1970s, and Apple itself is powerless to save you from the confusion this situation produces. I am going to try to get you through modem installation as painlessly as possible. Consult the "Warning signs for modem users" sidebar in case I succeed too well — and you become a modem junkie.

Warning signs for modem users

You can get into this modem stuff too deeply. Review these warning signs to make sure that you aren't turning into a wirehead.

✔ You hum dial tones in the shower.

✔ You can make modem sign-on noises with your nose.

✔ You remember which colors mean what on the phone jack's teensy wires.

✔ You absentmindedly reset the clock on a friend's VCR.

✔ The blinking lights on the front of your modem send secretly coded messages that only you can understand.

If any of these things happen, go to some live concerts to restore your equilibrium.

Determining What You Should Buy

Modem-buying calls for a little background. For historical reasons, modem speeds are based on funny multiples of 300 bits per second, and a half-dozen data compression formats are current. Manuals for modems tend to feature cable-connect pinouts, timing diagrams, arcane CCITT standards jargon, and tables of the time-honored Hayes AT commands.

In the Mac world, external modems are more common than internal modems. An external modem comes in its own case. An internal modem is a card that you stick into a slot inside the Mac. They don't differ much operationally, except that internal modems tend to be a bit cheaper. PowerBooks are a special case, as the following sidebar explains.

Power to the people

PowerBook owners should note that everything I say here applies to PowerBooks as well, with the provision that the same specs cost $100 more for PowerBook internal modems than for desktop Macs, a sort of surcharge for miniaturization engineering. Very small portable external modems (pocket modems) are also available, with the advantage that you can unplug them and use them with your desktop Mac.

Understanding What a Modem Does

Despite all these hardware considerations, a modem's job is really fairly simple: it takes output from your files or your keyboard and converts the pattern of zeroes and ones into an equivalent pattern of tones. The telephone line can handle the tones reliably, so the message gets sent.

The other common communications accessory is the fax machine, so these days modem makers tend to build fax capability into the modem. A fax/modem's job isn't much harder — it converts the document into a set of lines containing dark bits and white spaces (blocks of zeroes and ones) and performs the same tone conversion on this data.

The circuit boards inside these products reflect this simplicity. They usually contain just a few chips (and there are only a few popular chip vendors for data communications circuits) and other components. In portable modems, the holder for the nine-volt battery is often the biggest physical component. Because there's really not much in them, prices for modems fall steadily every year as the chips get cheaper. Yesterday's $600 modem is today's $99 bargain, and yesterday's mainstream modem is sitting on a closet shelf.

Is old stuff good enough?

Millions of 1200-bps (bits per second) modems are floating around, and if you plan to contact an on-line service only occasionally, you can get along with one of them. Frankly, you shouldn't *buy* one — try to cajole someone into giving you one instead. The typical Mac users group includes dozens of people who have upgraded their communications and may be willing to donate their old ones to you. You won't be happy downloading Internet files at 1200 bps.

Is not-quite-old stuff good enough?

You can still buy a 2400-bps modem without a fax as a basic communications system. Sometimes you find them bundled with introductory offers for national on-line services. As the following sidebar explains, they sometimes come bundled with your Mac.

Honest, they gave me this thing!

Apple sold at least a million Performa models with built-in modems and communications software. The catch in this arrangement is that the modems are 2400-bps units, for which Apple paid about $20. The built-in modem is fine for getting oriented to Internet services, but once you start doing anything serious, it's going to be out with the old and in with the new, modem-wise.

Although 2400 bps is a bit old-fashioned in terms of current chip technology, as of 1994, most bulletin boards and network connections have more local toll-free numbers for 2400 bps than for 9600 bps. Some commercial services also tack on a surcharge for 9600-bps connection. Major vendors such as Supra and Hayes sell 2400-bps modems for street prices of $60 to $100.

What should I buy?

To be happy with a modem connecting to the Internet, you should plan on buying a 9600-bps modem — or faster if you can afford it. The reason is simple. Once you get used to file transfers at 9600, using 2400 feels like you're wading though bean dip.

With a built-in fax, 9600 bps should cost a bit more than $100 in the next year. Modems that send data at 14,400 bps and also have 14,400-bps fax send/receive capability will replace their 9600 cousins over the next couple of years. They cost about $250 today, but that price will drop pretty quickly.

If you are the kind of person who wants a $3,000 trail bike and who bought a Power Mac the first day they appeared, you should know that 19,200-bps and 28,000-bps modems are also available (see Table 3-1). These modems work with special data-compression coding schemes that speed things up further by a factor of four. It's not clear which set of high-speed tricks will become universally accepted, so consider a modem faster than 14,400 bps as a sort of experimental investment.

Table 3-1	Modem Standards
The Standard	*What It Means*
V.22*bis*	2400 bps
V.32	9600 bps
V.32*bis*	14,400 bps
V.32terbo	19,200 bps
V.Fast	28,000 bps

CompuServe, for example, is installing 14,400-bps local numbers in large cities, but few on-line services are set up yet for this speed. In many areas, the phone service needs to be improved to allow fast modems to do their thing. So telephone systems themselves are being upgraded to carry more data — at 28,000 bps, the noise in ordinary voice lines becomes a big problem. Although lots of private bulletin boards with Internet connection have 14,000-bps lines, it's going to take a while for the big services to install the appropriate hardware.

Without Me You're Nothing: The Software Connection

The modem, of course, does nothing but sit there until a piece of software tells it what to do. (Also, make sure that it's turned on — believe it or not, I've been called out on consulting calls where pressing the On button was the issue.)

Three kinds of software are important for your Internet journey. First is the software provided directly by on-line services. If you're going to connect to Prodigy for Internet service, Prodigy sends you its own software disks. The second kind of software is represented by the special communications programs you have to use with direct Internet connection (I tell you about these programs in the next two chapters). Finally, basic communications software lets you connect to bulletin boards and on-line services that have a plain, vanilla, no-icon, text-style interface.

ZTerm, the last word

David Alverson wrote a terminal program called ZTerm that shows up (in earlier versions) on bulletin boards and in the software libraries of on-line services. If you have a PowerBook with an internal modem, the vendor probably gave you ZTerm (see Figure 3-1) as part of the package. In the *Macworld* August 1994 issue, the editors picked ZTerm as the best communications software. Computers, you see, are still a funny kind of business. One good programmer — for example Mr. Alverson, working by himself in Mason, Ohio — can do better work than a whole three-story building full of mediocrities on the West Coast.

Figure 3-1:
ZTerm is
fast, clean,
efficient,
and usually
free.

```
   File  Edit  Dial  Settings  Macros  Misc                    ⚙ ⑦ Z
                     Directory...        ⌘D  hone Numbers            
                     Save Setup                                      ⇧
   Enter choice <CR>  Dial Marked                                    
                     Hang Up            ⌘H                          
   Enter your full p                                                
     (example: 614 4  CompuServe                                    
   :707-431-7611     CompuServe Phone Numbers                       
                     DELPHI                                          
   From HEALDSBURG   GEnie                                          
                     Global BBS                                      
   Call (707) 579-15                                                
     Or                                                             
   Call (707) 257-0234  NAPA        [ CNS      ]                    
   Off at 01:27 EDT 30-Jun-94                                       
                                                                    
                                                                    
                                                                    
                                                                    
   Host Name:  _                                                   ≡
                                                                    ⇩
    0:50    24x102    1k    2400 N81                               
```

Microphone LT (for lovable terminalware)

A majority of new Mac modems ship with Microphone LT from Software Ventures Corporation (510-644-3232). It lacks the automation features and some of the high-end capabilities built into the full-scale version of Microphone, but it's certainly good enough for using your Mac as a text-based terminal. For signing onto a free Internet connection at a library or for any other dial-up Internet service that works on text command, it has everything you need.

If you know your modem's speed (see Figure 3-2) and the phone number for your connection, you can pretty much leave Microphone LT's default settings in place. Microphone LT also lets you specify VT-102 as the terminal type in a simple terminal settings window (see Figure 3-3). Lots of people on the Internet still use real hardware VT-102 terminals, so you're in good company.

One of this program's great virtues is that it keeps a record of your on-line session, and it's just about impossible to lose this record by accident. Instead of downloading files, often it's more convenient to read them on-screen and then later open the Microphone LT record of the session by using your favorite word processor. (See the coupon at the end of this book.)

Figure 3-2:
Microphone LT asks you to make only one or two setup decisions.

Edit

Communications Settings

Connection Settings

Method: MicroPhone Standard ▼

Driver: Standard ▼

OK

Cancel

Port Settings

Baud Rate: 2400 ▼

Data Bits: 8 ▼

Parity: None ▼

Stop Bits: Auto ▼

Flow Control: XOn-XOff ▼

Connection Port

Modem Port   Printer Port

Read Me!

11:14:29 PM

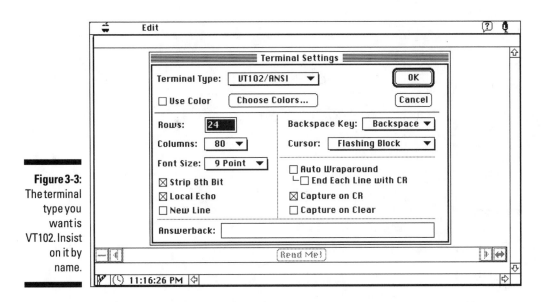

Figure 3-3: The terminal type you want is VT102. Insist on it by name.

ClarisWorks — I've seen better, I've seen worse

ClarisWorks, which is bundled with an amazing number of Macs sold through consumer channels, includes a communications module. It's neither as capable as Microphone nor as easy to use (see the dialog box in Figure 3-4); however, if you already own it, you can learn to live with it. It doesn't have as many friendly, built-in reminders as the best communications software and was clearly something of an afterthought to Claris, but if you use ClarisWorks all the time, it gets information into the other modules (word processing and database) conveniently.

Microsoft Works: Data communications for the Flintstones

You're a back-to-basics sort, right? No frills? Chip your own stone tools on weekends? Microsoft Works has a communications module just for you.

Somewhere far to the west, a brooding Bill Gates lies in bed and stares up at a vaulted ceiling in his giant mansion. What's keeping him up nights? The nagging thought that somehow, somewhere, someone got something for free from Microsoft. The word processor in Works is designed, for example, to force you to buy Microsoft Word from sheer frustration someday. Microsoft acquired the communications module from a third party in a no-cash-exchanged transaction essentially as a marketing consideration.

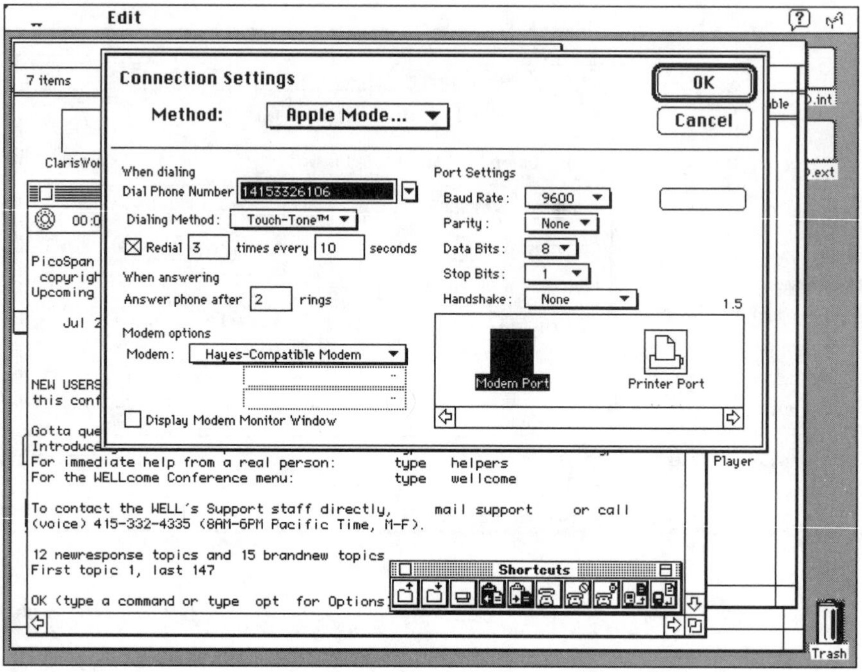

Figure 3-4:
ClarisWorks'
communi-
cations
module is a
bit fussier
than
Microphone's.

If you have Works, one of the first things you should do on the Internet is use it to download a better terminal program by using the screen shown in Figure 3-5. I tell you how later in this book.

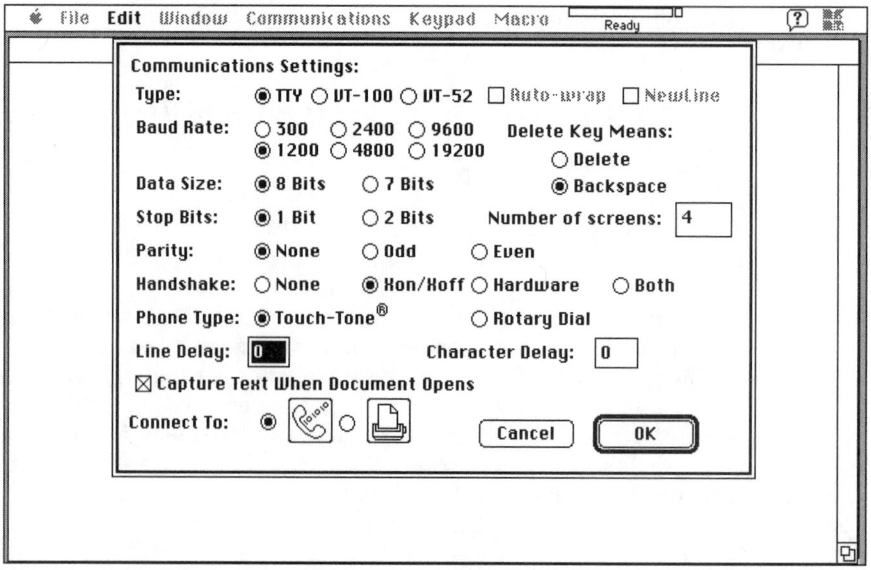

Figure 3-5:
This screen
isn't much
fun, but you
can use it to
download
ZTerm.

Fancy stuff

Figure 3-6, the sign-on screen from America Online, shows you what Mac communication software is supposed to look like. I don't show you the configuration and settings screens because usually you need to enter only modem speed and phone number, which often have been preset.

If, against All Odds, You Find Modems Fascinating

In this book, I only want to tell you enough modem stuff so that you don't buy something that's disastrously wrong. As you can see, the Internet itself is a big enough subject to occupy your attentions. The definitive work on modems is Tina Rathbone's *Modems For Dummies,* 2nd Edition, another fine IDG product. With these preliminaries out of the way, I show you how to communicate with everyone on earth in the following chapters.

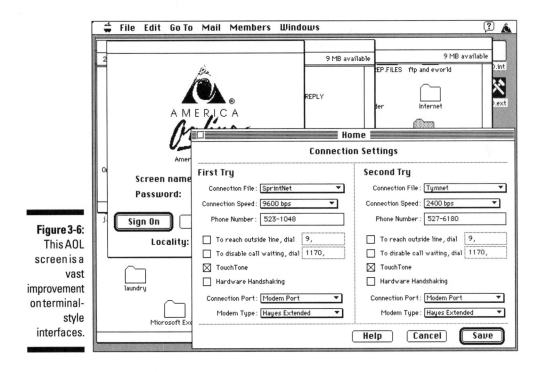

Figure 3-6:
This AOL
screen is a
vast
improvement
on terminal-
style
interfaces.

Chapter 4
E-Mail—Wired to the World

● ●

In This Chapter

▶ E-mail for beginners

▶ Putting e-mail to work

▶ Understanding how the other systems do it

▶ Doing it the Macintosh way

● ●

What's the Story on E-Mail?

You can send e-mail to any one of the Internet's 30 million users if

✔ You own a Macintosh and a modem.

✔ Your Mac is on a network, and the network has a modem.

✔ Your Mac is directly connected to a network that is an Internet *host*—a computer system with its own Internet numerical address. You don't even need a modem.

The first e-mail services open to the public (businesses have had in-house e-mail since the 1960s) were national organizations like MCI Mail and CompuServe. In the beginning, if you had an MCI account, you could send mail to anyone else with an MCI account, but you couldn't send mail out of the system. Actually, you could have had an MCI message delivered on paper to a regular street address for a discouragingly high fee.

By the early 1990s, however, everyone involved in the e-mail business had figured out that universal connection was the future of e-mail. If CompuServe, MCI Mail, and Prodigy became Internet hosts, then users could easily send messages from one service to another. It was obviously a good idea. Surprisingly, they actually followed through. Every commercial service that can afford to advertise in a magazine is now connected to the Internet.

Hosts, mailboxes, and you

Suppose that you sign up with a major Internet service provider, such as Netcom (408-554-8649). Netcom gives you a local dial-up phone number. You pick the name "Joe Cool," and you choose "joec" as your Net name. Your Internet address, then, is joec@netcom.com. Netcom is the *host,* meaning a computer system with its own Internet numerical address. You, in turn, are a user attached to that host, but you are not a host yourself.

As a service for outgoing e-mail, Netcom becomes the equivalent of the corner mailbox. You send a message to your pal Michael Nifty, miken@world.com. Netcom routes the message to the receiving Internet host, world.com. The receiving host acts like one of those big office mailbox systems with hundreds of pigeonholes. It finds miken, stores the message, and notifies your pal that he has new mail. Usually, he sees this notice the next time he logs into the world.com system.

Oh, there really is a world.com, provided by The World. It's another big-time commercial Internet service (based in Boston, it was one of the first), and you can reach it at 617-739-0202.

These connections work, in part, because the messages are primitive. The e-mail messages I'm talking about are plain text; these messages can be created on any type of computer and read on any other. And because they're just text, they're compact — a one-page color picture file is 500 times bigger than a file containing a page of text. That makes a difference when you use a relatively slow phone line (2400 bps) for Internet connection. Someday, you may be able to send systemwide sound-plus-picture messages across the Internet. Even now, it's possible to send sound and picture *files* with a few tricks (more on this subject later), but sounds and graphics are not generally available in Internet e-mail yet.

Dear Mr. President

Using only the simplest version of a mailing system, I'm going to give a little e-mail tour now. The way I show you is not the best way to do e-mail, but this simple way is common. Some national on-line services have convenient and intuitive mail systems, and you can use a Mac-specific mail program called Eudora if you are a host (or have a direct link to a host). But the typical Internet setup uses a plain, vanilla, UNIX mail program like the one in this chapter.

First step

You get an account and log into your system. All you need is your name, your password, and a phone number. Most likely, you'll use one of the communications programs described in Chapter 3 (most chapters in this book explain the details of signing on one way or another, so for now just come along for the ride). After you log in, you get a prompt (no menus here, folks); a common prompt is the %. That's right, the computer sends you this symbol — % — to assist you in figuring what to do next. Thanks for all the help.

If you read the manual, you know that at the prompt you can type

```
mail president@whitehouse.gov
```

to start the mail program. By the way, if you find yourself stuck using this kind of interface, at the % prompt you can also type

```
man
```

and the main system (the host system — it's the host, you're the user) fills your screen with pieces of the operating system's manual.

A piece of your mind

After you type **mail** and an address at the prompt, you're rewarded with something a bit more informative. Now you see

```
mail president@whitehouse.gov
 Subject:
```

You may as well compose a good general-purpose Internet presidential letter — one with a long shelf life. After you give a subject name and press Return, type this message:

```
mail president@whitehouse.gov
Subject: Such a Deal
The deficit in the Federal Budget is running nearly a billion
dollars a day. I have developed a spreadsheet in ClarisWorks
that can reschedule interest payments on the national debt by
half-day increments to save $10 billion a year, and I only
want payments of $1 million a day (it's a licensing arrange-
ment) for it. Look at it this way: I may even be right, and
$1 million a day is well within the range of accounting error
in your system. As far as you can tell, it wouldn't cost you
anything even if I were wrong!
Yours sincerely,
Joseph M. Cool
```

Now what? Well, if you read the manual, you know to press Ctrl-D (hold down Ctrl and D at the same time). The system sends you

```
EOT
```

for end of transmission.

Out into the Net

That's the end for you, but the computer system has just started working. It attaches an ID to your message and finds a path through the Internet to the target computer — in this case, a computer at the White House.

Sometimes this process is very straightforward, but the message path may go through a whole set of computers with their own weird Internet addresses.

At the receiving end, the president sees your message with a header that contains all sorts of system information. Actually, I'm just kidding about the president — it's a lead-pipe cinch that he won't see anything you send personally. But the header is there (see Figure 4-1).

Figure 4-1:
A typical Internet e-mail message, preceded by a header with more than you want to see.

```
Path:search01.news.aol.com!newstf01!cr1.aol.com!uunet!MathWorks.Com!europa.eng.gt
efsd.com!library.ucla.edu!csulb.edu!csus.edu!netcom.com!zzz
From: zzz@netcom.com (Louis Zzizz)
Subject: Re: Mac Ftp Mirrors
Message-ID: <zzzCqFHpC.AoC@netcom.com>
References: <2s1fq9$f8c@news.CCIT.Arizona.EDU> <fujii-260594031300@ts7-
38.upenn.edu>
Date: Sun, 29 May 1994 21:15:11 GMT

Subject: Re: Mac Ftp Mirrors
From: zzz@netcom.com (Louis Zzizz)
Date: Sun, 29 May 1994 21:15:11 GMT
Message-ID: <zzzCqFHpC.AoC@netcom.com>

>> Where else can I ftp to get the Umich and/or Info-Mac files?

Here are two sites that are updated every day:

ftp.univie.ac.at      131.130.1.4     mac/info-mac        1/1
ftp.ucs.ubc.ca        137.82.27.62    pub/mac/info-mac    1/1

Louis Zziz         zzz@netcom.com        San Jose, CA
```

If you make a mistake in the address, the message won't get through. Some systems tell you after a brief delay that the address isn't working. Typically, however, the message goes out on the Internet and gets bounced back to you much later — you'll find it returned the next time you connect to your host system. In other words, it's critical to get Internet addresses exactly right. Unlike the Post Office, the Internet has no way to work around your typos.

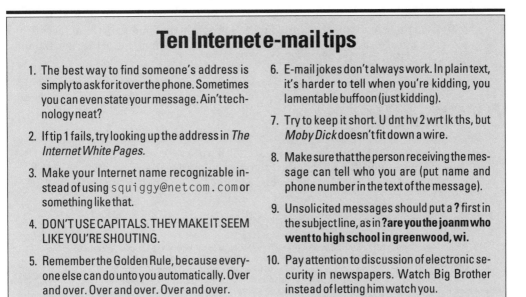

Ten Internet e-mail tips

1. The best way to find someone's address is simply to ask for it over the phone. Sometimes you can even state your message. Ain't technology neat?

2. If tip 1 fails, try looking up the address in *The Internet White Pages*.

3. Make your Internet name recognizable instead of using squiggy@netcom.com or something like that.

4. DON'T USE CAPITALS. THEY MAKE IT SEEM LIKE YOU'RE SHOUTING.

5. Remember the Golden Rule, because everyone else can do unto you automatically. Over and over. Over and over. Over and over.

6. E-mail jokes don't always work. In plain text, it's harder to tell when you're kidding, you lamentable buffoon (just kidding).

7. Try to keep it short. U dnt hv 2 wrt lk ths, but *Moby Dick* doesn't fit down a wire.

8. Make sure that the person receiving the message can tell who you are (put name and phone number in the text of the message).

9. Unsolicited messages should put a **?** first in the subject line, as in **?are you the joanm who went to high school in greenwood, wi.**

10. Pay attention to discussion of electronic security in newspapers. Watch Big Brother instead of letting him watch you.

Sorry about the UNIX Stuff

The Internet For Dummies includes a description of a somewhat-improved UNIX-based mailing system called elm. This program has a nice repertoire of commands and a full-screen editor. By UNIX standards, it's a big improvement. There are half a dozen other mailing programs, too.

But the fact is, they're all absolutely pitiful even compared to a simple Macintosh shareware mailing program. Nonetheless, only shareware programs are available for many kinds of basic Internet connections.

Here's why: Back when the Mac could run only MacPaint and MacWrite, UNIX was a highly evolved, nearly uncrashable operating system that could handle big networks. The best way to make a low-cost, multiuser system in the mid-1980s was to get a single, powerful UNIX computer and a bunch of cheap terminals that offered only character-oriented display. Hundreds of universities, government organizations, and businesses — the same ones that make up a big part of the Internet today — set up UNIX systems.

In the mid-1990s, therefore, Internet services often want you to take your lovely, graphics-oriented Macintosh, capable of QuickTime movies and stereo sound, and operate it as a character-oriented terminal. The machine at the other end of the wire thinks that you actually have a character-oriented terminal. Actually, I wish that some wise guy would write a program that mimics a terminal with a black screen and green dot-matrix characters to remind me of the time I spent as a child at a real VT-100 terminal.

BBS Are Bttr

Check out the mail system in Figure 4-2. It's a text-based but menu-driven system — you don't necessarily have to memorize the commands or keep a cheat sheet in your lap while you're typing because help is available at all times.

```
             COMMAND OPTIONS FOR USING EMAIL

mail userid  ...Send email to another WELL user.  You will be prompted for
             a "Subject".  Type a short subject header and hit Return.
             Then, enter the text of your message, hitting Return at
             the end of each line (about 70 chars wide).  To abandon
             the message without sending it, hit control-c twice.

             To send the letter, go to a new line, type a dot (.),
             and hit Return.

mail         ...Read your mail.  You will see a list of your mail items
             and a prompt which looks like this:  &   ...To read each
             consecutive mail item, hit Return at this "&" prompt.

             Type:  r    ...to respond to the current message.

             Type:  dt   ...to delete the current message.

             Type:  q    ...to quit email.
```

Figure 4-2:
This mail system isn't Mac software yet, but it makes a few concessions to the user.

The difference between this mail system and classic UNIX mailing systems, like so many things, has to do with money. In the stock UNIX situation, you had access to a computer system by using UNIX, and you took what you got. Don't like the mailing system? Then write people notes in purple crayon on paper towels.

A typical bulletin board system (BBS) or conferencing system wants you to sign up, wants you to be happy, and wants to charge you a fee. If the mailing system is intolerable, two problems arise: You don't want to write messages, so you won't stay connected (and the service usually charges an hourly fee). And eventually you quit, an even worse situation. Even if the BBS is free, the BBS operator pays for the software, so anyway you slice it, there's more incentive to offer a decent mailing system.

Mac Access

Two years ago, I would have felt compelled to offer a few pages full of UNIX mailing commands. Now, I propose to duck the whole, ugly mess. Even UNIX hotshots themselves are converting their systems wholesale to an interface called X Windows, which looks for all the world like a small-print version of a Macintosh screen.

You can get Internet e-mail access in lots of ways. You can use the plain, guess-your-next-command style that's standard with UNIX, or you can get a really friendly mail interface from America Online. Ironically, Internet e-mail access probably costs between $10 and $20 a month, whichever type of access you pick. Allow me to underline this distinction by presenting two mail-access screens (see Figures 4-3 and 4-4) back-to-back. Look, you had enough sense to pick a Mac in the first place — make your own decision.

Figure 4-3:
The traditional Internet mail interface.

```
Sun Mar 13 23:50:20 PST 1994
crl1% mail
Mail version SMI 4.0 Fri Jul  2 11:55:02 PDT 1993  Type ? for help.
"/usr/spool/mail/chseiter": 1 message 1 new
>N  1 wilson       Sat Mar 12 26 05:59  36/1103  Macworld note

& mail chseiter@aol.com
Subject: comm1
Hi. If you can read this, you're not having fun.

.
EOT

New mail has arrived.
crl2% mail
Mail version SMI 4.0 Fri Jul  2 11:55:02 PDT 1993  Type ? for help.
"/usr/spool/mail/chseiter": 1 message 1 new
>N  1 MAILER-DAEMON    Sun Mar 13 23:53  24/719
Returned mail: User unknown
& d 1
& quit
|
```

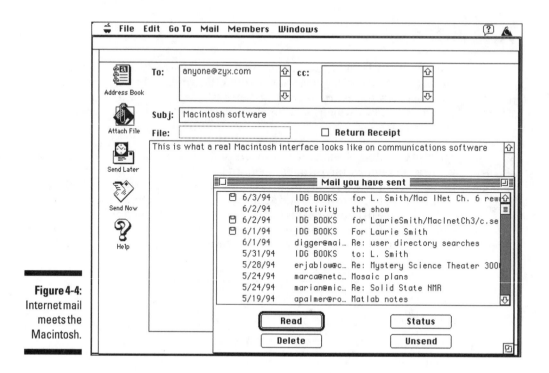

Figure 4-4:
Internet mail
meets the
Macintosh.

Names and Numbers

Once you're on the Internet and people know that you're a master of e-mail, you may find yourself called on to chitchat about esoteric topics. That is, I propose to get you up and running with minimal fuss, but if I don't fill you in on a few gory details, you won't be able to impress your friends. Already, Net old-timers are complaining that *anyone* can get on the Internet. In one plaintive newsgroup message I read recently, a hard-core Nethead complains that he just received a message from his grandmother!

A class system

Internet hosts have machine addresses composed of four numbers separated by dots. Thus the WELL in San Francisco is called

```
well.sf.ca.us
```

but other Internet machines know it as

```
198.93.4.10
```

The numbers between the dots range from 1 to 254. In other words, there are 254 x 254 x 254 x 254 possible addresses — about 4 billion.

A, B, and C

Because there are different ways to do the network address assignment, the people who assigned them made up three classes: A, B, and C. Class A networks can support about 16 million hosts (that's a big network!); class C networks can handle 254 hosts. Because a host computer on a network can handle several incoming lines, there's a lot of room out there.

Inside a big network, a method called *subnetting* simplifies addressing from one network to the next, and another method called *supernetting* lets organizations effectively address several smaller networks as though they were one big network. I wouldn't bother you with a word of this, except that it will come back to haunt you when I tell you how to make your Mac a host. Figure 4-5, for example, shows the setup screen from MacTCP. You have to know how to fill in the blanks, or you can't get connected.

Figure 4-5:
Class B?
Subnet
mask? It's
all part of
the Internet
fun.

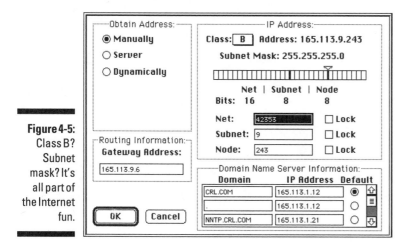

Chapter 5

Beyond E-Mail — The InfoSphere

Piles o' Files

E-mail contains everything that someone thought up yesterday and wanted to communicate. The rest of the Internet is everything that someone thought up *ever* and wanted to communicate.

The Internet currently has something like 100 gigabytes of text files that you can access with no special security clearance. This book is about half a megabyte of text, so I'm talking about roughly 200,000 books this size. Programs and pictures are available, too. In addition, gigabytes of information slosh back and forth between BITNET and USENET sites and thousands of bulletin boards.

Finding What You Want

The first problem you face is finding what you want. Thousands of big computers are on the Internet — so where's the good stuff? The next problem is hauling it back to your own computer. You actually have to transfer a file to your own hard drive to use it. Both problems have a standard Internet solution and a Macintosh solution.

TIP

The most common Internet tools for finding files are probably Archie, Gopher, and WWW (World Wide Web). I'll provide some basic exercises in these programs so you can see what a search is like. A program called FTP (*file transfer protocol*) is the standard tool for retrieving files.

The Macintosh equivalents are, as you may expect, even better than the originals. TurboGopher, Anarchie, and Mosaic (a program for hypertext searches of Internet databases) are just fantastic (see Figure 5-1). Fetch is a file retrieval program that makes users of other computers drool enviously. The catch, and it's not a small one, is that you need a direct Internet connection to use them. That means that either 1) you're a Mac user on a network host, 2) you're paying for an expensive full-time direct connection, or 3) you have bought a SLIP account (see the following sidebar).

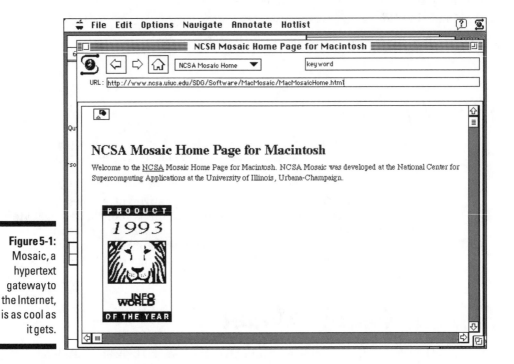

Figure 5-1: Mosaic, a hypertext gateway to the Internet, is as cool as it gets.

SLIPpery business

SLIP (Serial Line Interface Protocol), as implemented in the programs MacSLIP and InterSLIP, lets you connect directly to the Internet over an ordinary phone line. Get a fast modem (at least 9600 bps) and a SLIP account from an Internet service provider, and you can have your own Internet address number. You're a host!

SLIP service by phone involves a few minor difficulties. It's great for transferring files, but mail to your new address only works when you're on-line. If you hang up the phone line, as far as the rest of the Internet is concerned you're a "Host not responding" site. That's why most SLIP account users have another way to get mail 24 hours a day, through a national on-line service like CompuServe, or through a *shell* account (standard dial-up access) at the SLIP provider.

Another minor difficulty is that getting SLIP up and running can be frustrating. It's also likely that the customer support people at the service provider won't be Mac authorities. Sometimes these guys are a bit strange anyway. Here's an authentic hot-off-the-Internet joke:

Q: How do you recognize an extroverted network engineer?

A: He stares at *your* shoes when he talks to you.

Key to the Highway

At first, the assortment of Internet navigation tools can be somewhat bewildering. How are you supposed to figure out what tool to use when?

I'll tell you how. It's all very simple. It came to me in a blinding flash, after this book was 95% finished. I looked back over several chapters and realized that in fifteen different sections I was talking about the same thing. Here it is.

There is only *one* trick on the Internet. The trick is the ability to jump from one computer to the next. Everything else is just a file-management utility.

Two steps out

Here's the scenario. You get an Internet account and a password. You sign onto your host. There you are on your host computer, which probably has all sorts of interesting files itself. But let's face it. You want more. You want *power.* So you type the command

```
telnet fedix.fie.com
```

At this command, your own host computer then calls up a big computer network that's another Internet host (see the sidebar "Remote Possibilities"). This one is full of government databases. You see the dazzling display of character-based graphics in Figure 5-2.

```
Hello, Welcome to FEDIX on fedix...


Last login: Mon Jun  6 18:53:20 from uclink2.Berkeley
Up - Sat May 28 12:08:04 EDT 1994
SunOS Release 4.1.2 (FEDIX2) #1: Tue May 25 11:51:11 EDT 1993
          FFFFFFFFF EEEEEEEE DDDDDDDD  IIIII XXX   XXX
          FFF       EEE      DDD  DDDD  III   XXX XXX
          FFF       EEE      DDD   DDD  III    XXXXX
          FFFFFF    EEEEEEEE DDD   DDD  III     XXX
          FFF       EEE      DDD   DDD  III    XXXXX
          FFF       EEE      DDD  DDDD  III   XXX XXX
          FFF       EEEEEEEE DDDDDDDD  IIIII XXX   XXX


  **********************************************************************
  **********************************************************************

logged in on - /dev/ttyp5
Internet
```

Figure 5-2: Yikes! It's the Feds (sort of). But they're smiling!

Remote possibilities

Telnet is a standard UNIX command for connecting you to another computer network (you're on one now; it connects you to another one). Another command called **rlogin**, for remote login, is similar. If you type **!man telnet**, most systems give you a little manual about telnet to read.

If you don't have advance information, you usually won't know what to do at the login prompt. If you have to guess, use "guest" or "public" as your name and your Internet address as a password. A better approach is to get the information from your own host. Usually, if you read about an interesting telnet site in a magazine or newspaper, the login information will be provided.

Some networks you reach with telnet have prepared a lovely menu system to help you navigate. Some haven't. If you get into a network that just gives you a % prompt, try typing **ls** or **dir**. You should get a directory of files. If the directory doesn't make any sense to you, type **bye** or **quit** and read the rest of this chapter, like a good Net citizen.

You will be asked to log in, but fortunately this particular system tells you how:

```
Enter your FEDIX/MOLIS USERID, or NEW if you are a new user,
   or PRIOR if you have forgotten your USERID  > new
Logged in as new
```

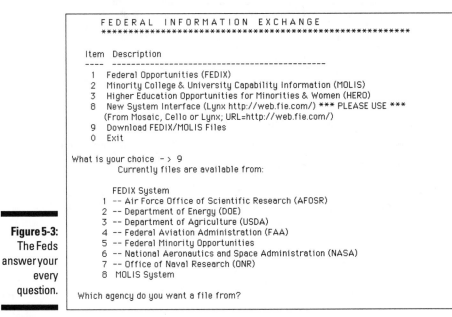

```
        FEDERAL  INFORMATION  EXCHANGE
        **************************************************************

     Item  Description
     ----  -------------------------------------------------
      1    Federal Opportunities (FEDIX)
      2    Minority College & University Capability Information (MOLIS)
      3    Higher Education Opportunities for Minorities & Women (HERO)
      8    New System Interface (Lynx http://web.fie.com/) *** PLEASE USE ***
           (From Mosaic, Cello or Lynx; URL=http://web.fie.com/)
      9    Download FEDIX/MOLIS Files
      0    Exit

What is your choice  - > 9
           Currently files are available from:

           FEDIX System
           1 -- Air Force Office of Scientific Research (AFOSR)
           2 -- Department of Energy (DOE)
           3 -- Department of Agriculture (USDA)
           4 -- Federal Aviation Administration (FAA)
           5 -- Federal Minority Opportunities
           6 -- National Aeronautics and Space Administration (NASA)
           7 -- Office of Naval Research (ONR)
           8  MOLIS System

Which agency do you want a file from?
```

Figure 5-3:
The Feds
answer your
every
question.

After this point, all you have to do is follow the menus. That's good, because there's a ton of material there — just look at the menus in Figure 5-3. You keep answering questions, the system keeps giving you choices.

One step back

You, the astute reader (hey, I figure you're all astute, since you had enough sense to get this book) may raise some questions at this point. How did I know *where* to telnet? Actually, I got the information from a list provided by my own Internet host as I experimented. Unless you have the worst service provider on earth, customer support at your own service can send you a list of telnet sites to try (send an e-mail message to customer support).

There's a Macintosh HyperCard stack called HytelNet that has a big directory of resources you can search off-line. You could also try sites from Table 5-1, my list of Ten Telnet Treasures.

Table 5-1	Ten Telnet Treasures	
Telnet to:	*Login as:*	*It holds*
fdabbs.fda.gov	bbs	The latest FDA warnings!
michel.ai.mit.edu	guest	A strange virtual reality world
sparc-1.law.columbia.edu	lawnet	Legal databases
coast.ucsd.edu	gopher	Everything about the oceans
nisc.jvnc.net	nicol	Directory of Internet resources
bbs.oit.unc.edu	bbs	General-purpose Internet facilities
hnsource.cc.ukans.edu	history	The login says it all
mb.com	mb	A shopping service
fedworld.doc.gov	bbs	Piles of government documents
nebbs.nersc.gov	new	K-12 education

As you might expect, there is an organized way to find stuff other than logging into one computer after another in search of gems. That's why the rest of this chapter is about searching.

Another "astute" question: how do I get those files from the big computer over there to my little Macintosh over here? That's the function of FTP (*file transfer protocol*), which is a sort of telnet-with-download-built-in that's the standard file transporter for networks on the Internet. I'll give you an FTP tour, too.

In fact, FTP is not just a good idea, it's the law, more or less. It does a high-speed file transfer from the remote computer to your Internet host. That lets other high-speed traffic pass you on the information superhighway. You can then get the file from your host to your Mac in your own quiet modem-based slow lane on the side. Most sites insist that you do your file transfers with FTP.

First You Search, and Then You FTP

A nice bunch of people at McGill University in Canada set up a computer that maintains lists of the files on a huge assortment of Internet networks. Instead of going around to computers one at a time by telnet and poking through the files, you just go to the computer at McGill. The computer is called an *Archie server*, since it maintains archives and lots of people can use it at the same time.

Archie in action

Other places, mostly universities, soon installed their own Archie servers. Figure 5-4 shows a sample search. As a demonstration, I looked for files with the name "MacTCP" in them. As a good citizen, I did the search on an Archie server in Finland at 4 a.m. Finnish time. There are only 4 million people in Finland, and even Finns have to sleep some time, so I figured the system would have room for me. The Finns were snoring, all right — I was doing the only search on the system.

Figure 5-4:
Archie goes
to Europe,
looking for
Mac
utilities.

```
OK : telnet archie.funet.fi
Trying 128.214.6.102 ...
Connected to archie.funet.fi.
Escape character is '^]'.

SunOS UNIX (archie.funet.fi)
      Finnish University and Research Network FUNET
                Information Service
Select service (gopher/www/wais/archie/exit) ? archie
Starting Archie ..

archie> set search sub
archie> prog MacTCP
# Search type: sub.
# Estimated time for completion: 23 seconds.

Host ftp.univ-rennes1.fr   (129.20.128.34)
Last updated 03:30  4 Mar 1994

   Location: /pub/Macintosh
     FILE   -rw-r--r--   51769 bytes  14:46  4 Feb 1994  MacTCP_2.0.2_->_2.0.x
     FILE   -rw-r--r--   68246 bytes  14:47  4 Feb 1994  MacTCP_Guide.sea.hqx
     FILE   -rw-r--r--   87986 bytes  14:47  4 Feb 1994  MacTCP_Watcher_1.1.0x
```

You can see the first part of the search results near the bottom of the figure. In 23 seconds, as advertised by the FUNET system, Archie found 200 sites with files on MacTCP (the other sites take 20 pages).

Figure 5-4 demonstrates two key points. Once again, you get into another network with telnet. That's what I meant when I said that telnet is really the fundamental Internet trick. The second point is that Archie by itself is a bit cryptic. It can manage all kinds of fancy searches, but it's not easy to use. That's why I'm going to tell you about Gopher.

CyberRodents, InfoBurrows, HyperMice, TeleDogs, InterCats...

AAAAAGGHH! Excuse me, please. I really dislike words with capital letters in the middle. And I hate cute names for programs. The one exception is Gopher (as TurboGopher for the Mac), which is so useful that they could have called it Mucus and it would still be one of my favorites.

Going pher it

Gopher is a menu system that directs searches at different Archie servers. You connect to a Gopher server, and make choices from the menus. That's it.

In the background, Gopher furiously telnets to different Archie servers, formulates searches, hauls the results back, and presents them to you. These Gophers are all connected to other Gophers, presumably with tunnels dug right through the earth. The Big Gopher in Minnesota is connected to all of them. If you have to start a search somewhere, telnet to `consultant.micro.umn.edu` and log in as "gopher."

In Figure 5-5, I connected to my own Internet host, and then telnetted to a Gopher site, this time in Australia. At this point, all I need to know is how to type what I want without misspelling it. In this sense, a Gopher search is better than doing Archie directly yourself. Not only does it require less planning from you, but it gets in and out of its own Archie connections thousands of times faster than you can, conserving Net resources.

Figure 5-5: The friendly, albeit text-based, world of standard Gopher.

```
OK : telnet info.anu.edu.au
Trying 150.203.84.20 ...
Connected to info.anu.edu.au.
|
|                    |Welcome to ELISA
|
| Welcome to the wonderful world of Gopher!
              Search Gopherspace: Jughead & Veronica

--> 1. Search GopherSpace: Veronica (AARNet, Australia) <?>
    2. Scope of AARNet Australian Veronica Server.
    3. Search GopherSpace: Veronica & Jughead (Other Servers)/
    4. About using the Veronica databases.
    5. About using the Jughead databases.
    6. FAQ: Frequently-Asked Questions about veronica  (1993-08-23).
    7. Archie (searching anonymous ftp sites) Via Texas A&M/
    8. How to Compose Veronica Queries.

+--------------Search GopherSpace: Veronica (AARNet, Australia)--------------+
|
| Words to search for  MacTCP
|
|                 [Cancel ^G] [Accept - Enter]
|
+---------------------------------------------------------------------------+
```

Too much fun?

What, you inquire sweetly, am I doing in Australia for this search? On the day I did it, I couldn't get into the Big Gopher, as it was too busy, nor yet the Gopher at infopath.ucsd.edu (my dear old *alma mater*, in fact). Neither could I reach the Gopher at scilibx.ucsc.edu, where one logs in as "infoslug" (the sports teams at UC Santa Cruz are inspirationally named after the banana slug — no kidding). The Internet is getting to be a crowded place.

But think of the snoring Finns and remember: it's always 4 a.m. somewhere, and the main users of a given network are still the locals. Pick a good time, and then get in and get out before they wake up!

FTP — Fetch This Phile!

Using Gopher, you can find all sorts of files out there on the Internet. Now you have to get them back to your Macintosh. That's when you use FTP.

Figure 5-6 shows a typical FTP session. There's really not much to it. You issue the FTP command followed by the name of the Internet host that has the files. That gets you connected, because, like practically every other Internet function, FTP has its own built-in analog of telnet. On some systems, it's more typical to sign on with this sequence:

```
OK: FTP
FTP> open
(to) archive.wherever.com
```

But your own Internet host is supposed to tell you all that.

```
OK: ftp mac.archive.umich.edu
Connected to mac.archive.umich.edu.
220 pogue.admin.lsa.umich.edu FTP server (ULTRIX Version 4.1 Tue Mar 19 00:38:1.

Name (mac.archive.umich.edu:chseiter): anonymous
331 Guest login ok, send ident as password.
Password:

230 Guest login ok, access restrictions apply.
ftp> get 00readme.txt
200 PORT command successful.
150 Opening data connection for 00readme.txt (198.93.4.10,52382) (5999 bytes).
226 Transfer complete.
local: 00readme.txt remote: 00readme.txt
6122 bytes received in 0.4 seconds (15 Kbytes/s)

ftp> bye
```

Figure 5-6:
This FTP session takes me to a big archive in Michigan.

In this case, I already knew that a plain text file called 00readme.txt was waiting at the Internet host in the main directory. If you don't know in advance which file you will be looking for, please read the sidebar on FTP tips and traps and then look at Figure 5-7. Screens like this are the main reason why this edition of *The Internet For Macs For Dummies* is an extended plea for using national on-line services to get the 500 favorite Mac files. Right now, you and I are treated to the Internet equivalent of a guy with a free airline pass flying to Sydney to buy a Coke. Think globally, act locally (or at least act on your local network, if possible).

```
OK: ftp wuarchive.wustl.edu
Connected to wuarchive.wustl.edu.
220 wuarchive.wustl.edu FTP server (Version wu-2.3(1) Fri Apr 8 14:26:26 CDT
19.
Name (wuarchive.wustl.edu:chseiter): anonymous

530-Sorry, there are too many anonymous FTP users using the system at this
530-time.  Please try again in a few minutes.
530-
530-There is currently a limit of 200 anonymous users.  Yes, there REALLY are
530-that many users on wuarchive -- this message is not the result of a bug.

530 User anonymous access denied.
Login failed.
```

Figure 5-7:
Uh-oh.
Internet
logjam!

Digging Deeper

Of course, there's more to life than finding and retrieving files. Hey, even *I* think so, and file-hunting is about all I've done for the past six months. You may want some information and not have much idea where it might be stored. The information you want might be stored under a funny filename that doesn't tell much about what's in the file.

As the Internet has expanded to the point where it's barely searchable even by a Gopher, two new tools, described in the following sections, have emerged from the laboratories of various advanced thinkers. Actually, this business is very important — the tools are a model for retrieving electronically-stored information in general. In the next few decades, that will mean practically all information.

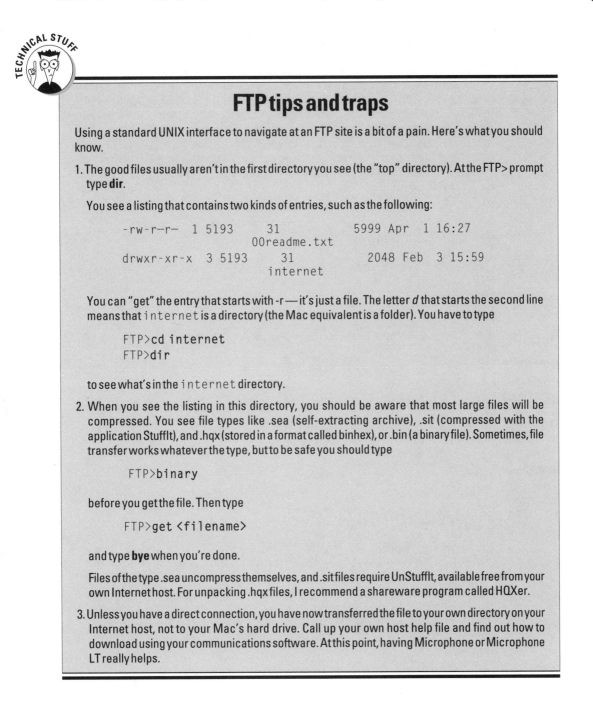

FTP tips and traps

Using a standard UNIX interface to navigate at an FTP site is a bit of a pain. Here's what you should know.

1. The good files usually aren't in the first directory you see (the "top" directory). At the FTP> prompt type **dir**.

   You see a listing that contains two kinds of entries, such as the following:

   ```
   -rw-r--r--  1 5193      31        5999 Apr  1 16:27
                       00readme.txt
   drwxr-xr-x  3 5193      31        2048 Feb  3 15:59
                       internet
   ```

   You can "get" the entry that starts with -r — it's just a file. The letter *d* that starts the second line means that internet is a directory (the Mac equivalent is a folder). You have to type

   ```
   FTP>cd internet
   FTP>dir
   ```

   to see what's in the internet directory.

2. When you see the listing in this directory, you should be aware that most large files will be compressed. You see file types like .sea (self-extracting archive), .sit (compressed with the application StuffIt), and .hqx (stored in a format called binhex), or .bin (a binary file). Sometimes, file transfer works whatever the type, but to be safe you should type

   ```
   FTP>binary
   ```

   before you get the file. Then type

   ```
   FTP>get <filename>
   ```

   and type **bye** when you're done.

   Files of the type .sea uncompress themselves, and .sit files require UnStuffIt, available free from your own Internet host. For unpacking .hqx files, I recommend a shareware program called HQXer.

3. Unless you have a direct connection, you have now transferred the file to your own directory on your Internet host, not to your Mac's hard drive. Call up your own host help file and find out how to download using your communications software. At this point, having Microphone or Microphone LT really helps.

Info from everywhere with WAIS

The first tool is WAIS, for *wide area information server*. A WAIS database is an index of keywords in the text of its files, so you can search what's *inside* those files. Figure 5-8 shows an edited transcript of a plain-text WAIS search — the main point is that the search turns up lots of sources of information where the keywords turn up in the *description* of the files, rather than just the file names. Most of the time, when you call up a Gopher server, you'll see a WAIS option (our Australian adventure included one). Using WAIS requires no special skills, so if you find yourself with access to a WAIS server, just jump in and start answering the prompts.

```
OK: telnet quake.think.com
Trying 192.31.181.1 ...
Connected to quake.think.com.

login: wais
Welcome to swais.

SWAIS                          Source Selection              Sources:  1
  #             Server                    Source                Cost
001: * [    quake.think.com]  directory-of-servers            Free
Keywords: bootstrap  statistics
Found 13 items.
SWAIS                          Search Results                Items: 13
  #    Score     Source                    Title              Lines
~~~~~~~~~~~~~
006:   [ 858] (directory-of-se)  bit.listserv.cdromlan            22
007:   [ 858] (directory-of-se)  cool                            108
008:   [ 858] (directory-of-se)  queueing-literature-database    157
009:   [ 858] (directory-of-se)  sas-archive                      14
010:   [ 858] (directory-of-se)  spss-archive                     15
011:   [ 858] (directory-of-se)  statfaqs                         17
~~~~~~~~~~~~~
```

Figure 5-8:
WAIS gets
the *inside*
information
on file
sources.

Hyperactivity: WWW

A very ambitious project called WWW (*World Wide Web*), uses another search technology. WWW is essentially a database made of linked hypertext documents. You call up a starting screen, and some of the words on the screen are highlighted or underlined. Select a word (in the clunky plain-text version, you do this with arrow keys), press Return, and you get a new screen. Of course, to the poor old Netheads who have been using UNIX for years, this technology seems pretty futuristic. If you're a longtime Mac user, you'll be harder to impress.

During 1994, the WWW sphere absolutely exploded. When the first edition *of The Internet For Macs For Dummies* was sent to press in July, the WWW still had only a handful of servers. Now it has hundreds. By mid-1995, it should have thousands. WWW is becoming *the* repository of information for business and science and computing, and information for goofing around. That's why this book (from your friends at IDG, the organization that never sleeps) now has a whole chapter (Chapter 8) of the main WWW browser, a program called Mosaic.

Back to the Mac

So far, I've been using the Mac as if it were just a VT-102 terminal. No Finder, no folders, no icons, no menus, no mouse — you may as well be computing in 1975.

Here is a short preview of Internet navigation with real Macintosh software. Right now, the problem is that you need some kind of direct connection to the Internet to use Mac software: either you're direct-wired to an Internet host at work or at a school, or you have a SLIP account with a service provider.

This access situation will change during the next year. Merry elves at the major national on-line services are diligently cannibalizing the best features of these Mac products, and you're going to be able to get most of the cool real-Mac features of the programs here just by signing up with a service. If you're a student at the University of Minnesota, this won't matter much, but if you're an individual Mac user in Dayton, Ohio, it's big news. Meanwhile, compare a few of these screens to what you've seen earlier in this chapter.

Archie? How about Anarchie instead?

Figure 5-9 shows an Archie search using the brilliant shareware program Anarchie. Send a nice e-mail message to peter.lewis@info.curtin.edu.au, and ask him for his current mailing address so you can send him $10 if you've downloaded Anarchie.

To use Anarchie: Type your search terms, click find, and you get a lovely, completely specified list of matching files. It still uses UNIX search terminology, but it's so fast (and has built-in search limiting) that you can just experiment until you get the hang of it.

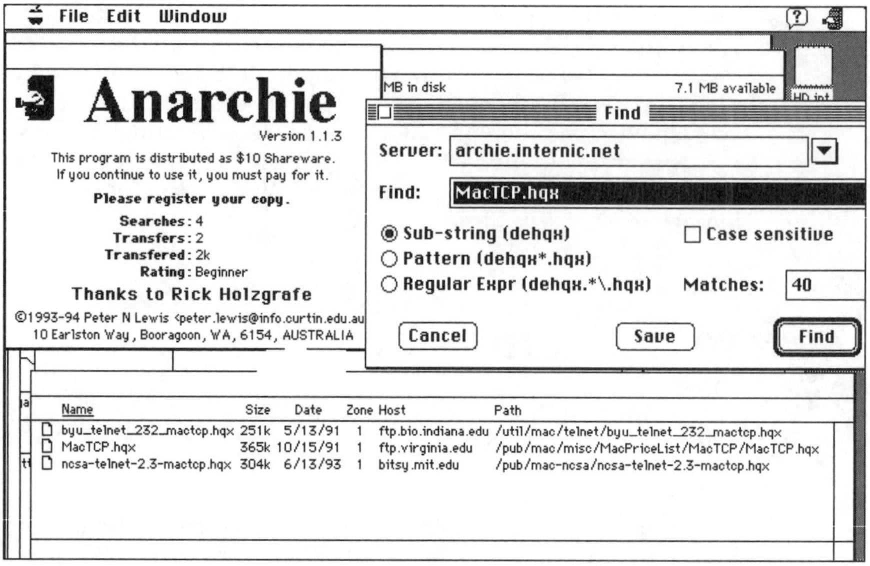

Figure 5-9:
Anarchie,
file-finding
at warp
speed.

TurboGopher, the runnin' rodent

This program, from the University of Minnesota, practically turns the rest of the world into one big directory. It's preloaded with the most useful Mac software sites, so it knows the right places to look when you start it.

As Figure 5-10 shows, you can operate this program if you know how to open a folder on your Mac. When it's working, a hilarious little cartoon of a Gopher scampers along on your screen. These people invented Gopher stuff, and this product is king of the Gophers.

Fetch: the super retriever

Fetch, from Dartmouth University, is a Mac replacement for FTP (see Figure 5-11). That's an understatement. If you've been stuck poking your way through UNIX directories on remote machines, Fetch will knock you flat — it brings back everything but a Frisbee. Like TurboGopher, it already knows where to look, so it doesn't have to nose through sites with hundreds of UNIX utilities you'll never need. You click Get File, and you get the file. It was supposed to be that way all along.

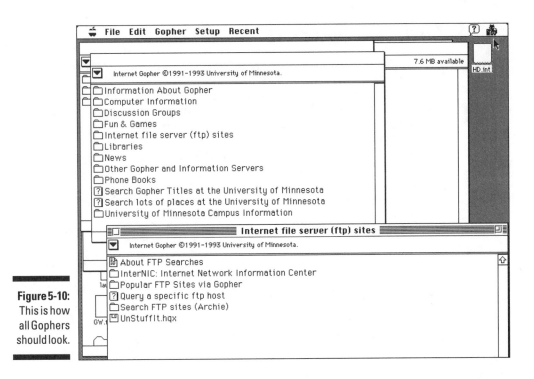

Figure 5-10:
This is how
all Gophers
should look.

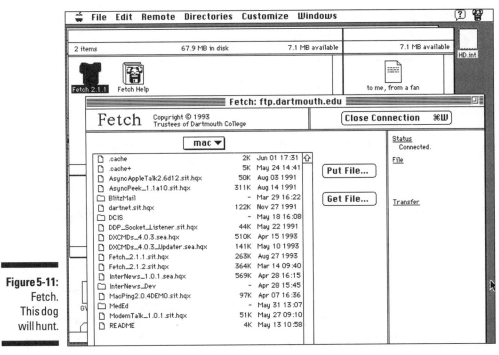

Figure 5-11:
Fetch.
This dog
will hunt.

Easy WAIS to do it

WAIS, even standard WAIS, is pretty easy because all you do is follow menus. MacWAIS, shown in Figure 5-12, requires that you double-click the MacWAIS icons and then type in your search terms in the dialog box and click the Ask button. This little gem of a program logs itself onto the appropriate host, finds everything, and reports back to you in a few seconds. MacWAIS is shareware, so send some e-mail to mac-shareware@einet.net for the latest information. If you're really interested in WAIS searches, you'll want this program.

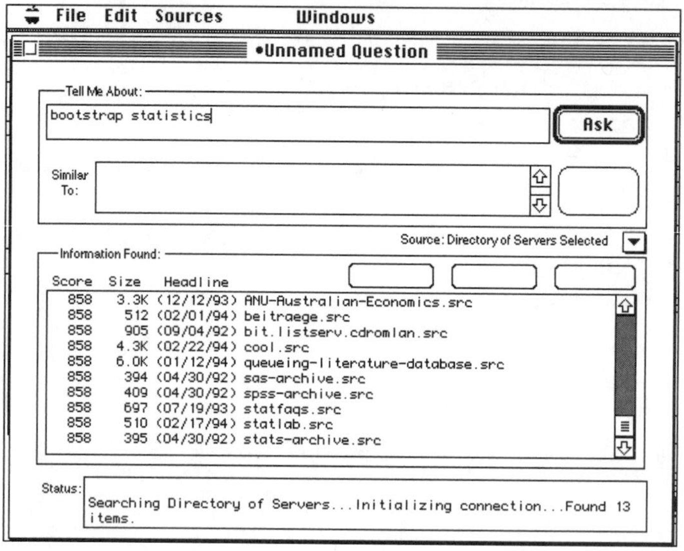

Figure 5-12:
MacWAIS
delivers the
goods.

Something for everyone

You may have noticed that every individual UNIX command seems to have turned into a whole Macintosh program. Is there any way to get most Internet features in a single package?

Yes, briefly. That's why IDG included a disk in this book for the all-in-one, real Internet service from Intercon. In the next chapter, I show you how to sign on and get started so that you can try all the Internet facilities in this chapter and e-mail besides.

The other way, which I explore in Chapters 9 through 11, is to take on-line services that already exist and see what combination of Mac features and Internet services you can find on each one. The Internet aspects of most services used to be pretty limited, but, by late 1994, they started to offer what even grudging Net old-timers were forced to admit was the "real thing." People wanted it, and someone delivered — it works for pizza, it works for the Internet. (Actually, in many communities you can order pizza on the Internet!)

Part II
Internet via Pipeline and Mosaic

The 5th Wave — By Rich Tennant

"All through High School he wouldn't talk to anyone-hardly said a word. Now he's graduating from an Ivy League college with an advanced degree in communications."

In this part...

1n this part, you'll finally find out about Pipeline, TCP Connect II, and Mosaic, the king of browsers. Here, you'll enter the world of cyberspace and gopher your way through discussions of hypertext, MacTCP, and InterSLIP as you try not to get caught (unexpectedly) in the World Wide Web.

Chapter 6

Pipeline

Transitions

This chapter gives you a survey of Pipeline, one of the software applications included with this book. Pipeline was founded by the science author James Gleick, mainly because Gleick saw a need for a simpler kind of Internet access than was available in 1993. He also, earlier than most observers, saw the need for a commercial service that preserved some of the altruistic spirit of the original Internet pioneers.

Pipeline was an immediate success. It was so successful that handling the details of signing up new members and providing customer support became somewhat overwhelming. The people at InterCon (developers of TCP Connect II Remote) thus formulated a deal with Pipeline involving customer-support management and software licensing rights, presumably giving the beleaguered Mr. Gleick and his associates a chance to sleep at night again.

As this was written, it wasn't clear whether this service would continue to be named Pipeline or whether InterCon would provide service through a renamed gateway called InterCon Online. But, although a company can buy a service in a few months and change its name in a week, it takes years to develop content. So the *description* of this Internet service and how it works will be valid no matter what arrangement the lawyers produce. Check the ReadMe file on the Pipeline disk for the latest hilarity on this count.

Making Things Click

What Gleick realized was that the standard UNIX command-line interface could be replaced by icons and dialog boxes, both in the Mac and Windows versions of Pipeline. The big computer at the other end of the wire doesn't know that you are simply clicking icons — if you could intercept the stream of characters flying out of your modem you would find that you are actually issuing UNIX commands as fast as you can click. The interface programming thus reduces to a translation task, and the Pipeline team did a brilliant job of it.

Follow the instructions in the Pipeline ReadMe file and look up your local phone number in the SprintNet file. Double-click the Pipeline icon to get started (see Figure 6-1). Under the Internet menu is the Connect command. Select this command and note that the Show settings for: scrolling list is where you stash most of your setup information. The phone number goes in the Phone dialog box, modem speed goes in the Connection box, modem type is selected in the Modem box, Sprint vs. direct dial goes in the Access box, and Session contains your Login name and Password.

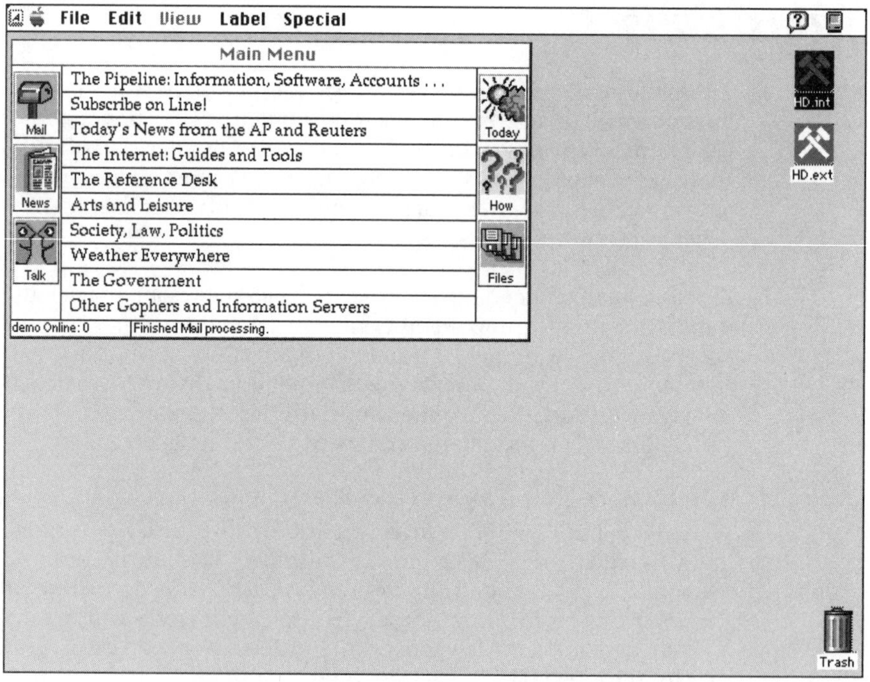

Figure 6-1:
Pipeline's
main menu:
simple but
powerful.

By the way, you might want to use the New York number 1-212-267-8606 for the first two or three sessions. It's not that expensive if you do it late at night and only sign on for a few minutes, and you can make sure everything's working properly before you start using your SprintNet local number. That is, if you can't get on through the New York number, it means you have to do some reconfiguration. If you start directly with Sprint, you often won't know whether there is some funny business in your Sprint connection or whether you have a problem with your Pipeline account itself.

Stuff Central

Einstein said that in science, everything should be made as simple as possible, but not simpler. That's the situation with Pipeline. These simple menu selections lead you to the whole rest of the Internet.

Look at The Reference Desk, just one of Pipeline's proprietary services (see Figure 6-2). It leads to the services of an Internet hyper-library, where electronic journals and reference books and directories are all available, up to and including the catalog of the Library of Congress.

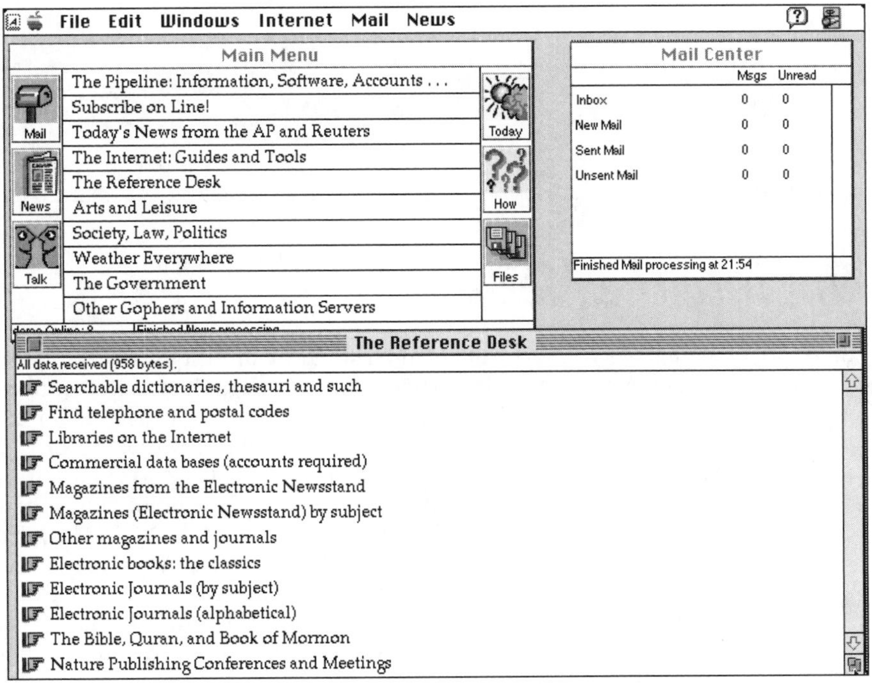

Figure 6-2:
Newspapers,
magazines,
dictionaries,
and more.

The mail system is also the ultimate in simplicity (and an e-mail address at
`pipeline.com` has rather more cachet than an address at a Here-Comes-
Everybody national on-line service. You get a little dialog box giving you your
mail status (see Figure 6-3), and you write your e-mail in a standard form that
looks a bit like a telegram. Just double-click on the New Mail line to read your mail.

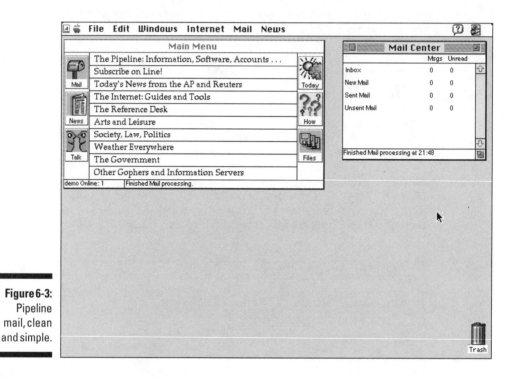

Figure 6-3:
Pipeline
mail, clean
and simple.

Out into the Net

Pipeline lets you reach out to most standard Internet services. The deceptively
unassuming menu choice Other Gophers... might just as well be named "everything else on the Net." For starters, you can get to the original Gopher service at
the University of Minnesota (see Figure 6-4). If you're looking for files you have
read about in the burgeoning world of Internet literature, you can take a site
and filename directly into Pipeline's Archie/FTP combination (see Figure 6-5)
instead and fetch the file. (That's one easy way to get NCSA Mosaic 2.0 from the
site `ncsa.uiuc.edc`) You can also get to other Gophers and search services
(see Figure 6-6) from this menu at `umn.edu` or as a choice from the Internet
menu from the Main Menu. In other words, from Pipeline you can get the same
Gopher services you would get from TurboGopher and a SLIP connection,
without the software setup adventures.

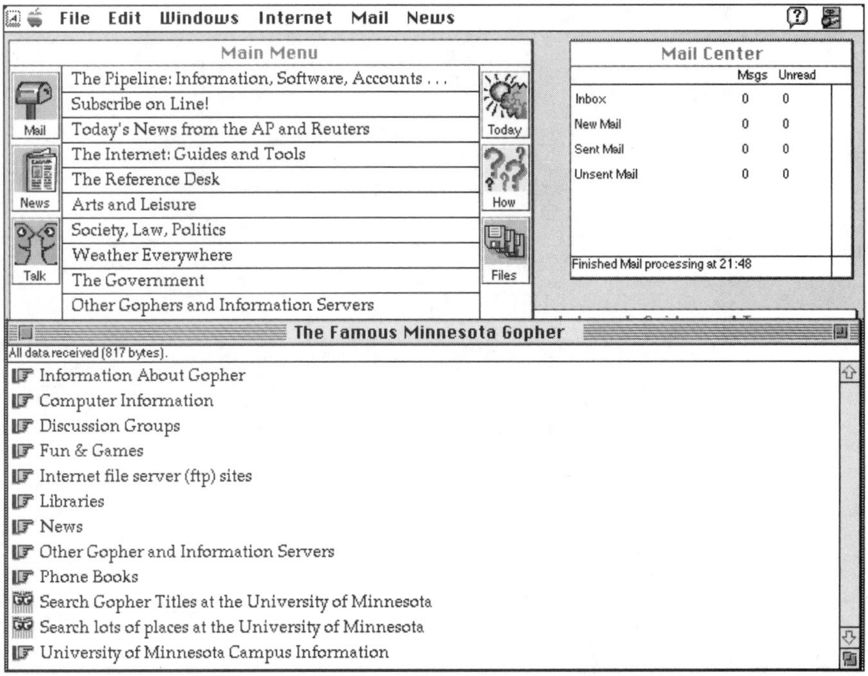

Figure 6-4:
Go Gophers!
Minnesota
via Pipeline.

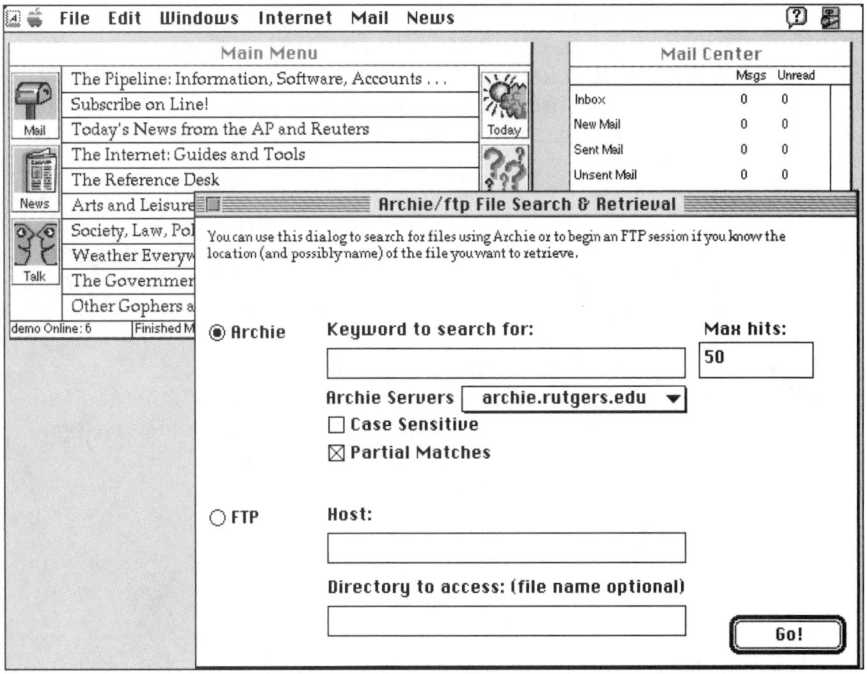

Figure 6-5:
An
accessible
Archie, a
fabulous
FTP.

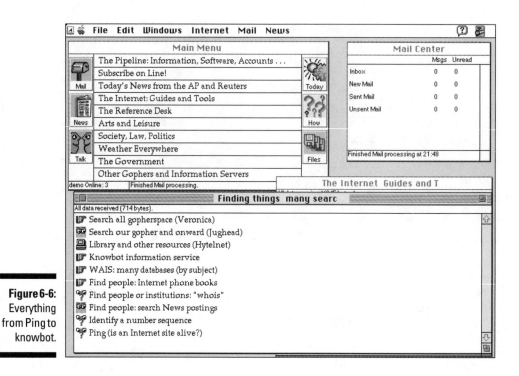

Figure 6-6:
Everything
from Ping to
knowbot.

One of Pipeline's big information advantages is that because James Gleick is affiliated with the New York Times, he set up this service with better traditional and non-traditional news links than most. There's a separate Internet news service (see Figure 6-7) in the Internet menu, and you can also check out Wiretap (see Figure 6-8), a major repository of weirdness and adventure.

You are likely to have more questions about navigation than any other topic, so Pipeline is preloaded with helpful navigation facts. At any time, just click the Internet Guides and Tools topic (see Figure 6-9) for Internet tutorials, or, better yet, click the How? topic to get a set of short guides to finding your way in the world's largest maze (see Figure 6-10).

Please note that it is quite possible to get lost on the Internet and, worse, lose track of time. Unless you have opted for Pipeline's Unlimited Time plan, this could get expensive. It's always a best bet to formulate a navigation plan with How? before actually setting forth.

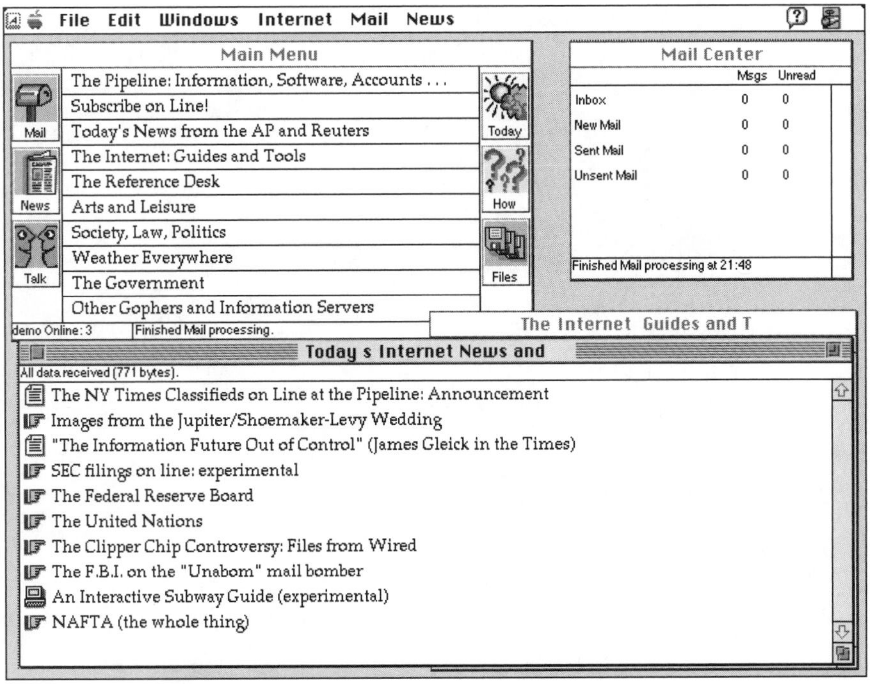

File   Edit   Windows   Internet   Mail   News

	Main Menu		Mail Center
	The Pipeline: Information, Software, Accounts . . .		Msgs Unread
Mail	Subscribe on Line!	Today	Inbox 0 0
	Today's News from the AP and Reuters		New Mail 0 0
	The Internet: Guides and Tools		Sent Mail 0 0
News	The Reference Desk	How	Unsent Mail 0 0
	Arts and Leisure		
Talk	Society, Law, Politics		
	Weather Everywhere	Files	Finished Mail processing at 21:48
	The Government		
	Other Gophers and Information Servers		

demo Online: 3   Finished Mail processing.

The Internet Guides and T

Today's Internet News and

All data received (771 bytes).

- The NY Times Classifieds on Line at the Pipeline: Announcement
- Images from the Jupiter/Shoemaker-Levy Wedding
- "The Information Future Out of Control" (James Gleick in the Times)
- SEC filings on line: experimental
- The Federal Reserve Board
- The United Nations
- The Clipper Chip Controversy: Files from Wired
- The F.B.I. on the "Unabom" mail bomber
- An Interactive Subway Guide (experimental)
- NAFTA (the whole thing)

Figure 6-7:
Internet
news,
including
the latest
from Mr.
Gleick
himself.

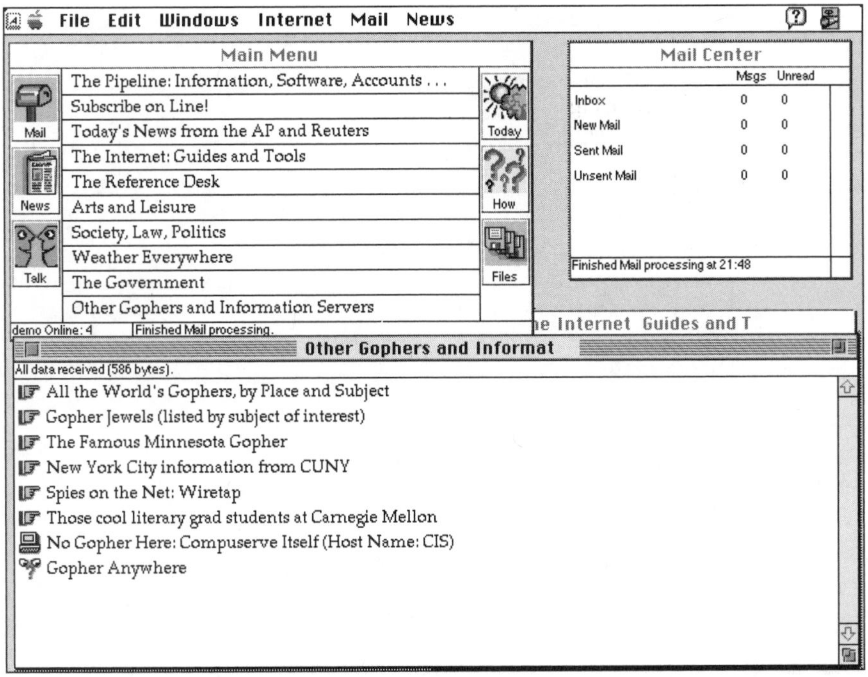

File   Edit   Windows   Internet   Mail   News

	Main Menu		Mail Center
	The Pipeline: Information, Software, Accounts . . .		Msgs Unread
Mail	Subscribe on Line!	Today	Inbox 0 0
	Today's News from the AP and Reuters		New Mail 0 0
	The Internet: Guides and Tools		Sent Mail 0 0
News	The Reference Desk	How	Unsent Mail 0 0
	Arts and Leisure		
Talk	Society, Law, Politics		
	Weather Everywhere	Files	Finished Mail processing at 21:48
	The Government		
	Other Gophers and Information Servers		

demo Online: 4   Finished Mail processing.

he Internet Guides and T

Other Gophers and Informat

All data received (586 bytes).

- All the World's Gophers, by Place and Subject
- Gopher Jewels (listed by subject of interest)
- The Famous Minnesota Gopher
- New York City information from CUNY
- Spies on the Net: Wiretap
- Those cool literary grad students at Carnegie Mellon
- No Gopher Here: Compuserve Itself (Host Name: CIS)
- Gopher Anywhere

Figure 6-8:
Walk on the
wild side
with
Wiretap.

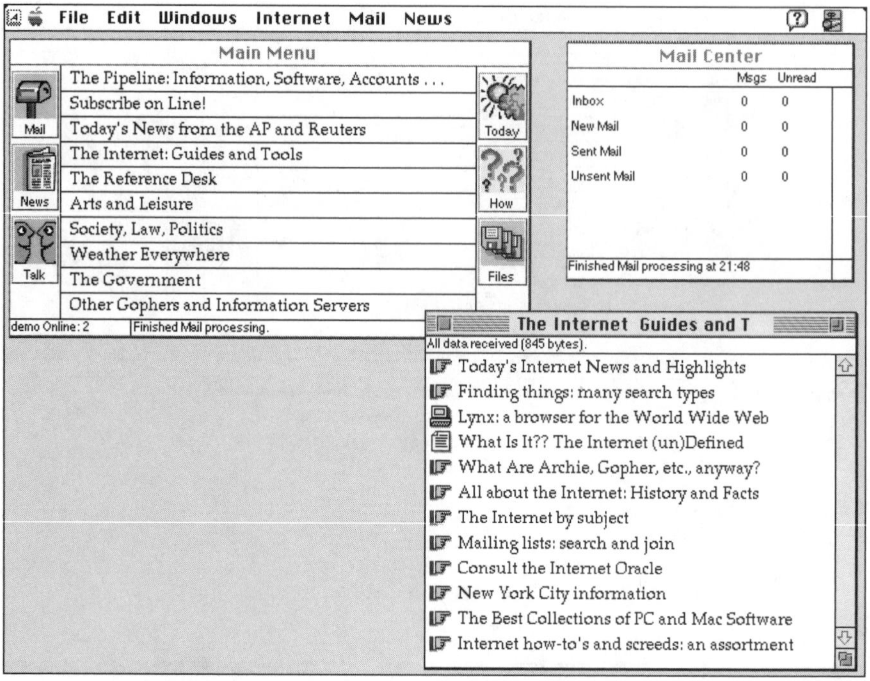

Figure 6-9: The Internet Guide, an instant refresher course.

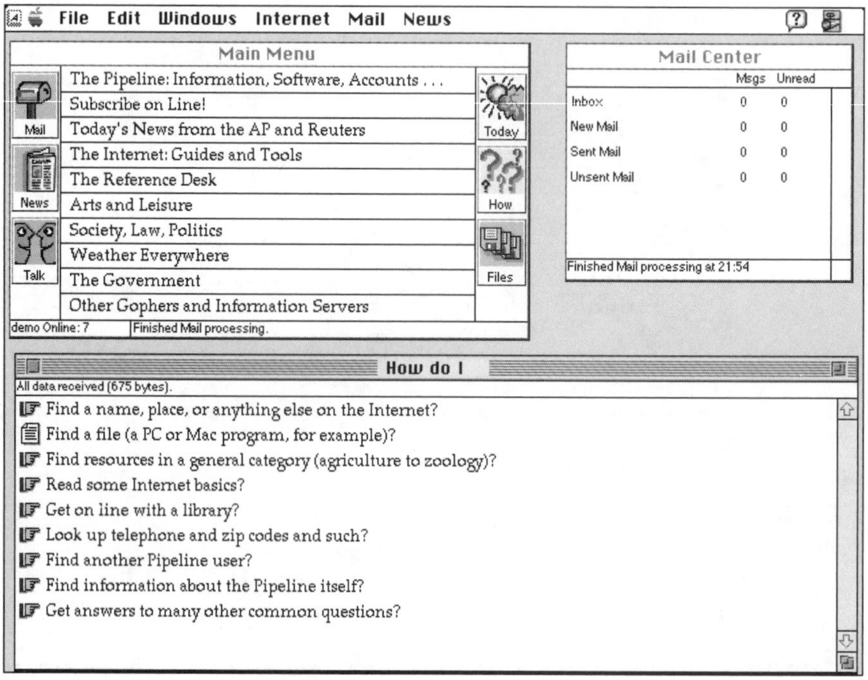

Figure 6-10: Pipeline How?, a superior help system.

Short-Order Menu

Some of the nicer features of Pipeline are arranged as their own menu areas. You could find most of this material by diligent navigation and Gopher burrowing, but Pipeline has brought it right to the surface. The Government (see Figure 6-11) takes you right to the White House, the Senate, and—above all—the giant FEDIX service, official database of the ominously named FedWorld. (I personally find the name FedWorld to be a more potent nightmare-inducer than Dracula movies.)

You can also get an assortment of the top news stories on the Associated press wire (see Figure 6-12). As a little experiment, you can sign onto Pipeline fifteen minutes before the national news goes on TV in your area. Then check out the top five or six stories, and see which ones don't make it onto TV. For fast-breaking news stories, you can examine the evolution of the story over a 24-hour period. After a bit of this, you'll realize that you could do a perfectly competent job of being your own news service.

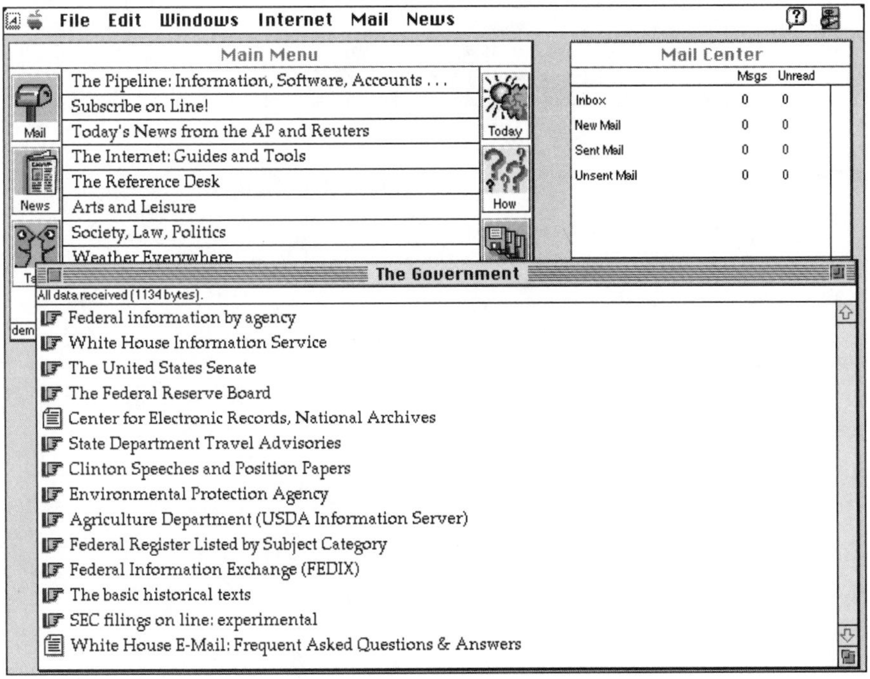

Figure 6-11:
The Feds
get Net-
ready.

Pipeline, although it's an excellent general-purpose entry point to the Internet, still has a sort of high-brow, New York Times Review of Books flavor. The Arts and Leisure service (see Figure 6-13) includes sports schedules and games, but there's an emphasis on more cultural pursuits. As the concept of virtual art galleries and virtual museums comes to be more widely embraced, you may find that a Pipeline connection in Tonopah, NV gives you a cultural life that previously would have require a residence somewhere in the East 60s in Manhattan.

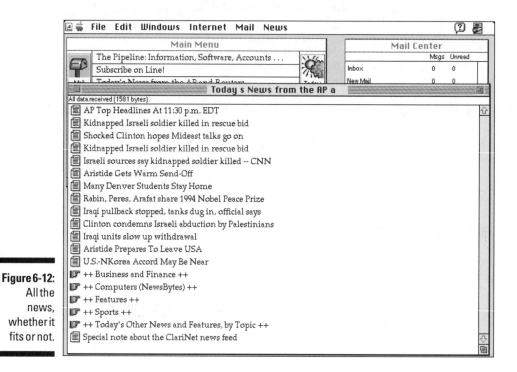

Figure 6-12:
All the news, whether it fits or not.

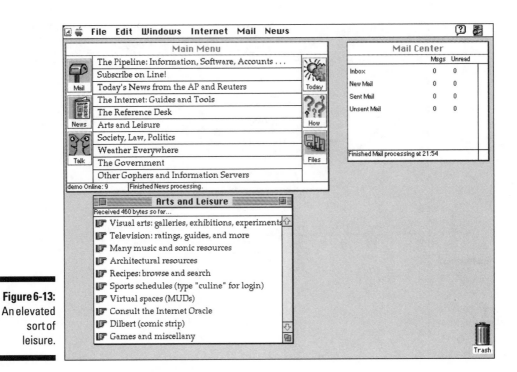

Figure 6-13:
An elevated
sort of
leisure.

Mosaic on Pipeline?

Well, not just yet exactly. Using Pipeline's Lynx program (see Figure 6-14), you can get all the information that's on the World Wide Web, and at standard modem speeds, this character-based approach is often preferable to the full bells-and-whistles approach of Mosaic. Nonetheless, it obviously has not escaped the attention of Mr. Gleick and his top-notch software staff that a Mosaic-clone Web browser is going to be a big priority for users, and a Web browser that includes pictures and sounds will probably be ready in early 1995.

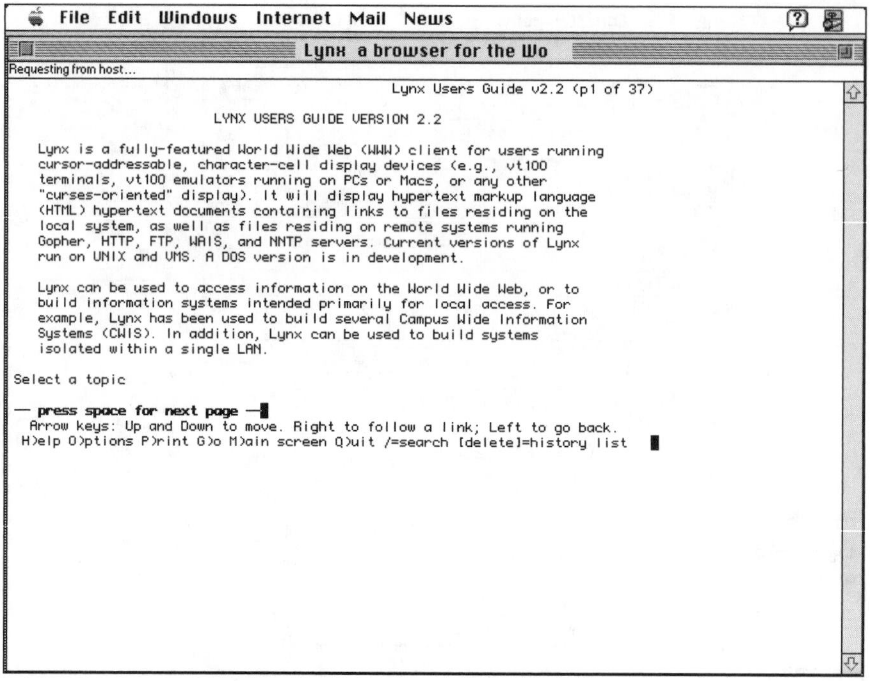

```
   File   Edit   Windows   Internet   Mail   News                    ⑦ 圝

                       Lynx  a browser for the Wo

Requesting from host...
                                        Lynx Users Guide v2.2 (p1 of 37)

                        LYNX USERS GUIDE VERSION 2.2

     Lynx is a fully-featured World Wide Web (WWW) client for users running
     cursor-addressable, character-cell display devices (e.g., vt100
     terminals, vt100 emulators running on PCs or Macs, or any other
     "curses-oriented" display). It will display hypertext markup language
     (HTML) hypertext documents containing links to files residing on the
     local system, as well as files residing on remote systems running
     Gopher, HTTP, FTP, WAIS, and NNTP servers. Current versions of Lynx
     run on UNIX and VMS. A DOS version is in development.

     Lynx can be used to access information on the World Wide Web, or to
     build information systems intended primarily for local access. For
     example, Lynx has been used to build several Campus Wide Information
     Systems (CWIS). In addition, Lynx can be used to build systems
     isolated within a single LAN.

Select a topic

— press space for next page —▮
  Arrow keys: Up and Down to move. Right to follow a link; Left to go back.
 H)elp O)ptions P)rint G)o M)ain screen Q)uit /=search [delete]=history list  ▮
```

Figure 6-14:
Lynx, facts
without the
flash from
WWW.

Chapter 7
TCP Connect II

● ●

In This Chapter

▶ InterCon's design philosophy

▶ Installing and configuring TCP Connect II

▶ Connect's built-in services

▶ MacTCP and InterSLIP

● ●

One-Stop Shopping

InterCon is attempting to do something interesting for Mac users, and IDG Books is trying to encourage this noble endeavor. The attempt is this: to make a *single* program that works with *any* service provider and performs *all* Internet services.

Here's the problem, to which I allude fairly obliquely in Chapter 5. If you get a SLIP (or PPP) connection, you have your choice of fabulous Internet programs. Fetch from Dartmouth is a fabulous FTP program. TurboGopher is a fabulous Gopher program. Eudora is a fabulous e-mail program.

BUT THEY'RE ALL DIFFERENT PROGRAMS!

Every time you want to do any named Internet activity, you have to switch programs. In a better world, you could check your mail and FTP from the same program, obviously, because FTP and Telnet and e-mail are all closely related network activities.

InterCon has developed TCP Connect II Extended (and Remote) to solve this specific problem. Connect (I'm going to call it Connect from now on, with due deference to InterCon Marketing's delicate sensibilities) has nearly every type of Internet facility built right in to this single program.

But...

The one thing Connect can't quite do is run Mosaic by itself. Mosaic was designed to work with MacTCP, so InterCon includes it in the Connect Extended package. With the Installer on the disk, MacTCP and InterSLIP are automatically filed in the right places in the System folder, so all you will need to do is provide a phone number and IP address from your service provider.

 Currently, InterCon is working on a Web browser that will work from within Connect, and it should be ready by January 1995. In fact, since software in books like this is continuously updated, you can expect the new version of Connect II included here in Spring 1995 to have its own Web connection. For that matter, the Pipeline staff is furiously working on a graphical Web browser for Pipeline users.

When Mosaic first appeared it seemed magical, but like many magic tricks, once you see how it works you can do it yourself. Expect half a dozen World Wide Web programs, as good or better than Mosaic, to be available during the coming year.

The Pipeline style, where a provider provides a real graphical version of every service, or the InterCon style, where a software vendor makes a general-purpose program that works with any provider, both have a place on the Internet. And either of these styles is likely to prevail over the original Internet mode, in which shareware for specific functions glued users into the Net. Lots of people will miss the free-for-all old ways of the Net, but these days it's simply become too important to be an all-volunteer activity.

First Steps

When you open the Connect folder and double-click the application icon, you should see a screen like Figure 7-1. One interesting point to note is that little buttons for text size and style are available on the tool bar. That's because this package supports MIME, a set of extensions to standard plain-text Internet e-mail that lets messages include font information, sound and pictures.

Connect will require a bit of configuration information. Under the Edit menu, the last choice is Configure, which will call up a scrolling list of icons of various services. The mail configuration (you get it by clicking the little picture of an envelope in the list) is shown in Figure 7-2 and the FTP configuration is shown in Figure 7-3. You could try to puzzle out the data to fill in these dialog boxes, but hey! this ain't shareware. There's a working customer support number at which cheerful technicians will hand-hold you through the whole process.

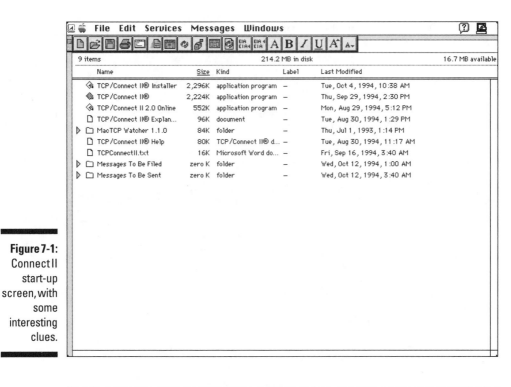

Figure 7-1:
Connect II
start-up
screen, with
some
interesting
clues.

Figure 7-2:
Connect's
mail
configuration,
which
expects you
to get an
Internet
address
from a
provider.

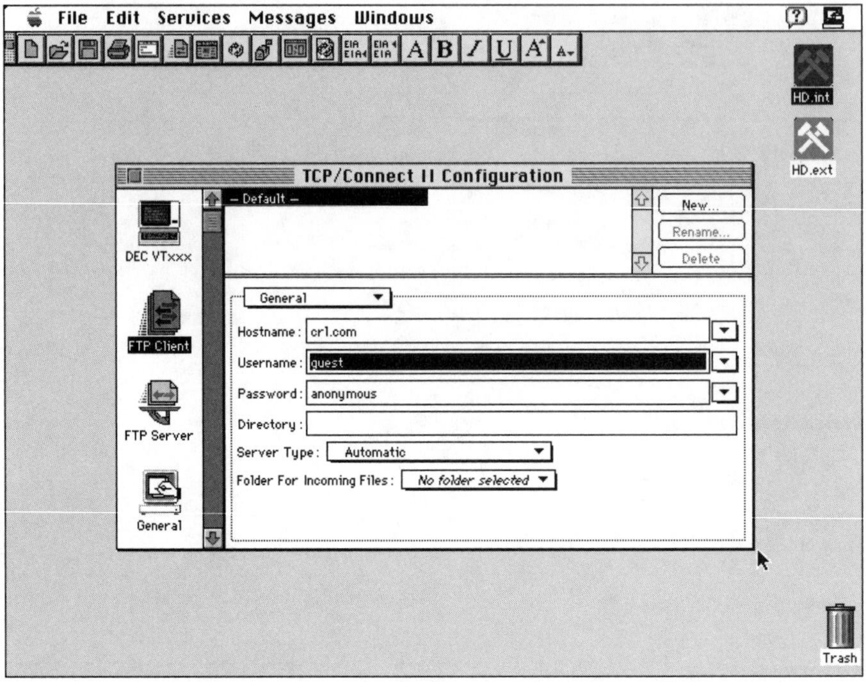

Figure 7-3:
Connect's
FTP
configuration.
You're the
client, your
service
provider is
the host.

Another advantage of the real-commercial-software approach is that the on-line help in this product is also pretty educational (see Figure 7-4). Not only does it cover configuration in detail, but it explains how to use all the built-in services (the mail explanation is particularly good).

Check out the explanation of Network configuration (see Figure 7-5) before you call InterCon, just so you'll understand what the technician is telling you. Getting a SLIP connection running from scratch isn't really a "for Dummies" activity, but it's no harder than setting up a database in Filemaker Pro, for example.

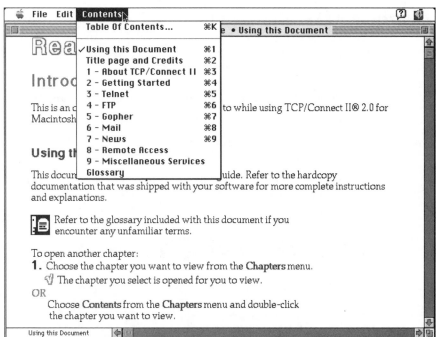

Figure 7-4:
Excellent
on-line
documen-
tation of
Connect is
included.

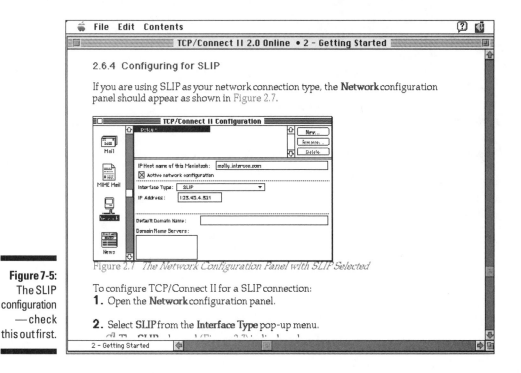

Figure 7-5:
The SLIP
configuration
— check
this out first.

Hooking Up

When you've entered the handful of configuration numbers, it's time to see what Connect can do for you:

1. **Choose Terminal from the Services menu (see Figure 7-6).**

2. **Pick Serial Port from the scrolling list of possible sessions (see Figure 7-7).**

3. **Click the Connect button, and you get the black serial-port terminal screen of Figure 7-8.**

4. **Turn on your modem, type** ATDT **to wake it up, type the phone number of your service provider (see Figure 7-9), and press Return.**

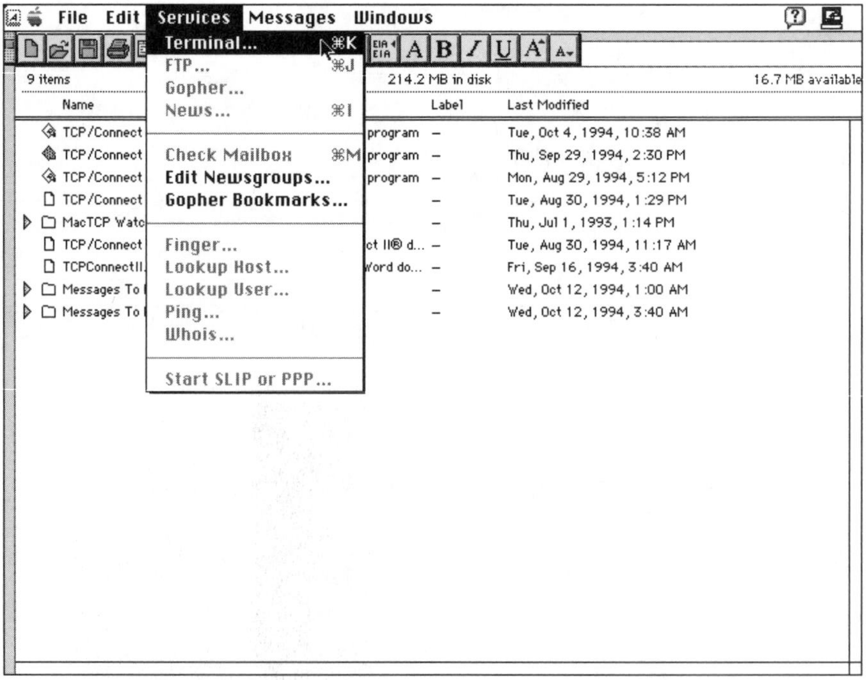

Figure 7-6:
Connecting
step 1:
Choose
Terminal.

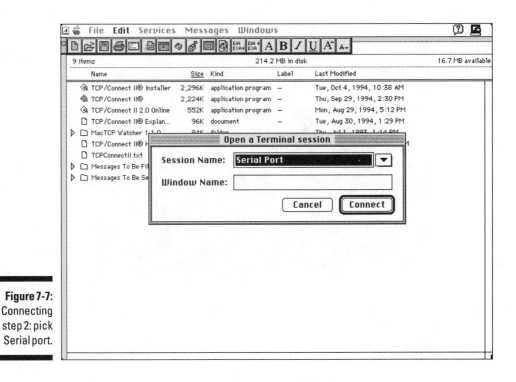

Figure 7-7:
Connecting
step 2: pick
Serial port.

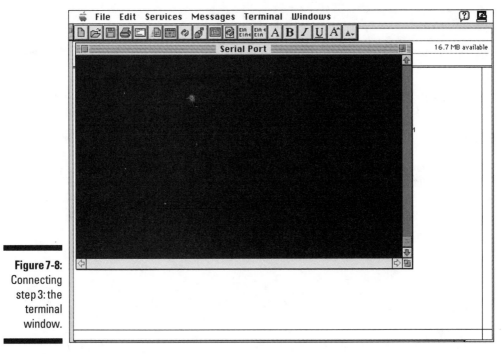

Figure 7-8:
Connecting
step 3: the
terminal
window.

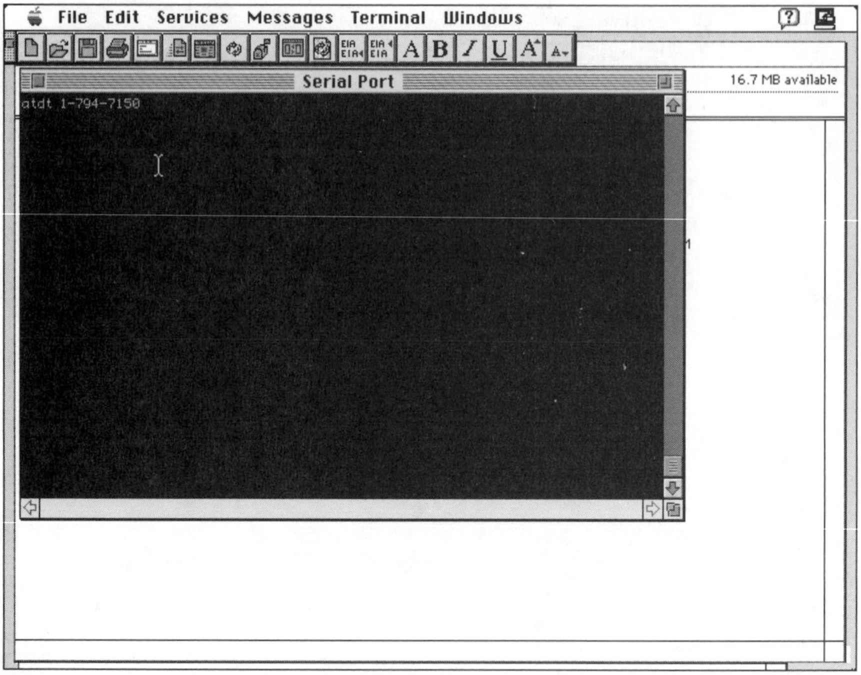

Figure 7-9:
Connecting
step 4:
Dialing the
service.

How about Some Service?

Connect II dials into the service provider, where you sign in with your screen name and password, typically (see Figure 7-10).

After you're connected, choose Start SLIP (see Figure 7-11) under the Services menu.

Now when you consult the Services menu, instead of grayed-out mush, you see the whole glorious range of Internet possibilities (see Figure 7-12), soon to include WWW as well as the older services. Connect II provides all the most useful Internet services in this one program, and typically you can connect to a SLIP provider. (PPP, Point-to-Point Protocol, is also available in Connect, although most providers are still more familiar with SLIP.)

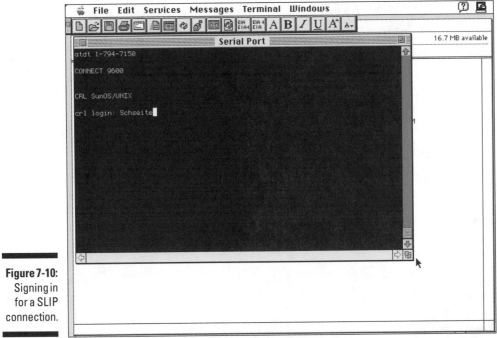

Figure 7-10:
Signing in
for a SLIP
connection.

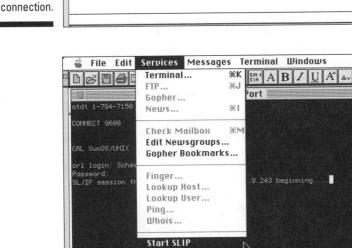

Figure 7-11:
Start SLIP,
and the real
action starts.

```
   File   Edit   Service   Messages   Windows                        ⑦ ▣
 ┌──────────────────────────────────────────────────────────────────────────┐
                     Terminal...     ⌘K   EIA◄  A  B  I  U  A⁺ A▾
                     FTP...          ⌘J   EIA
 9 items             Gopher...            214.2 MB in disk        16.7 MB available
       Name          News...         ⌘I        Label   Last Modified
      TCP/Connect                        program  —    Tue, Oct 4, 1994, 10:38 AM
      TCP/Connect    Check Mailbox    ⌘M  program  —    Thu, Sep 29, 1994, 2:30 PM
      TCP/Connect    Edit Newsgroups...    program  —  Mon, Aug 29, 1994, 5:12 PM
      TCP/Connect    Gopher Bookmarks...            —   Tue, Aug 30, 1994, 1:29 PM
   ▷  MacTCP Watc                                   —   Thu, Jul 1, 1993, 1:14 PM
      TCP/Connect    Finger...            ct II® d... — Tue, Aug 30, 1994, 11:17 AM
      TCPConnectII.  Lookup Host...       Word do... — Fri, Sep 16, 1994, 3:40 AM
   ▷  Messages To    Lookup User...                 —   Wed, Oct 12, 1994, 1:00 AM
   ▷  Messages To    Ping...                        —   Wed, Oct 12, 1994, 3:40 AM
                     Whois...

                     Stop SLIP
 └──────────────────────────────────────────────────────────────────────────┘
```

Figure 7-12:
Real
Internet, in a
convenient
Connect
package.

Each Internet service in this scheme has its own Connect dialog box — this is
in contrast to the one-program one-service approach in which you use a whole
collection of shareware. Note that this service doesn't have an Archie entry,
in recognition of the gradual replacement of Archie by Gopher as the main
Internet file search facility. Select FTP, and a simple dialog box (see Figure 7-13)
asks you for the site you wish to browse. This type of program is the future of
Internet software.

Using Mosaic with TCP Connect II

Mosaic was written with the expectation that MacTCP would be present on
your Mac. Since MacTCP was written by Apple, not InterCon, it doesn't set itself
up automatically, although the Installer on your disk has put it in the right
place.

To get Mosaic running with the software in this book (assuming you have a
copy of Mosaic, downloaded from Pipeline) or to use your included copy of
MacWeb (which in my humble opinion is slightly better than Mosaic), you have
to get MacTCP and InterSLIP configured.

Here's what you do — it's the standard SLIP drill:

1. **Find a service provider and get the customer support number.**

   Either use one of the providers shown on a coupon at the back of this book (I admit that CRL is my favorite, and I've checked them out on this routine), or find a provider by looking in a local computer tabloid. Lots of companies say "Internet"; look for one that says "SLIP" also, and hopefully, "Macintosh."

2. **Make photocopies of Figures 7-13, 7-14, 7-15, and 7-16.**

3. **Fax these figures to customer support at the service and ask the support to fill in the right numbers in the blank spaces (including where to set the little slider for Subnet Mask in Figure 7-14).**

4. **Ask customer support to fax the whole set of figures back to you with all this information marked.**

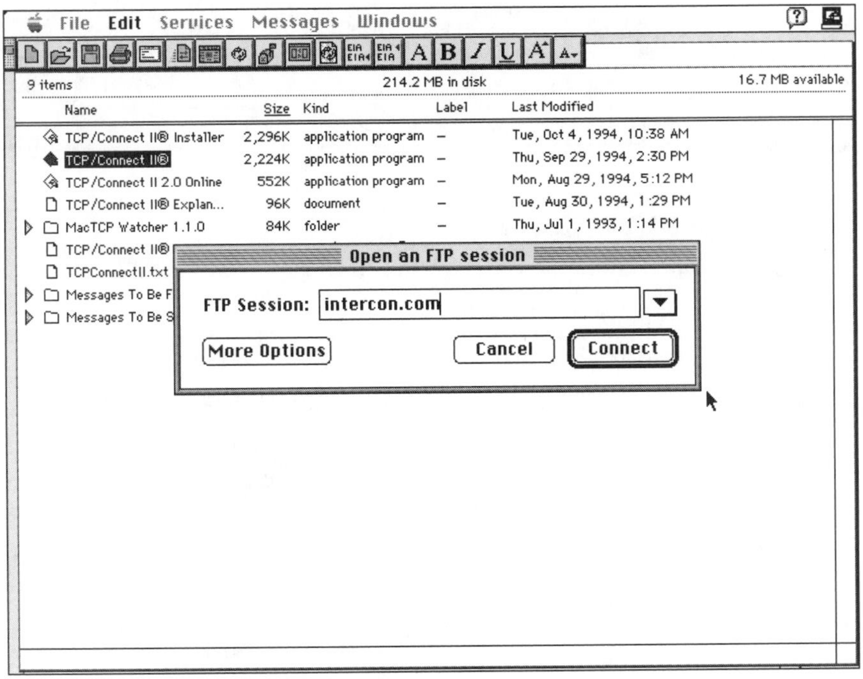

Figure 7-13:
The MacTCP
Control
Panel.

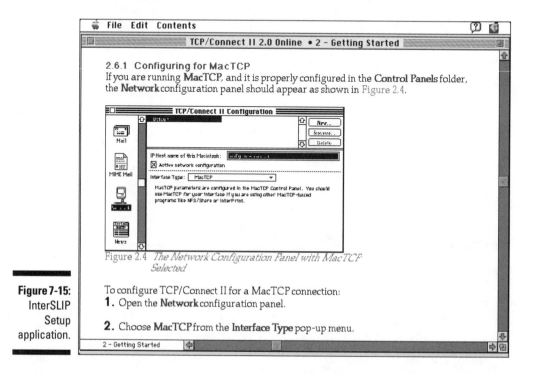

File   Edit   Options   Navigate   Hotlist

Commercial Services on the Net

URL: http://www.directory.net/

Welcome to Open Market's directory of commercial services, products, and information on the Internet.

You can access this directory in several ways:

- See **What's New** (last updated October 14)

- Enter a word or two that describes what you are looking for:

    [   ] [**Search**]

- Browse the **alphabetical listing**

See also:

- About the directory
- How to submit listings
- List of commercial servers

Do you have any comments or suggestions? Please send us your feedback!

Copyright (c) 1994, Open Market, Inc.

Figure 7-14:
MacTCP
set-up data
page.

File   Edit   Contents

TCP/Connect II 2.0 Online • 2 – Getting Started

2.6.1 Configuring for MacTCP
If you are running **MacTCP**, and it is properly configured in the **Control Panels** folder, the **Network** configuration panel should appear as shown in Figure 2.4.

TCP/Connect II Configuration

Mail

MIME Mail

News

IP Host name of this Macintosh:
☒ Active network configuration
Interface Type: MacTCP

MacTCP parameters are configured in the MacTCP Control Panel. You should use MacTCP for your interface if you are using other MacTCP-based programs like NFS/Share or InterPrint.

New...
Rename...
Delete.

Figure 2.4 *The Network Configuration Panel with MacTCP Selected*

Figure 7-15:
InterSLIP
Setup
application.

To configure TCP/Connect II for a MacTCP connection:
1. Open the **Network** configuration panel.

2. Choose **MacTCP** from the **Interface Type** pop-up menu.

2 - Getting Started

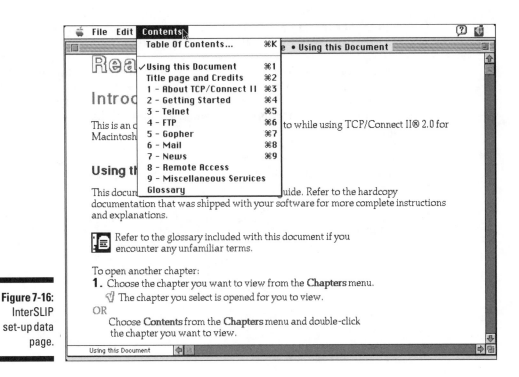

Figure 7-16:
InterSLIP
set-up data
page.

Now go through these check-out steps:

1. **Find Control Panels under the Apple menu and double-click to open it.**

   Find the MacTCP icon and double-click it. Do that now, and then come back and type in the IP Address.

2. **Double-click on the More... button.**

   Fill in the information the service gave you for Figure 7-14. Make sure you have the Obtain Address button set properly and move the Subnet Mask slider to the position the service recommended. Fill in the Domain Name Server data at lower right and pick the default.

3. **Your version of SLIP may show nothing in the scrolling list area yet.**

   Just pick New from the File menu and fill in a name in the dialog box. When you're done, click back to the window in Figure 7-15 and then double-click on your new filename. You get to a screen that looks like Figure 7-16.

4. **For Gateway, pick Simple Unix/Telebit, since you're not a direct connection.**

   Pick Hayes... under Dial Script, and pick your modem's speed. Every other bit of information should be on your back-fax of Figure 7-16.

Now double-click the InterSLIP Setup icon to get to a window like that in Figure 7-15. Click the Connect button, and InterSLIP will make your connection.

Watch the top of the window. You'll see the message change from Idle, to Dialing, to Signing In, to Connected. Sometimes you'll see it pop back to Idle. It's a good idea to check the "Speaker on" box in Figure 7-16 so you can hear whether your dial-up number is busy, or whether (as often happens) there just isn't a line.

If you have problems for more than one day, call customer support. You'd be amazed how often a service itself can make set-up mistakes that it will need to fix (get your password wrong, for example).

Once InterSLIP indicates that you're connected, just double-click your copy of the MacWeb application (or Mosaic if you prefer) and you should find yourself on a WWW home page, with plenty of topics to explore. That's the subject of the next chapter!

Chapter 8

Mosaic and the World Wide Web

- -

In This Chapter

▶ The World Wide Web and hypertext

▶ Mosaic, king of the browsers

▶ Getting and using Mosaic

▶ Roaming the Internet with Mosaic

▶ Alternatives to Mosaic

- -

Hypertext

Everyone who thinks deeply about information retrieval has agreed for decades that hypertext is an effective and friendly way to search for things. Early glimpses of this appeared in the works of Dr. Ted Nelson (who, in the optimistic dawn of computing, wrote a book called *ComputerLib*) and later in HyperCard itself. The biggest hypertext project on the planet, a direct result of these first efforts, is the World Wide Web. (It's also called WWW, "the Web", and sometimes W3.)

At CERN in Geneva (the name stands for Nuclear Research Center for Europe, but since the real name is in French, the acronym reads backwards), diligent workers created the first big World Wide Web site. They took reams of physics data and other text information and laundered it in *HTML* (*h*ypertext *m*arkup *l*anguage), the WWW's native dialect.

HTML is a set of formatting directives that define hypertext *links*. Links take you from one WWW page to another when you click on an underlined keyword. They also created HTTP, the *h*ypertext *t*ransport *p*rotocol, to specify WWW connections. Just as there's an FTP (*f*ile *t*ransfer *p*rotocol) and a SLIP (*s*erial *l*ine *i*nterface *p*rotocol), there's an HTTP.

When you fire up software to browse the Web, you open a URL (*u*niform *r*esource *l*ocator) and give it a resource such as `http://www.commerce.net/`. Your browser then connects you to a world of HTML pages.

This sounds a bit dry so far, and text-based WWW was not setting the world on fire. But this system has two big advantages, just waiting to be exploited:

1. **It knows where you're going.**

   The links contain information for automatically telnetting to other WWW sites. In the old style of "surfing the Internet", you needed to know all your destinations in advance. This was more like skateboarding a construction site than surfing — unless you were good at jumping and knew the terrain, you wouldn't get far. In contrast, once you're on a WWW site, all you do is click.

2. **It's got pictures.**

   Graphics are, of course, generally cool, but they're essential if you want people to order garden equipment over the Internet. A big part of the rush to expand the WWW in the mid-1990s was the drive to put business on the Internet, with catalogs, order forms, annual reports, even employment offers. All these work better with a text/graphics mix than with text alone.

Mosaic Takes Over

In the last chapter I explained how to get a copy of the current version of NCSA Mosaic. As a point of interest, I should say that you joined the company of the several thousand people *each day* who get their own copies of Mosaic. At one point, the WWW/Mosaic situation looked like a chicken-and-egg problem — the WWW didn't have much material, so browser demand was low. But the original NCSA Mosaic was just so much fun to use that nearly a million people downloaded it, creating a big window on the WWW. So all sorts of universities, businesses, and other organizations began furiously filling the WWW with material.

When you activate your TCP/IP connection and double-click the Mosaic icon, you automatically connect to the NCSA *home page*, shown in Figure 8-1. (Every entity on the WWW has a *home page,* a place to start exploring.)

Where do you go from here? Try scrolling down this page to the What's New section (Figure 8-2), because the WWW has more genuinely new stuff every week than all the national TV networks have produced since the day you were born. I've been following the Internet since the whole thing was still called ARPANET. The most impressive development I've ever seen is the WWW explosion in the summer of 1994.

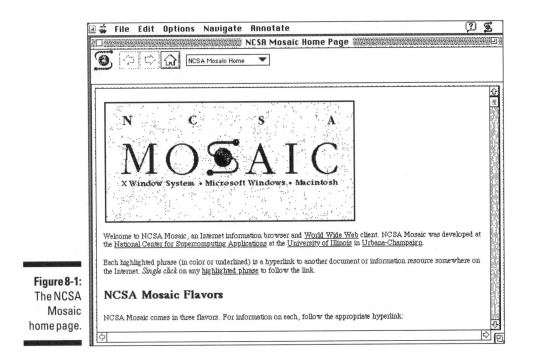

Figure 8-1:
The NCSA
Mosaic
home page.

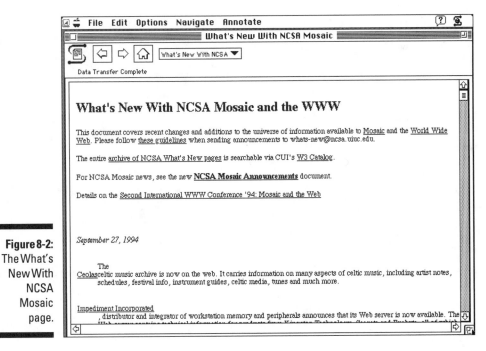

Figure 8-2:
The What's
New With
NCSA
Mosaic
page.

As a navigation exercise, I scrolled down to the first entry and clicked on the name Ceolas (the underlined terms — the hyperlinks — in the color version are blue, and a little mustard-colored rectangle appears over the term when you select it). This page leads to a gateway (see Figure 8-3) to the rainy, wind-swept shores of Europe's Atlantic fringe.

When these guys say Celtic music, they're not kidding — they have reports on bands not just from Ireland and Scotland, but from Brittany and Galicia, too (didn't know they used bagpipes in northwestern Spain, eh? Or you just *hoped* they didn't have bagpipes in Spain? Or maybe you just hoped that bagpipes would stay the heck in Ireland and Scotland?)

Even if tin whistles aren't your thing, this exercise shows you why the Mosaic approach to the Internet is so fascinating. I haven't typed anything, I've just clicked terms. Yet I find myself in this interesting corner of the cultural universe. Compared to a laborious single-shot FTP to an archive to retrieve a text file, Mosaic really is the big time.

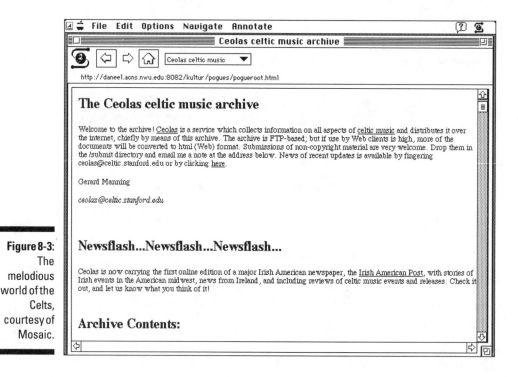

Figure 8-3:
The melodious world of the Celts, courtesy of Mosaic.

Roaming Around on the Web

To return from the Celtic realms to the What's New page, I pull down the list that appears next to the Home icon at the top of the page, and choose the item for the What's New page. I could also use the right and left arrows at the top of the page, or click the Home icon to start over. When you do this yourself, you'll be relieved to find that Mosaic has "cached" or stored enough material to show you something right away.

Since some Web documents are not just long, but full of graphics, it can take a long time to get results, even at 14.4 kbps. Rather than just scroll through new topics (even though doing so can entertain you for days), check the CUI W3 Catalog (Figure 8-4). This catalog, which will have more than 10,000 entries by the time you get to it, is typical of the hefty files lumbering around the WWW. For example, the recent changes link is a 250K download.

Even though the WWW is wide open to mere mortals like ourselves, the wireheads still firmly control administration of advanced services. The optimal way to search this catalog is to write some regular expressions in Perl. *Regular expressions* are a bizarre way of expressing things logically. *Perl* is a somewhat esoteric programming language. Surely you're not going to disappoint me by saying that you can't even program in *awk*, much less Perl.

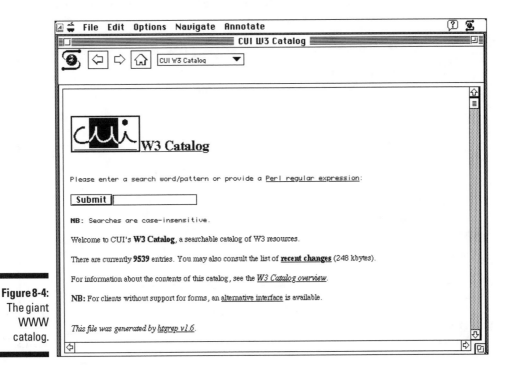

Figure 8-4:
The giant
WWW
catalog.

You say you wait a long time while your computer and modem download screen updates from Web sites? This is because NCSA didn't really consider users like you when they wrote Mosaic.

Remember, NCSA stands for National Center for Supercomputing Applications. These guys were wired to a Cray supercomputer server over the fastest direct-wired networking setup available. Speed wasn't a problem. On the worst day they ever saw, they got screen updates twenty times faster than you with your modem-SLIP connection. In the meanwhile, faster Mosaic clones have become available. Some are described a little bit later. So just be patient and performance will improve.

One of the first things you'll find when you dip into the CUI W3 Catalog is that We Are Not Alone. Living in North America, a giant land mass with thousands of miles of cold salt water at either side, it's easy to forget that the rest of the world is real. On the WWW, the rest of the world jumps right down your modem wire and splashes on your screen.

Look at the first entries (Figure 8-5) in the new part of the catalog — they're postings from math departments at Portugese and German universities. That's because the WWW is rapidly supplanting traditional research journals as a means of distributing papers. All sorts of transnational scientific collaboration is now possible through the Internet, so it's a convenient coincidence that most of the Cold War barriers to collaboration disappeared just as the Net started to explode.

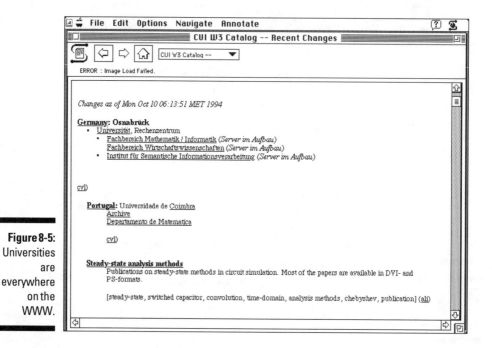

Figure 8-5:
Universities are everywhere on the WWW.

Even though a lot of this international material is provided in the originating languages (I have a friend who has managed to learn rudimentary written Finnish simply from logging on the FUNET server for a year), services looking for wider audiences offer translations. Figure 8-6 shows the language menu of Deutsche Welle, roughly the German equivalent of the BBC. Most services that want an international audience will have to provide similar language menus.

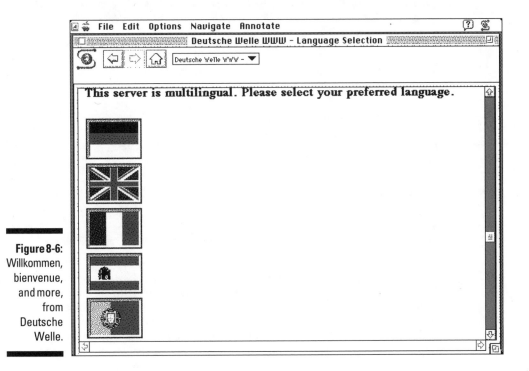

Figure 8-6:
Willkommen,
bienvenue,
and more,
from
Deutsche
Welle.

WWW...Fun, Fun, Fun

I suspect, although I cannot prove, that most readers of this book are not fired up about Mosaic because it gives them access to Portuguese-language math papers from the University of Coimbra, one of the oldest universities in Europe. (I could be wrong.)

You probably had something a little lighter in mind. How about the official site for the world's most profitable geriatric rock collective? There they are in Figure 8-7, costing you about five extra minutes on-line to download all those little tongues and other icons. I can't tell whether they're demons or just Keith Richards in his seldom-seen Bozo the Clown haircut.

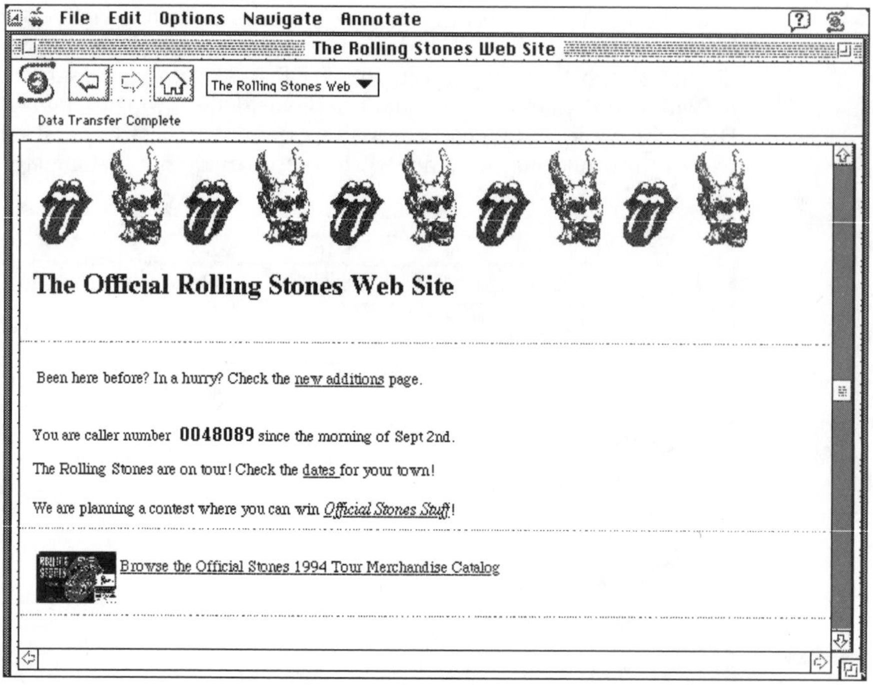

File   Edit   Options   Navigate   Annotate   ⌘

The Rolling Stones Web Site

The Rolling Stones Web ▼

Data Transfer Complete

The Official Rolling Stones Web Site

Been here before? In a hurry? Check the <u>new additions</u> page.

You are caller number **0048089** since the morning of Sept 2nd.

The Rolling Stones are on tour! Check the <u>dates</u> for your town!

We are planning a contest where you can win <u>*Official Stones Stuff*</u>!

<u>Browse the Official Stones 1994 Tour Merchandise Catalog</u>

Figure 8-7:
I've seen
these guys
somewhere
else.

Besides letting you order T-shirts and so forth on-line, this page leads you to a schedule page (Figure 8-8). Because real information is being transferred, it's time for lots of text in 9-point Monaco. The Rolling Stones aren't the only band to have a Web site for schedules and such — if you drill down through the links in the Ceolas home page, you'll find that even such intransigent, semi-non-profit ne'er-do-wells as the Pogues have this part of their act together.

Consider this not just a trend, but a now-permanent fixture of the music business. Sound clips are also posted on the WWW, but they're an uncomfortably long slog of a download.

But enough of these ruffians! Let us fly, you and I, across the Web and through the sky, to the City of Light. Check out the Paris home page (available in French through a click on the tiny language version link). How did I find this? How did I find the Stones, for that matter? They were all on the original What's New page at NCSA, and I just scrolled down with the scroll box to find them.

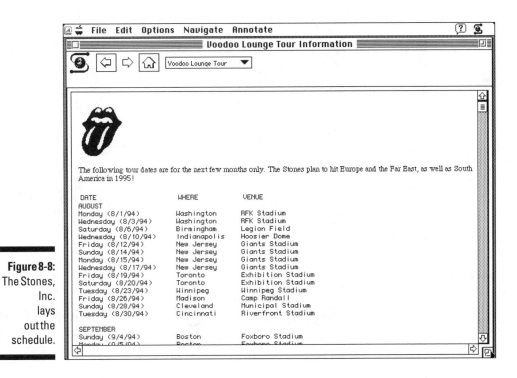

Figure 8-8:
The Stones,
Inc.
lays
out the
schedule.

The Paris site has complete, gorgeous, full-color tours, along with tons of other, more standard information. This site is a real *tour de force*, as I believe Parisians themselves used to say in the pages of American high-school textbooks. If the Paris resource were the only site available on the Web, it would be worth getting a copy of Mosaic just to look at it. (I'm very proud to say this material was assembled at my old school, UCSD, and one of my math professors,

Dr. H. Halkin, provided some of it!)

Another new site you may want to visit, especially if you want to justify the time you spend on-line, neglecting your job, family, and community obligations is, The Well Connected Mac (Figure 8-9), which has connections to other sites, to vendors, and to mailing lists. It also makes a beginning attempt at doing e-mail through the WWW. Find this in the NCSA What's New section (until March 1995 or so) or send e-mail to elharo@shock.njit.edu for more information. This site is a one-stop shopping center for all sorts of Mac stuff. It lets you find what you need quickly so you can spend hours doodling around the Net's endless by-ways.

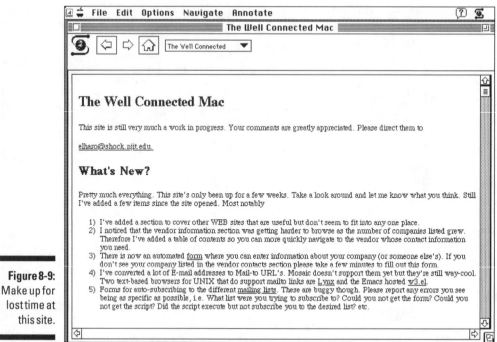

Figure 8-9:
Make up for
lost time at
this site.

Other Ways to the Web

As fine a product as Mosaic is, perfectly good alternatives are available. Mosaic was the first graphic WWW browser, and its developers deserve a world of credit, but it's not going to be the final word.

I particularly like MacWeb, available from `FTP.galaxy.einet.net` and from every national on-line service's software libraries. MacWeb is fast, efficient, and compact, and it has one impressive advantage—the `galaxy.einet.net` home page (Figure 8-10) from which it starts never seems to be crowded.

One of MacWeb's key features is that it, by default, shows graphics icons where they're present but does not download the graphics unless instructed. In the Rolling Stones page, for example, you would see all the tongues only if you were feeling naughty and insisted on opening the graphics files. In timed experiments with standard WWW files, I consistently get files about three times faster with MacWeb than with Mosaic.

A page of text takes about 2K of file space, and a page of 8-bit color takes several hundred K. That's pretty compelling logic for keeping graphics files buttoned up until you decide you want them. The trivial visual differences between Figures 8-11 and 8-12 make a noticeable difference in display time.

Figure 8-10:
Arrows, a
little house,
a URL
window—
deja vu!

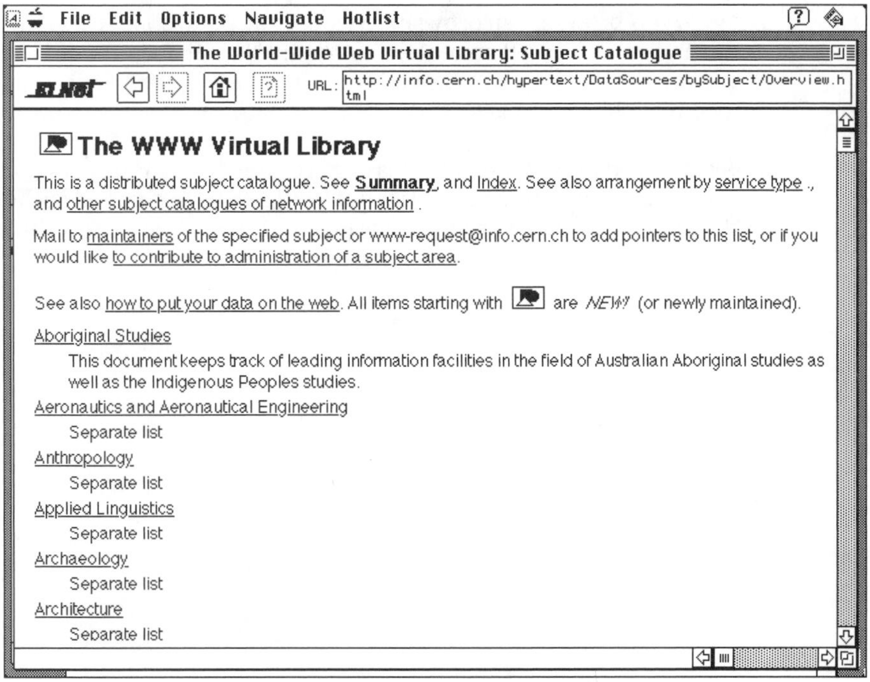

Figure 8-11:
MacWeb
graphics as
icons.

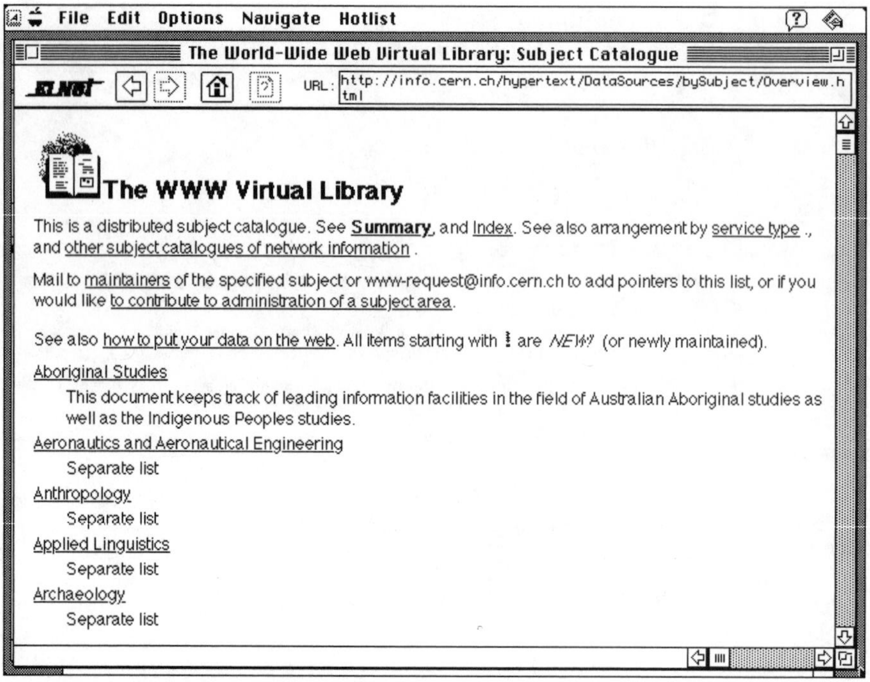

File   Edit   Options   Navigate   Hotlist

The World-Wide Web Virtual Library: Subject Catalogue

URL: http://info.cern.ch/hypertext/DataSources/bySubject/Overview.html

The WWW Virtual Library

This is a distributed subject catalogue. See **Summary**, and Index. See also arrangement by service type ., and other subject catalogues of network information .

Mail to maintainers of the specified subject or www-request@info.cern.ch to add pointers to this list, or if you would like to contribute to administration of a subject area.

See also how to put your data on the web. All items starting with ! are *NEW!* (or newly maintained).

Aboriginal Studies
> This document keeps track of leading information facilities in the field of Australian Aboriginal studies as well as the Indigenous Peoples studies.

Aeronautics and Aeronautical Engineering
> Separate list

Anthropology
> Separate list

Applied Linguistics
> Separate list

Archaeology
> Separate list

Figure 8-12:
MacWeb
graphics
unpacked.

Any WWW browser can browse anywhere, of course, but EINet is a very good starting point. You get connected in the middle of the afternoon Texas time, and you can find lots of trivial and serious material very quickly (MacWeb's speed encourages cruising).

Because computer books like this one are often written late at night (the phone stops ringing and the Net empties out a bit), I have become an authority on the kind of material in the Archive X file (see Figure 8-13), including the fan club page here for the Canadian vampire show *Forever Knight*.

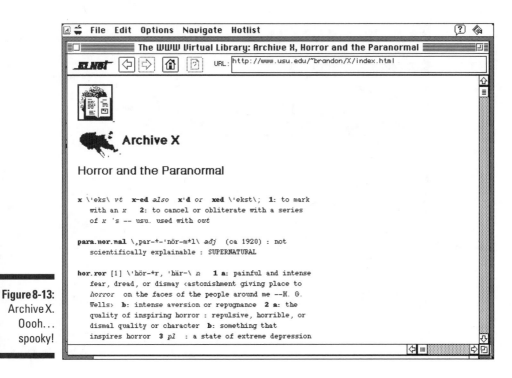

Figure 8-13:
Archive X.
Oooh...
spooky!

Just to show that MacWeb is not actually graphics-averse, I have included the Chance database home page in Figure 8-14, showing merry mathematical revelers trying to beat the odds in its title bar. You owe it to yourself to peruse Chance. Use the URL tag

```
http://www.geom.umn.edu/docs/snell/chance/welcome.html/
```

If you ever feel the need to interpret for yourself all these strange studies that appear in newspapers, claiming that toasted almonds cure glaucoma or that second-hand smoke rots your tires, perusing Chance every week is a good place to start.

Meanwhile, look into this Web site.

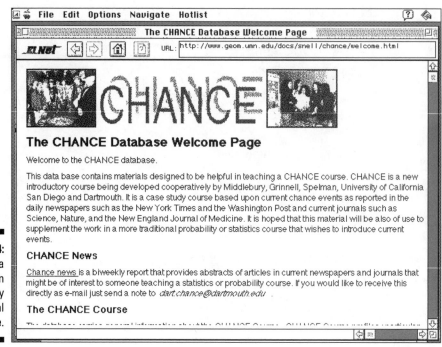

Figure 8-14:
Take a
Chance on
this highly
educational
site.

Other organizations (see sidebar: Mosaic for business) have also produced WWW browsers. Spyglass, Inc. has an official license to make OEM versions of Mosaic, for example.

But 1995 (and beyond) will bring a profusion of browsers. Some of them will be custom programs for national on-line services, some will be commercial software (InterCon, the disk source for this book, will have its own browser by early 1995), and some will be shareware. The reason is that the real heavy lifting in the WWW project was in defining structure and the mark-up language. Writing a browser is nowhere near as grand a challenge as defining the WWW was.

Mosaic for business

You may find that you're working for a company with a site license for a special version of Mosaic from Spyglass, Inc. Spyglass is a scientific software firm with deep connections to NCSA and has been officially licensed by NCSA to produce a commercial version of Mosaic for internal use on large networks. There aren't many operational differences between the version of Mosaic I'm describing here and the Spyglass Enhanced Mosaic edition. Spyglass's product is more compact, faster, has better Help, and has a snappy Power Mac version. But the main difference is that you'll be using it on a network at work. So all my intemperate whining about slow downloads doesn't apply.

Part III

Internet via National On-Line Services

"I'M SORRY, BUT MR. HALLORAN IS BEING CHASED BY SIX MIDGETS WITH POISON BOOMERANGS THROUGH A MAZE IN THE DUNGEON OF A CASTLE. IF HE FINDS HIS WAY OUT AND GETS PAST THE MINOTAUR, HE'LL CALL YOU RIGHT BACK."

In this part...

*A*ll the big national on-line services have figured out that they aren't viable any more without a good Internet connections. So they're scrambling as fast as they can to offer Internet services with a friendly Mac face to lure you on-line.

In this part, I'll compare the services from the point of view of their own content and their Internet readiness. This area is rapidly evolving, but it's possible to see what's going to happen. Think of this part as a shopping tour for your Internet connection.

Chapter 9
Internet from America Online

● ●

In This Chapter

▶ AOL puts a Mac face on the Internet

▶ Easy mail links to the whole planet

▶ Here comes everybody — AOL and newsgroups

▶ Watch Gopher burrow through the on-line universe

▶ Finally, FTP and "real" Internet

● ●

They Said They'd Do It, and They Did It (Almost)

In 1993, reading the handwriting on the wall, not to mention the hype in the Wall Street Journal, America Online decided to begin moving into Internet service. Through the first part of 1994, Internet e-mail service was introduced, and then a "toy" version of Gopher, and then a few newsgroups, and by June 1994, America Online users had access to thousands of newsgroups as the system operators gradually added to the list.

In the America Online Internet user group area, the AOL operators have promised telnet and FTP capabilities for many months and have endured heaps of abuse about delays. FTP finally arrived; it's as easy to use as AOL's other services. It takes these people a while, but they do keep their promises. In fairness to AOL, software development for a large on-line service is not a trivial task. And the oldest rule in computing is that software always ships late (the software for *this book* shipped late).

One last service to be added is an AOL equivalent of Mosaic. Until AOL gets lots and lots of 14.4 kbps service signed up, there's not much point in perfecting a graphical Web browser. But the inside scoop is that an AOL World Wide Web service will probably be appearing by early 1995, at which point AOL will have a pretty impressive "Internet for Beginners" package.

Pioneers Are The Ones With The Arrows In Their Backs

If you wanted to get to California in time for the Gold Rush, you had to risk life and limb on a leaky boat or cross the whole hostile country in a wagon train. On the other hand, to get a chance to make a fortune in the earliest movies (the second Gold Rush, really), you could take a train from Chicago. It makes sense, to me anyway, to let services like AOL fix up the Information Superhighway and put in a few rest stops. I've done Internet the hard way and I've done it the easy way, and easy is better. That's why this book includes a trial copy of Pipeline, the easiest complete Internet service.

AOL as an Internet Tool

Yes, the Internet is cool. The Internet contains a huge amount of information and allows easy communication with millions of people. But the fact is *every* large on-line service provides lots of the same features.

The main advantages of the Internet include access to more esoteric information, weirder fan clubs, international users, and more serious research databases. But if you want to download game software, all the good stuff is on AOL. Shareware and on-line magazines? They're here, too. Interactive on-line games? AOL has them. For that matter, so do most on-line services and even local bulletin boards.

What I'm proposing is this: The Internet is wonderful, and you and I can keep it wonderful by using it for real Internet tasks. Only you can prevent forest fires, and only you can keep the Internet from becoming an unusable electronic trash heap. If you want stock quotes, if you want to chat in real-time with people in Chicago, or if you want to download finance templates to use with a spreadsheet, simply use AOL.

From the standard archives at Stanford and elsewhere, the service has already retrieved nearly all the Mac-specific shareware you could want (see Figure 9-1). The stock quotes are up to the minute. You can tap into brilliant and idiotic opinions of users who happen to be logged onto the network at the same time as you are. So if you're looking for a job as a historian, by all means use the Internet to look up the academic jobs database at the University of Kansas [listserv@ukanvm.cc.ukans.edu]. But if you're just in a mood to flame about bugs in Microsoft Word 6.0, do it on AOL instead.

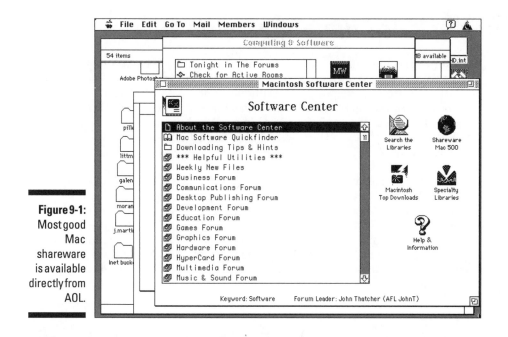

Figure 9-1:
Most good
Mac
shareware
is available
directly from
AOL.

Just Do It!

America Online has the best Macintosh interface of any of the national services currently operating. Place a call to America Online customer service at 800-827-6364, and a few days later you will get in the mail a disk with instructions. Every few months, you will find an introductory offer for AOL with some free on-line time bundled with a copy of *Macworld*, too. In either case, insert the disk, double-click the installer icon, and you get a screen like the one in Figure 9-2.

Figure 9-2:
If the AOL
installer
works, you
see this
folder.

What AOL Is Like: A Personal Tour

After you type in your password, the software, which has been configured to
run your modem at the highest speed available, connects you automatically to
AOL. AOL provides you with a local phone number for calls. It took AOL a while
to get 9600 bps local access numbers available in most areas, and it will
probably take until late 1994 for 14.4 Kbps or 19.2 Kbps service to appear.
(Kbps means a thousand bps, so 14.4 Kbps is 14,400 bps, as described in
Chapter 3.)

When you sign on, you see the screen in Figure 9-3. As a newcomer, you should
check the icons on the right and at the lower left of the screen. By double-
clicking on the Discover AOL icon, you can guide yourself through a tutorial. By
double-clicking on the letter icon (which is the No mail icon in Figure 9-3), you
can enter a sophisticated e-mail system that can access Internet mail. The icons
at the right are usually topics that AOL management thinks are newsworthy.
Right now, I'm displaying this screen so that you can admire the amazingly
clean design.

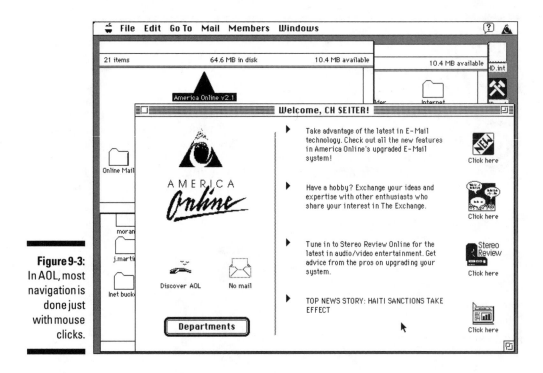

Figure 9-3:
In AOL, most
navigation is
done just
with mouse
clicks.

AOL has a real Mac interface

In most on-line services, you have to perform a significant amount of idiotic grunt labor, calling up menus and answering questions. Often you find yourself arguing with the service menus as different commands become available or unavailable, depending on the last menu you were shown. This problem is in direct contradiction to the style of all the other Mac software you use in daily life. If the services want my money, they gotta do better than that!

So AOL did better. Instead of expecting thousands of on-line users to pound away at their keyboards and scroll through menus, trying to work around the deficiencies built into an interface, AOL hired a handful of programmers to code a proper point-and-click, Apple-interface-guidelines front end for AOL services. There is great efficiency — which saves *you* precious time — in the AOL on-line screen design. At any point, you can figure out your next move just by inspecting the icons or scrolling the lists presented to you on-screen. You think this would have occurred to somebody else, but it didn't.

Too much fun!

Even in its currently incomplete form, AOL is one of the few ways to get going on the information superhighway without getting lost in traffic. This list covers some top points in support of AOL:

- ✔ The people at AOL know you're lazy — and they *like* it that way.
- ✔ AOL e-mail is easier than licking stamps.
- ✔ You can use a screen name, such as Zorro or Bambi.
- ✔ AOL people don't censor your flames.
- ✔ AOL's Internet administrator has the patience of Mother Teresa.
- ✔ The AOL Gopher is so cute that you just have to click him.
- ✔ AOL runs thousands of Usenet groups, even the strange ones!

The icons speak

The first thing you hear is a voice announcing that you have mail. AOL packs some amusing sound files into the interface program it sends you on disk. The message itself isn't sent through your modem — a flag in the sign-on data plays the sound at your end of the connection. At this point, you can read the latest headlines or double-click on some new service — but you're going straight to the Internet.

You can get to the Internet area by clicking the Departments button and then picking your way through more icons, but it's faster to pull down the Go To menu, pick Keyword from the choices, and type **internet** in the Enter keyword text box in the Go to Keyword dialog box (see Figure 9-4). The screen then changes to the glorious vista presented in Figure 9-5.

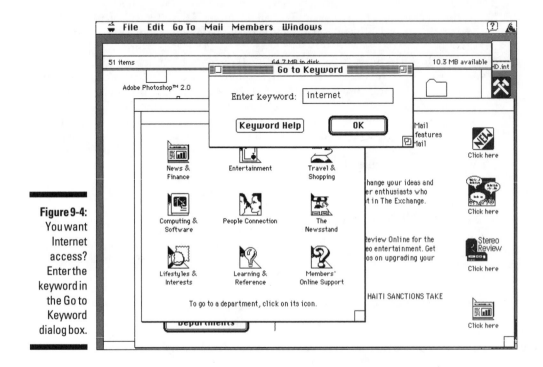

Figure 9-4:
You want
Internet
access?
Enter the
keyword in
the Go to
Keyword
dialog box.

Keyword: Internet

The list at the left of the Internet Center window in Figure 9-5 contains an amazing amount of material. For example, it contains Zen and the Art of the Internet, Brendan Kehoe's admirable information file, arranged in searchable form. If you don't like my explanations, you can try one of his, although the file is mostly a guide to old-style UNIX telecommunications.

If you double-click on About the Internet Center, you get AOL's own explanation of its services. Double-clicking the Mac Communications Forum gets you into the Apple Professional Exchange, a legal group, and "nomadic" computing discussions.

Another interesting bunch in this forum is the Electronic Frontier Foundation, an organization that's trying its best to keep information transfer free and unmonitored. At present, the U.S. government is desperately trying to maintain its right to "wiretap" e-mail when it thinks it's necessary, and the EFF doesn't like this invasion of privacy, to put it mildly.

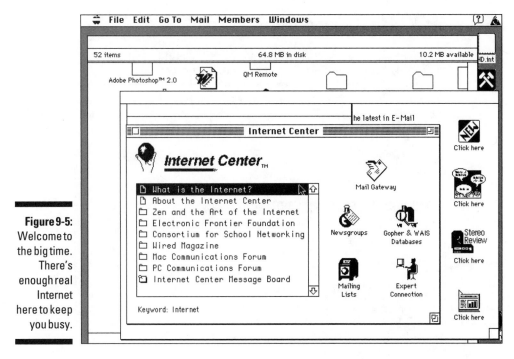

Figure 9-5:
Welcome to
the big time.
There's
enough real
Internet
here to keep
you busy.

The Internet Center Message Board, shown in Figure 9-6, is where you see announcements of new services. It's also where you see AOL management being mercilessly slagged by impatient users. To AOL's credit, it doesn't censor any of its on-line criticism. These AOL people get flamed plenty.

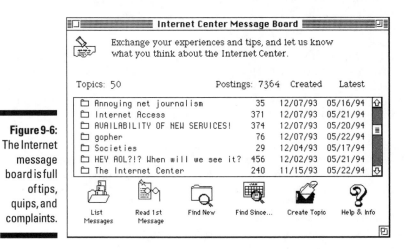

Figure 9-6:
The Internet
message
board is full
of tips,
quips, and
complaints.

AOL Mail Gateway

I now leave the flames, change out of my fire-resistant pajamas (decorated, in fact, with little appliqués of gophers), and put on a business suit. I click back through the main Internet Center window (a fast way to do so is to give the Keyword command Internet) and click the Mail Gateway icon, which gets me to the window in Figure 9-7.

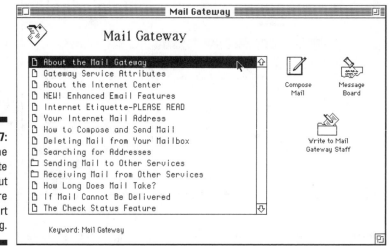

Figure 9-7: Read the etiquette note about mail before you start posting.

While you're in the Mail Gateway window, read the Internet Etiquette message. *Etiquette,* in this sense, doesn't really have much to do with Miss Manners; instead, it refers to being careful about addressing messages so that they don't clog up the wrong e-mail mailboxes.

Early in 1994, for example, two lawyers in Arizona sent out messages soliciting business to tens of thousands of Internet addresses, and by now they have received close to a million flames (not to mention death threats) in return. Just when you thought the much-maligned legal profession couldn't disgrace itself any further, these guys have started a whole new category of e-mail lawyer jokes.

Next, read the document called Your Internet Mail Address. Check this out! You now have your own Internet address, even though you did nothing more than follow a few Mac menus. Sending and receiving mail are handled automatically by AOL, and you can put your new Internet address on your business cards.

If you click the Compose Mail icon, you get a screen like the one in Figure 9-8. Because the America Online software is a real Mac application, you can actually compose your letters in a Macintosh word processor and simply cut and paste text into the message area. Similarly, you can cut sections of messages you receive and paste them into standard documents in other applications. In the

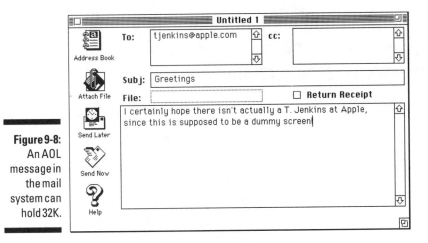

Figure 9-8:
An AOL
message in
the mail
system can
hold 32K.

To box, at the top of the form, you can list an Internet address in the same way you list an AOL internal address (a screen name, in AOL lingo).

Using AOL doesn't get much easier than this. In fact, it's hard to see how it *could* be much easier than this. But there are still two problems with AOL Internet mail as it stands today. First, messages are currently limited to 32K. If the system could handle longer text messages, people could send you files with a sort of trick called FTP mail, in which a text file is sent to you as a mail message.

Second, the nifty Attach File feature — very useful for sending files of pictures or sound or bits of database to other AOL users — doesn't work for messages to other services.

Despite these problems, AOL's e-mail messaging system is convenient and inexpensive (you get ten on-line hours per month for your monthly fee). Later in this book (see Chapter 13), I show you what e-mail is like in a traditional UNIX-based system — the comparison is a shocking argument for AOL.

Newsgroups on AOL

E-mail is certainly useful. It offers a major justification for getting an Internet connection. But it's not all that entertaining, and just using e-mail doesn't make you a "real Internet" user. So it's time to get cool. Close the Mail Gateway window and you're back at the Internet Center. If you click the Newsgroups icon in the Internet Center window, you get a personal gateway to the thousands of newsgroups on Usenet, BITNET, and WhatNotNet (OK, I made up the last one). Figure 9-9 shows what these newsgroups look like on-screen.

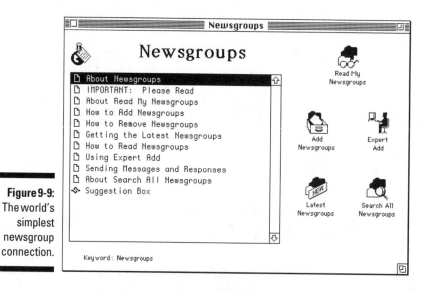

Figure 9-9:
The world's
simplest
newsgroup
connection.

The list of groups is so huge that AOL doesn't even offer to show you the whole list. Instead, you pick topics of interest and search for newsgroups that match. When you first start the AOL service, "your" newsgroups are a short list of six or seven newsgroups that AOL thinks may be of general interest.

To add to this list, you can find newsgroups by searching or by using the Expert Add icon. To add a newsgroup with Expert Add, you need the exact name of the newsgroup you're joining. I list some groups in Appendix D, and you can join the group news.lists to see the whole list. Actually, using AOL's search procedure is the easiest way.

My own list (trimmed down for this book) is shown in Figure 9-10 and includes both serious stuff (magnetic resonance) and the resolutely silly (the Mystery Science Theater 3000 list Alt-Tv-Mst3k).

A key point to watch is the sheer number of messages that crop up in an active group. The group Alt-Tv-Mst3k, for example, discusses a show that appears on the Comedy Channel, and it picks up nearly a hundred messages a day! (A lesson from the Internet: The world is big — one percent of a million people is a lot of people.) You're not going to get around to reading most of the messages unless you feel like spending hours every night on-line and making AOL ridiculously rich.

Fortunately, AOL shows you the subjects (see Figure 9-11), so you can scan them and pick out a few favorites. Then click the icon that says "Mark As Read." Otherwise, you would drown in a week, even with a rigorously austere list.

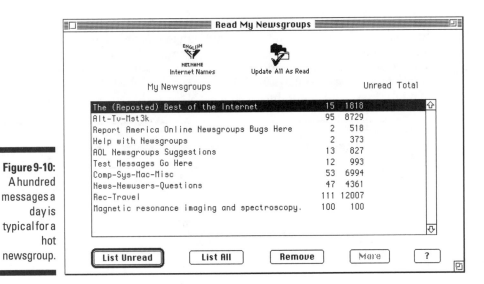

Figure 9-10:
A hundred
messages a
day is
typical for a
hot
newsgroup.

Figure 9-11:
A modest
sample from
an
"alternative"
newsgroup.

All these newsgroup correspondences are conducted in plain text. However, you're going to need to know just a bit of Internet code, such as BTW and IMHO, to read and respond to newsgroup messages. A standard set of abbreviations has been developed over the years; Table 9-1 provides a minimal list of these abbreviations so that you know what's going on when you see them. To convey some sort of accent to the text, symbols that look like cartoon faces soon appeared, too; Table 9-2 contains a smattering of these symbols, called *smileys*, and their interpretations.

I predict that within three years, Mac Internet interfaces will have improved to the point that you can annotate messages with sounds and pictures for impact — a sort of smileys-on-steroids. But for now, these abbreviations and smileys are standards. If you poke around in the AOL communications forums, you can find whole dictionaries of smileys (various jokers have concocted about 500), which may interest you for cultural anthropological reasons.

Table 9-1	Short Takes
Code	*It Stands For*
IMHO	In my humble opinion
BTW	By the way
FYI	For your information
LOL	Laughing out loud
GMTA	Great minds think alike
RTFM	Read the f*&^% manual

Table 9-2	Keep On Smilin'
On the Keyboard	*What It Says*
:)	Smile
;)	Wink
: *	Kiss
: (	Bummer!
: >	Fiendish grin

Getting Listed

Mailing lists are just collections of Internet e-mail addresses. The mailing list system evolved mainly as a way for researchers at widely separated institutions to keep in touch. The biggest set of mailing lists, in fact, evolved separately from the Internet on BITNET, although there's considerable crossover.

The window in Figure 9-12 shows some mailing lists turned up by clicking on Search and entering the word *politics* in the text box (when you click the mailbox icon in the Internet Center window, search is one of your options). In AOL, you can sign up to join any of these discussion groups just by adding your name to the list, and you can quit a group just as easily.

```
▓▓▓□▓▓▓▓▓▓▓▓▓▓▓▓ Search Internet Mailing Lists ▓▓▓▓▓▓▓▓▓▓▓▓▓▓▓▓
```

Internet Mailing Lists

Type words that describe what you are looking for, then click List Articles. For
example, "politics or motorcycles." Click Help & Info for more instructions.

```
politics
```

Items 1-13 of 13 matching entries.

```
act-up
home-ed-politics
LIBFEM
new-orleans
Oglasna Deska
POSCIM
Spojrzenia
WELSH-L: Welsh Language and Culture
ALTINST: Alternative Institutions
TIBET-L: Tibet Interest List
KENTUCKY: Kentucky Civic and Political Discussion
SPECPRESS: Spectrum Press News and Discussion
UNITED: Labor Union Discussions
```

[**List Articles**]   [More]   [**Help & Info**]

Figure 9-12:
AOL has set
up an
Internet
mailing list
search.

These lists are amazingly interesting and entertaining, but there are a few
precautions you should be aware of. The first is that when you join a list, you
should probably monitor it every day for the first few days to get an idea of the
traffic volume. When anyone on your list sends a message to the rest of the list,
it appears in your mailbox. If you sign up for lots of active lists, you will find that
your AOL mailbox limit (550 messages) can be reached quite rapidly. It's not
hard to join so many lists that your mailbox blows out in a single day!

The other precaution is that you should read the messages for a week or so to
determine whether you really have a contribution to make to the other list
members. The Internet gives you, in effect, an introduction to most of the
research and special-interest groups in the world. I don't want to sound like too
much of an old grump on this point, but please think about whether you'll be
wasting your own time and someone else's time by getting involved in an
endless series of messages.

Having pointed out the precautions, I still want you to believe that mailing lists
are a fantastic way to keep in touch with individuals who share your interests.
Somewhere out there in Flatville, Illinois, there's probably someone who's
fascinated with Minoan archaeology, and now she can read daily reports from
researchers doing field work in Crete. That's wonderful!

Finding Stuff in the Internet Jungle: Gopher and WAIS

There's so much information available on the Internet that special sets of searching tools (I describe them in Chapter 5) have evolved. One standard tool is Gopher (named for the mascot of the University of Minnesota, home of the Golden Gophers and a pioneer Internet software site). There are hundreds of Gopher sites all over the planet, and they maintain menus of files available on different topics. You give a Gopher some possible file titles of interest, and the Gopher tells you what's available. WAIS, for *w*ide *a*rea *i*nformation *s*erver, searches the contents of files rather than just file titles.

In "full" Internet access, you could connect to any Gopher server (a server is just a computer, generally big and fast, set up as a central resource for "client" computers, like yours). To connect to another Gopher server, you find a Gopher list for yourself and Gopher Internet addresses. On AOL, none of these procedures and details really matters.

AOL hides the search details

AOL has done something a bit different. First, it evaluated dozens of Gopher sites for reliability. Most of these are noncommercial sites maintained as a public service, and some of them are as flaky as a basket of crescent rolls. AOL then wrote an interface in which you, the end user, can't always tell whether you're getting information from a Gopher site or a WAIS server. You get the information — you don't get the search path or the Internet details. Unless you're an experienced on-line searcher, you get better results the AOL way than you get poking around on your own.

From the Internet Center screen, just click the Gopher & WAIS databases icon. Figure 9-13 shows some of the available topics, and in AOL, you can click in these folders to carry out a search. At present, AOL has loaded a large array of topics into what appears to be its own site so that searches are fast and don't usually connect you to other computers.

Searching absolutely everything

To find specific subjects, you can also perform a Veronica search over all available Gophers. Just click on the Search All Gophers icon in the Gopher and WAIS window, and you'll see a window like the one in Figure 9-14. I searched on the word *analytical* because I design analytical equipment for biochemistry, so I used this keyword to tell AOL how much material to access. (By the way, I did this search because I already knew what was available from doing searches

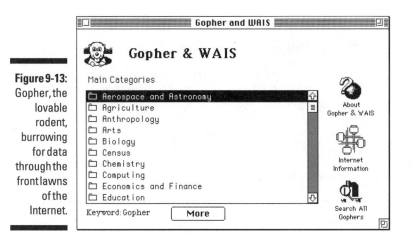

Figure 9-13:
Gopher, the
lovable
rodent,
burrowing
for data
through the
front lawns
of the
Internet.

with full access to all known Gophers and WAIS databases.) At present, my guess is that AOL databases probably have between 20 and 30 percent of all text files on this topic that are available worldwide, but the list is expanding fairly quickly as AOL adds behind-the-scenes access to more Gophers.

Figure 9-14:
A Veronica
search pulls
out the
details.

Whimsy in cyberspace

Archie is a program that lets you search over files that you can find on the Internet and is basically an index of archived software, hence the name. Later, a more powerful search program was named Veronica, for *very easy rodent-oriented netwide index to computerized archives. Rodent-oriented* means that the program works with Gophers, but the name Veronica was cooked up as a reference to Archie and Veronica comic books. There is also a program for Archie-searching called Jughead, meaning that a program called Betty can't be too far away. I explain these programs merely because many Internauts are probably too young to have seen any of these harmless relics of a bygone comic-book age (the age cutoff seems to be about 21).

Gossip Hot Line!

To learn more about the direction the Internet is taking, including new kinds of searching systems, you can click back to the main Gopher screen and then click on the Internet Information icon. Figure 9-15 shows the fairly complete set of AOL Internet informational files, including material on InterNIC, a prime resource on Internet operations. At this point, if you want to impress your friends with your totally cool, leading-edge status among Internauts, go and read the items in the Heard on the Net Electronic Newsletter. Even though you haven't spent more than a minute suffering through "real Internet" commands, you'll have all the gossip just as if you were a lifelong UNIX communications hacker. Seems like cheating, doesn't it?

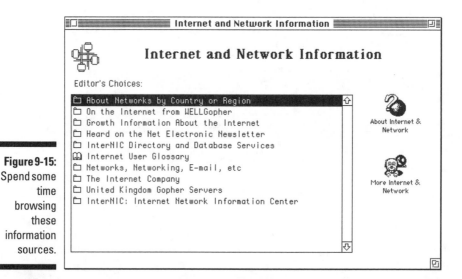

Figure 9-15:
Spend some time browsing these information sources.

Is AOL for You?

AOL is taking its time about expanding services to full Internet. Many users have found this frustrating, but in their defense, every time the AOL programmers add a service, they're dumping a million new users into that service, so they have to be careful. If you find AOL's approach restricting, go and buy IDG's *The Internet For Dummies*, 2nd Edition, by John Levine, and do the funky UNIX thing, or stick with Pipeline.

Anyway, AOL has done a not-perfect but very good job of making the Internet Mac-accessible to people just starting out in communications. It's not a full Internet service like Pipeline, but it's got a lot to recommend it.

As Long As You're Here

AOL has mountains of non-Internet material. I'll just show you a few choice bits, and you may find that a lot of what you've been told is out there on the Net is already on AOL.

Buy something

AOL is a commercial service. There is no squeamishness about serving businesses on-line. The only point you may need to investigate is whether your interests qualify as mere shopping or whether they constitute a lifestyle. If you want to buy airline tickets or roses, for example, you're just an AOL shopper (see Figure 9-16).

If you are fascinated by gadgets, on the other hand, that's a lifestyle (see Figure 9-17). It's no trouble to find what you want on AOL (you can usually do with a keyword), but the logic of classification is sometimes quite amusing. I'm sorry to say that nearly everything I do is apparently part of a lifestyle, a humiliating bit of stereotype because I live in the Wine Country in California and remember the ratings

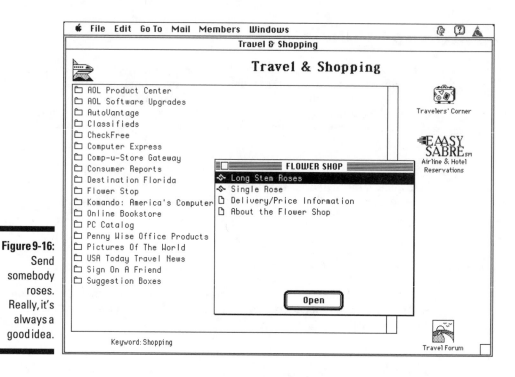

Figure 9-16:
Send
somebody
roses.
Really, it's
always a
good idea.

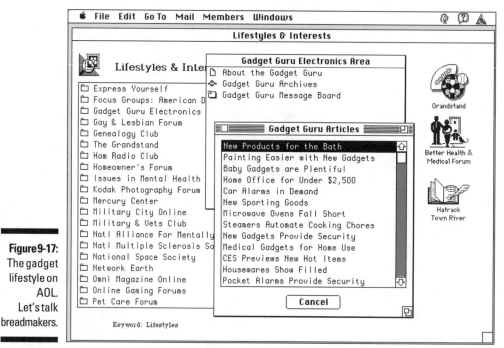

Figure 9-17:
The gadget
lifestyle on
AOL.
Let's talk
breadmakers.

Get mellow

Fans of the Grateful Dead have always been one of the best-organized groups, electronically (see figure 9-18). The brilliant journalist Mary Eisenhart (editor of *MicroTimes*), for example, used to maintain an electronic bulletin board for Deadheads, following them to every conference appearance with a laptop. And she was doing this 12 years ago, when there probably weren't more than a handful of musicians who could identify a modem. The AOL Grateful Dead Forum is a real little hot spot — and a whole universe for fans.

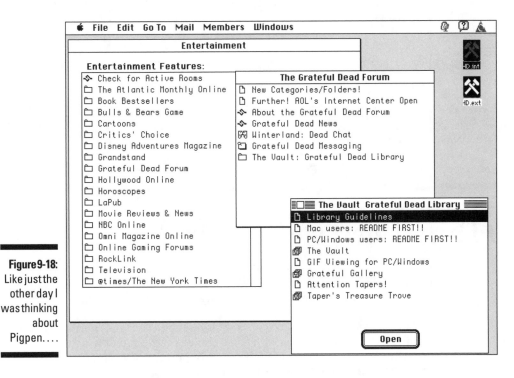

Figure 9-18: Like just the other day I was thinking about Pigpen. . . .

Stay informed

Figure 9-19 shows the huge list of on-line magazines available on AOL. As soon as you start cruising this area, you'll discover that on-line magazines are better as a way to find specific topics than as a way to browse. There are no ads, and the information is stunningly fresh — I usually see the final version of my own *Macworld* reviews here three weeks before I get the magazine in my mailbox.

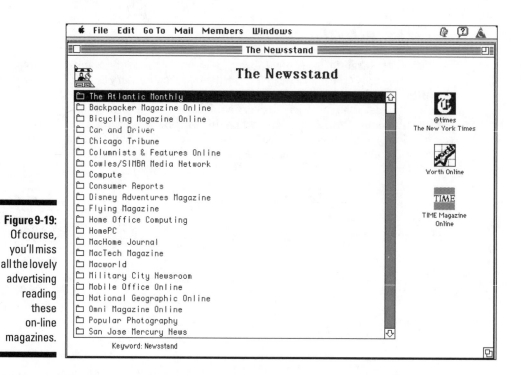

The Newsstand

The Newsstand

🗀 The Atlantic Monthly
🗀 Backpacker Magazine Online
🗀 Bicycling Magazine Online
🗀 Car and Driver
🗀 Chicago Tribune
🗀 Columnists & Features Online
🗀 Cowles/SIMBA Media Network
🗀 Compute
🗀 Consumer Reports
🗀 Disney Adventures Magazine
🗀 Flying Magazine
🗀 Home Office Computing
🗀 HomePC
🗀 MacHome Journal
🗀 MacTech Magazine
🗀 Macworld
🗀 Military City Newsroom
🗀 Mobile Office Online
🗀 National Geographic Online
🗀 Omni Magazine Online
🗀 Popular Photography
🗀 San Jose Mercury News

@times
The New York Times

Worth Online

TIME
TIME Magazine
Online

Keyword: Newsstand

Figure 9-19:
Of course,
you'll miss
all the lovely
advertising
reading
these
on-line
magazines.

FTP, the Latest and Greatest

In response to incessant demand, AOL got its version of FTP up and running in October 1994. Although FTP will be integrated into the Internet keyword area soon, in the Preview version it has its own keyword (Figure 9-20).

In the FTP area (the little disk icon is wearing shades because it's totally cool - Figure 9-21) you get a screen with some choices of explanation of the service and icons for action. The explanations are important, since for many AOL users this will be the first glimpse of FTP.

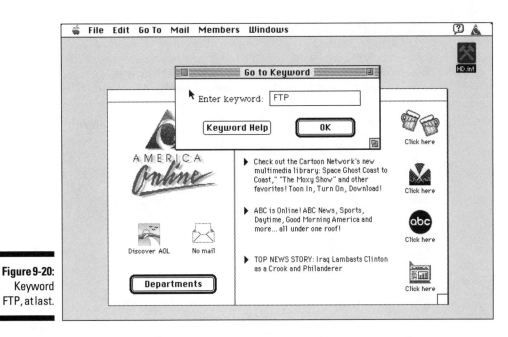

Figure 9-20:
Keyword
FTP, at last.

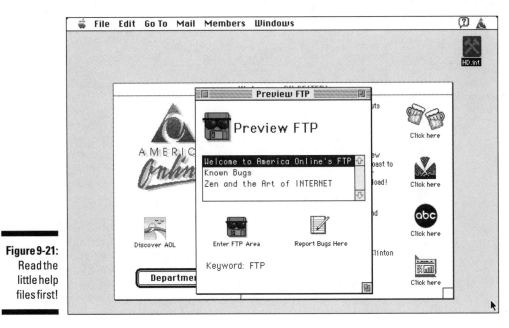

Figure 9-21:
Read the
little help
files first!

In Figure 9-22 you also see a bit of AOL cleverness. Rather than telling you to learn Archie and locate files before starting your FTP, AOL has built in a proprietary search system, and I'll bet it runs on an index maintained on AOL's own computers. Technically this means AOL is its own Archie server and it uses a custom front end. All you have to know is that it's easier than the traditional way.

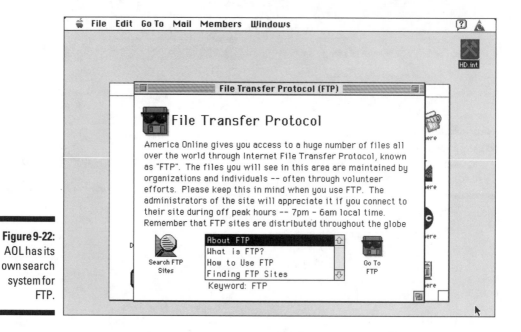

Figure 9-22: AOL has its own search system for FTP.

AOL has pre-loaded its Gopher service with a bunch of starting points, and the same is true for FTP (Figure 9-23). By the way, the note in the previous figure strongly encouraging off-peak-time usage of FTP is serious business — AOL users could bring the poor old VAX at Dartmouth to its little electronic knees if they all started jamming on 2 PM on the same day.

Just for fun, try the White House site (Figure 9-24). You'll find all sorts of briefing papers, the President's daily schedule (with enough detail to give a Secret Service agent security nightmares) and pieces of the wit and wisdom of Al Gore. Think about it — you can get up every morning and download the President's schedule into your own electronic Day-Timer. Pseudo-interactive fantasy adventures like this are a big part of the fascination of the Internet!

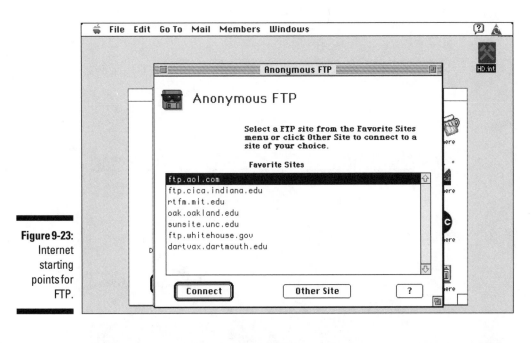

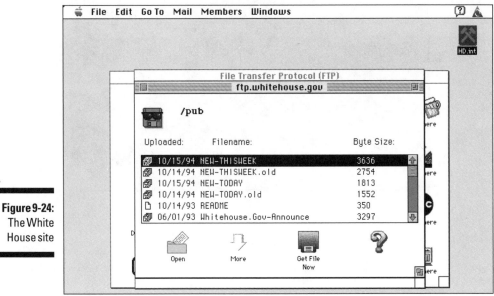

Chapter 10
Internet from Delphi

- -

- -

*E*very now and then — probably because of our pressing national shortage of marketing MBAs (just kidding, just kidding) — an organization runs advertisements that accurately represent the organization's services. Yes, this honesty in advertising does actually happen.

For more than a year, Delphi has been filling the back covers of computer magazines with an offer of a free, five-hour Explore The Internet! service. Remarkably — given that Delphi operates in a world where Internet access in an ad can often mean a badly designed e-mail interface and nothing more — Delphi delivers the goods. Jolly good show, Delphi!

Complete Internet Service

Delphi is, of course, not the only longtime, full-service Internet provider. Plenty of places have offered shell accounts for several years. With a *shell account*, you have a user name, a password, and the right to dial in as a terminal on (typically) a UNIX network. If you're happy with UNIX commands, you'll like the shell game. You should then also buy a copy of the original *The Internet For Dummies*, 2nd Edition, and see a psychologist about reconciling your left-brain UNIX personality with your right-brain Mac side.

Ordering from the menu

Delphi has gone far beyond shell account service. Walt Howe, Delphi's Internet system operator, has designed a menu-driven front end for the Internet service so that all you have to do is be able to type out responses to menu prompts. Look at the password procedure in Figure 10-1, for example. Think you can handle it? You bet you can. And the rest of Delphi is just that easy.

Figure 10-1:
As easy as
1-2-3.
Actually,
easier than
Lotus 1-2-3.

```
Greetings, and welcome to the DELPHI Guided Tour.

Before using DELPHI the first time, you should select a new password. Your new
personal password should be different from the one you were initially assigned
and have just used to log on. Your new password should consist of six or more
letters and numbers and should be somewhat cryptic; your name, nickname, or
other obvious information is not appropriate as it may be possible for someone
else to happen upon it.

You will first be asked for your old password (the password you just used when
you logged on) and then your new password. When prompted for the verification
of your new password, type the same new password again.

Old Password:

New Password:
```

Asking Howe to do things

Normally, in the Dummies universe, all relevant questions can be answered by reference to another . . . *For Dummies* book. I have every confidence that IDG will publish a *Genetic-Algorithm Software Design For Dummies* book by the year 2000. *Home Brain Surgery For Dummies*, another example, is actually under contract right now and should be ready soon.

In the matter of Mr. Howe, we have a special case. If you have signed up for Delphi, you can order, on-line, a Delphi-specific, Internet-specific manual by Walt Howe and Steve Lambert that runs to 480 pages. You'll be a happy little Delphi camper with that document, I can promise you, because if there's anything in the book you don't understand, you can e-mail a question to Walt (see Figure 10-2).

For reasons of page allotment and preservation of sanity, this chapter covers the principal highlights of Delphi Internet. For horrible, niggling little what-went-wrong-here questions, ask Walt.

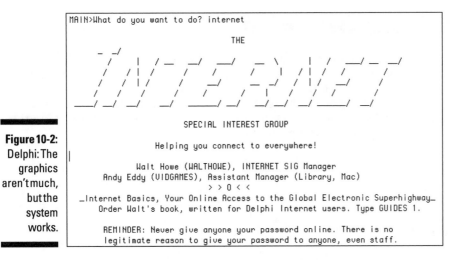

```
MAIN>What do you want to do? internet
                            THE
    _ _/
      /  /_ _ _/    _/    _ \    | /    _/ _ _/
     / |\| \    /       /   \    |/    /      /
    /  | \  \  /       /  _/ \   |    /      /
   __/ _/ _ _/   __/  _/ _/ _/ _/    _/  __/  _/

                 SPECIAL INTEREST GROUP

             Helping you connect to everywhere!

         Walt Howe (WALTHOWE), INTERNET SIG Manager
      Andy Eddy (VIDGAMES), Assistant Manager (Library, Mac)
                     > > 0 < <
   _Internet Basics, Your Online Access to the Global Electronic Superhighway_
      Order Walt's book, written for Delphi Internet users. Type GUIDES 1.

      REMINDER: Never give anyone your password online. There is no
      legitimate reason to give your password to anyone, even staff.
```

Figure 10-2: Delphi: The graphics aren't much, but the system works.

Plain Text

The only downside to Delphi Internet service is that these people don't mean the same thing by *menu* that you or I or the folks at Apple mean. Delphi is strictly a text-oriented service. No color pictures. Just characters. You press Control-C to stop. Nothing on-screen looks right (or, at least, looks like the screen shots in this chapter) unless you display all your text in the Monaco font, where all letters have the same width.

An advantage of this text-oriented service is that you can use any old communications software to reach Delphi. A disadvantage is that all the way-cool Macintosh software I was showing off in Chapter 5 can't be used here. To use this fancy software, you need a separate *serial-line-interface-protocol* (SLIP) account on another service. There is also no indication that Delphi intends to "iconize" its interface, probably because Macintosh users are a small minority on Delphi.

Later in this chapter, I'll describe a partial fix-up, called D-Lite, for this deplorable situation. There are rumors that a real Mac interface will be available soon. But for now, it's just as my third-grade teacher told me, "Charles, you simply can't have everything your own way!"

Delphi: The Real Thing

How do you find the Internet service on Delphi? You can't miss it. I have highlighted it in Figure 10-3, just for emphasis. You can't highlight words on-line in this graphically pitiful terminal-style system, so italic and bold are indicated by underscores that are located before and after the word(s) to be highlighted, such as in the following example: _drama_. Dramatic, no? To get to the Internet, type **internet** at the prompt, and you get to the special Internet menu.

Figure 10-3:
Go ahead.
Pick one
from
Column A.

```
MAIN Menu:

Business and Finance      News, Weather, and Sports
Computing Groups          Reference and Education
Conference                Shopping
Entertainment and Games   Travel and Leisure
Groups and Clubs          Using DELPHI
Internet Services         Workspace
Mail                      HELP
Member Directory          EXIT
```

The menu in Figure 10-4 is full of possibilities. It contains not only every Internet buzzword I have mentioned so far in this book, but it also contains a convenient menu to back up each buzzword. It's the whole Internet, fresh off the high-speed national fiber-optic link.

Figure 10-4:
Yep, looks
like it's all
there, all
right.

```
Internet SIG Menu:


About the Internet    Help
Conference            Exit
Databases (Files)
EMail                 FTP
Forum (Messages)      Gopher
Guides (Books)        IRC-Internet Relay Chat
Register/Cancel       Telnet
Who's Here            Utilities (finger, traceroute, ping)
Workspace             Usenet Newsgroups
```

Unfiltered

Delphi doesn't censor on-line material. In fact, Delphi offers so much material that it couldn't possibly censor it. A case in point is Internet Relay Chat, a kind of global Internet conference call in which a virtual "roomful" of people type their comments on a topic in a running dialogue.

Some of these chat groups are, um, remarkable (see accompanying figure). Some are amateur radio operators trading tips on upgrading equipment. Some of them are "adult" chat groups — with a variety of specialty interests — describing activities that I'm pretty sure no one could actually do (hey, after all, you can't see anyone in a plain-text interface). I have a friend who spent years in the Navy seeking out the least elegant entertainment imaginable near every U.S. Navy base in the Far East, and he turned pale and left the room after looking over my shoulder while I let a particular chat group scroll past.

Uncensored adult entertainment is one of the aspects of the Internet that gives fun-for-the-whole-family services, such as America Online and Prodigy, fits. Family services just *can't* let the kiddies point and click their way into some of these discussions. Wouldn't work. No way.

```
***    #malang:      4  Cangkruk dul, Jagongan Dul!

***    #DogWorld:    1  Cats: enter at your own risk!
***    #aposoc:      6  Alpha Phi Omega National Co-ed Svc Fraternity
***    #dementia:    2  Weird Al, Dr D., Tom Lehrer, and other demented music!!!
*** #Demon's_L*      1  What evil lies in the hearts of Men? The DemoN knows!
***    #kun:         1  Welcome to the KUN: Katholieke Universiteit Nijmegen

*** #Doom(201):      2  ANYONE IN 201 AREA WANNA PLAY D O O M ?

***    #freenet:    14  Freenet Finland

***    #math:        5  what is mathematics?
***    #BotFree:     2  IRC Astrology /sign (your sign here)
*** #machscafe:      5  Marry me and be my Love for always!
***    #anime!:     16  Japanese Animation and Comics (manga)
***    #vampires:   |7  If you are going to be offended by the exchange of ideas,
                                       IRC isn't for you
*** #macintosh:     11  http://disserv.stu.umn.edu/~thingles/macintosh.html
***    #depeche:     7  THE DEPECHE MODE CHANNEL
***    #nippon:     15  kokoh nihonjin ryuugakuseitachi no tamariba
```

Telnet, if you must

Telnet is the most basic Internet function. Therefore, you should, in my humble opinion, use telnet only when it's the only way to do the job. If, for example, you have been assigned a real user account at a remote computer and you want to run UNIX programs on that computer for some reason (this happens all the time in science), you have to use telnet. If you just want to poke around on a remote site to see what may be there, you will use up everyone's resources and patience scrolling through the directories.

Here's how to do your homework before setting out with telnet. Instead of going directly to the Internet conference, type **computing** at the opening menu and then type **mac**.

This set of commands gets you to the choices in Figure 10-5. Delphi usually has 99 percent of the files, fonts, and information a Mac user will want right here in the Macintosh group. Usually, you can save yourself plenty of time and frustration by looking through this section before sailing out into the vastness of the Net. Remember my Uncle George's proverb: "Just because you have a swimming pool doesn't mean you have to practice holding your breath."

Figure 10-5: These Delphi areas have tons of interesting material.

```
APP - Applications Sig      ENT - Entertainment Sig

DAT - ICONtact Files        COM - Communications Sig

DEV - Developer's Sig       FOR - ICONtact Forum

UTI - Utilities Sig         INT - Mac Internet GOPHER

USE - USENET Groups
```

At this point, the INT command gets you the deliriously detailed menu in Figure 10-6. And thar she blows, mateys, at number 11. These are the sites, all right. If you fetch the site list by recording the on-line session in your communications software, you can review it on paper and make yourself a little telnet guide with all the current Mac sites. This, in fact, is probably the only telnet plan that will work by mid-1995 because sites pop on and off the Internet with alarming regularity. Another Delphi source of telnet information is HytelNet, a hypercard stack with a catalog of sites (it's in the TOOLS&UTILITIES area of DATABASES in the Mac interest group).

Figure 10-6: Bingo! You've landed on Delphi's Macintosh treasure barge.

```
Macintosh ICONtact Gopher
Page 1 of 1

1    PERSONAL FAVORITES                          Menu
2    A DIRECT FTP INTERNET CONNECTION            Menu
3    ABOUT DELPHI'S GOPHER SERVICE               Text
4    ARCHIVES OF MAC FILES                       Menu
5    DOCUMENTATION, ETC FOR MACS                 Menu
6    FAQ'S, MAC INFO, HELP FOR YOUR MAC          Menu
7    FONTS FOR THE MAC                           Menu
8    GRAPHICS OF ALL FLAVORS                     Menu
9    INTERNET SEARCH UTILITIES                   Menu
10   MAC BBS'S ON INTERNET                       Menu
11   MACINTOSH TELNET SITES                      Menu
12   MISC. FILES FOR THE MAC                     Menu
13   PRODUCT INFO ON MACS                        Menu
14   TOOLS FOR YOUR MAC                          Menu
15   UTILITIES FOR YOUR MAC                      Menu
16   WEATHER INFORMATION                         Menu
17   DELPHI'S MAIN GOPHER (INTERNET SIG)         Menu
```

Delphi — being pretty much a model of good Internet service and the only other service that's as Mac-friendly as America Online — has collected everything you may want in this fantastic Gopher menu. There's enough stuff here to keep you busy for weeks.

When you launch telnet from Delphi, Delphi provides you with a set of useful definitions and commands right after the prompt. In most communications software, you can scroll back to these commands if you get lost or need further advice. This ability to go back to the commands is helpful because plenty of the telnet sites have only primitive or nonexistent help. Again, I think that for souvenir collecting and such, telnet is actually the last resource you should use (Gopher is more efficient), but Delphi at least makes it as easy as possible to use it when you must.

FTP, if you like

There is also a menu item for FTP in Figure 10-6. If you have a file in mind that hasn't already been downloaded to some area on Delphi, you can get it with FTP. This is *real* FTP, of course, not the FTP-by-mail operation required at some other services.

Figure 10-7 shows an FTP session (the commands I typed in are highlighted in bold — you can do the same). I logged onto the giant Mac collection at Stanford, and I'm ashamed to say I did it in broad daylight because I was in a hurry. It's usually better to try a less popular "mirror" site (a copy of the original collection) as a point of netiquette, but your chances of getting into the Stanford sumex-aim site during the day are about as good as your chances of getting admitted to Stanford's freshman class as a high-school dropout.

Figure 10-7:
Straight
FTP, with a
little Delphi
hand-
holding.

```
Internet SIG>Enter your selection: ftp
Enter destination INTERNET address: sumex-aim.stanford.edu
Enter username (default: anonymous): anonymous

To get a binary file, type:  BINARY and then GET "remote filename" myfilename
To get a text file, type:    ASCII  and then GET "remote filename" myfilename
  Upper and lower case ARE significant; use the "quotes" shown above.
To get a directory, use DIR.
To type a short text file, use TT for myfilename
To get out, type EXIT or Control-Z.

Enter password [XXYYZZ@DELPHI.COM]: XXYYZZ@DELPHI.COM
220 SUMEX-AIM FTP server (Version 4.223 Thu Jun 24 16:42:58 PST 1994) ready.
331 Guest login ok, send mail address (user@host) as password.
230 Guest connection accepted. Restrictions apply.
FTP> ls

200 PORT command successful.
150 Opening ASCII mode data connection for /bin/ls.
info-mac
226 Transfer complete.
```

Watch out for file extensions

Again, as in the telnet example, you can scroll back to look at Delphi's hints about commands. Most sites that have interesting material have a combination of binary files and ASCII text files, so pay attention to the file extension (.BIN and .SIT are binary; .TXT and .HQX are ASCII).

You're not quite home yet

The file you request in an FTP transfer to Delphi leaves the remote computer and lands on Delphi's computer. You don't have it yet on your Mac. It's in your *workspace*. There's a WORKSPACE command available at the Internet menu. Just type **workspace** and then get your bearings in workspace-land by typing **help**.

If you look at the directory of your workspace, you should see whatever files you have FTP'd to Delphi. Just type the download command and follow the instructions to receive the file on your own computer.

Gopher, the right way to go

The world of the Internet is a world of choices. You can find them all by telneting to one site after another. In one perspective, this is "surfing the Net," and it has some entertainment value for people who want to feel like they're hacking. The problem, of course, is that if enough people decide to explore the Internet in this way, the situation will have more in common with a logjam on a river in British Columbia than surfing on Maui.

Fortunately, all sorts of diligent, kindly, and clever people have set up Gophers for you. Gophers are simply-structured menus that have all the resources of the Internet neatly classified. Just pick your way through all those remote computers by selecting menu choices. At the end of the menu trail, you usually get down to text files or programs. By using Gopher instead of FTP, you will notice a prompt asking you if you want to download the material — the Gopher already knows whether the file is binary or ASCII.

Just look at the lovely Gopher menu in Figure 10-8. How about the choice ALL THE WORLD'S GOPHERS? Is that good enough for you? It's your assurance that if you are willing to work in Gopherspace, you are going to find essentially everything that's out there.

```
Internet SIG>Enter your selection: gopher

Internet SIG Gopher
Page 1 of 1

1    PERSONAL FAVORITES                                    Menu
2    "ABOUT DELPHI'S GOPHER SERVICE"                       Text
3    *** FAQ: FREQUENTLY ASKED QUESTIONS *** (REVISED 5/25) Menu
4    ALL THE WORLD'S GOPHERS                               Menu
5    BUSINESS AND ECONOMICS                                Menu
6    COMPUTERS                                             Menu
7    FREE-NETS AND COMMUNITY ACCESS                        Menu
8    FTP: DOWNLOADABLE PROGRAMS, IMAGES, SOUNDS            Menu
9    GAMES AND MUDS, MUSHES, MUSES, AND MOOS               Menu
10   GOVERNMENT AND POLITICS                               Menu
11   HEALTH AND MEDICINE                                   Menu
12   INTERNET INFORMATION                                  Menu
13   LAW                                                   Menu
14   LIBRARIES AND RESEARCH GUIDES                         Menu
15   SCHOOLHOUSE (K-12)                                    Menu
16   SEARCH UTILITIES (INCLUDING WORLD WIDE WEB)           Menu
17   SUBJECT MATTER MENUS                                  Menu
18   THE GRAB BAG (WITH WHAT'S NEW 6/21)                   Menu
```

Figure 10-8:
Gophers to
everywhere
and
everything!

I know I have this paragraph labeled with a Tip icon, but this remark is a tip the way "Do unto others . . ." is a tip. It's really a plea, an approach to things, a way to *be*. I realize that Archie (also available on Delphi), FTP, and telnet are honorable Internet commands of long standing and are greatly beloved by the UNIX guys who put the Internet together. Using them with suitable ingenuity, you can do all sorts of neat things on the Internet. However, *you should always try Gopher first. It's powerful and easy to use, and it's designed to conserve Net resources.*

I know there is always a temptation to stray away from the tour group and start exploring directly on your own, but if you're new to the Net, you're going to get better results with Gopher. If you need anything — from aerospace engineering files to multiuser dungeon on-line games — this Gopher will lead you to the right place. It's true that it takes all the mystique out of the Internet, but you don't have to tell anyone you use it. Do your searching with Gopher and *pretend* you have hundreds of telnet site addresses memorized along with scads of UNIX commands.

E-mail, of Course

If using the Gopher on Delphi is that simple, can you imagine what e-mail is like? Well, you're right again. There's almost nothing to be said about it, as you'll find out if you accept Delphi's free trial offer. To use Delphi e-mail, you just pick MAIL from the main menu and follow the directions. To send Internet mail, you put INTERNET first in the address. People will send you e-mail at [yourname]@delphi.com. That's it.

Because Delphi is real-thing Internet, you don't have to bootleg services through e-mail. You used to have to manage Usenet newsgroup access through Delphi e-mail, but there's a gloriously effective NEWSGROUP choice now in the Internet menu.

D-Lite: It's Mac and It's Fast

Nothing you have seen so far, although it may have been first-rate Internet access, looks much like real Mac software. However, there is a third-party Delphi interface for the Macintosh called D-Lite (see Figure 10-9), a semi-mandatory-payment shareware product that costs $29 to register and is worth considerably more.

D-Lite is a Delphi equivalent of CompuServe Navigator. D-Lite is designed to let you run a Delphi session faster than you can possibly type by logging requests in advance and then playing them into the service. It logs on, does everything you want at blinding speed, and then logs off. For sessions of any level of complexity at all, it's ten times faster than you are.

In D-Lite, you can prepare all your outgoing e-mail messages off-line (see Figure 10-10). You can write them in your favorite word processor and just paste them in the message space. D-Lite signs on Delphi, collects your mail, jams your messages into the system, and then ends the session. You can set it to collect all the new messages in your interest groups; you can assign it to scan your newsgroups; and it can manage an automated FTP session. It's very, very good.

Figure 10-9:
D-Lite, a bright idea for Delphi users.

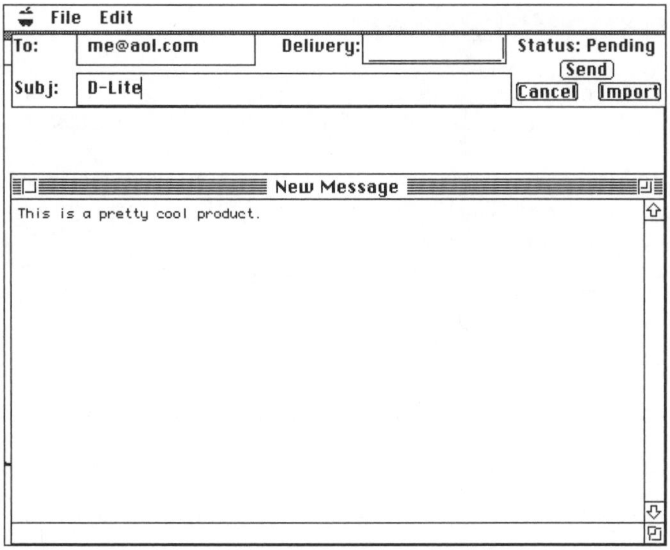

```
  ~   File   Edit
┌──────────────────────────────────────────────────────────────┐
│ To:  │ me@aol.com     │ Delivery: │        │ Status: Pending  │
│      │                │           │        │      (Send)      │
│ Subj:│ D-Lite│        │           │        │ (Cancel) (Import)│
│                                                                │
│  ┌────────────────────── New Message ──────────────────────┐  │
│  │This is a pretty cool product.                        ⇧  │  │
│  │                                                         │  │
│  │                                                         │  │
│  │                                                         │  │
│  │                                                         │  │
│  │                                                         │  │
│  │                                                      ⇩  │  │
└──────────────────────────────────────────────────────────────┘
```

Figure 10-10:
The D-Lite
e-mail
system
saves loads
of time.

D-Lite is not as cool as the America Online interface, in which all you need to do is point and click, but it certainly enhances Delphi for the average Mac user. In this book, I've been making a big point of efficient use of Internet resources, and D-Lite is a key program for efficiency. It's like windsurfing the Net with a 60 mph wind.

Delphi Does It All

To write this book, I signed onto every kind of Internet access and on-line service. I have monthly on-line charges on my credit card that look like Honolulu mortgage payments. A few months after publication, I'll be cutting back a bit.

But I won't cut Delphi. This service is a keeper. It's simply more useful for most Mac users than a shell account, and the Macintosh is a big part of Delphi rather than an afterthought. Hey, it's got to be worth a five-hour free trial!

As Long As You're Here

For a nice practical thing to do with a text-based interface, try this little mortgage calculator (Figure 10-11) in the Business forum available from the main menu.

Delphi also has some unusual options because it's a relatively highbrow service compared to the rest. The Dictionary of Cultural Literacy (Figure 10-12) is available on-line under the Reference menu, reminding you of the basics (in my opinion, this dictionary has some shocking non-Western omissions).

Figure 10-11:
A sample
mortgage
calculation,
with
optimistic
numbers.

```
BUSINESS>Which service? MORTGAGE

This program does mortgage, loan or lease calculations.  Default entries are
shown in brackets like [this].  Enter Control-Z to exit.

What would you like this program to calculate?

Term, Interest, Principal, or Payment (? for help) [PAYMENT] ?PAYMENT

Will compute PAYMENT.

Term of loan, in years [15] ?20
Interest rate, in percent [10] ?8.5
Principal (amount borrowed) [10000] ?125000

Term of loan          20.00 years.
Interest Rate          8.500% per year.
Principal        125,000.00
Monthly Payment    1,084.78
```

Figure 10-12:
This
dictionary is
strong on
Western Civ
basics.

```
The Dictionary of Cultural Literacy
Copyright (c) 1988 by Houghton Mifflin Company
All rights reserved.

Search for: AESCHYLUS

1  AESCHYLUS

(ES-kuh-luhs, EES-kuh-luhs)

An ancient Greek poet, often considered the founder of TRAGEDY. He was
the first of the three great Greek authors of tragedies, preceding
SOPHOCLES and EURIPIDES.

References for AESCHYLUS
--------
    1  EURIPIDES
    2  SOPHOCLES
    3  TRAGEDY
```

The collaborative novel project (Figure 10-13), in the Writer's forum, is another Delphi intellectual adventure (uh-oh, Toto, something tells me we're not in Prodigy anymore). You pick a novel and make a contribution. This figure shows just a few choices out of several hundred in progress. This activity is strongly addictive, though a pretty demonstrable waste of time.

Figure 10-13:
The collaborative novel project lets you create without dealing with editors.

```
WRITERS Menu:

Announcements          Poll
Collaborative Novel    Set Preferences
Conference             Topic Descriptions
Databases (Files)      Who's Here
Entry Log              Workspace
Forum (Messages)       Classified Ads
Member Directory       Help
MAIL                   Exit

WRITERS>What do you want to do? COLLABORATIVE

List of novels:

PLANET TONUCISH
BILLY
ALL THINGS EARTHLY
FAIRYTALES FROM A BROKEN HEART
A WEEKEND AT CEDARWOOD
GILLIAN'S ISLAND: A TV SCRIPT
MUFFY AND THE SKINHEADS
```

Chapter 11

Internet from GEnie

GEnie is a national on-line service that can call on the rather deep pockets of General Electric to finance its expansion. For most of the 1980s, GE managed networks for large corporations — Apple's own AppleLink was operated by General Electric Information Services. Now GEnie is what those "in the know" call a major player in the struggle for the hearts and minds of America's computing public. GEnie has local access numbers all over and a growing list of features. One of the new features, under development in the summer of 1994, is a decent Macintosh version of the service, at long last.

A Mild Complaint

Before I launch into the story of GEnie's many virtues — and indeed they are many — I am going to complain about the way this service has been presented to Mac users. *Macworld*, my own magazine, has been running advertisements in which America Online and CompuServe are represented by pairs of broken nerd-glasses held together by tape. GEnie is then described against a colorful mock generation-X graphic with the slogan, "The most fun you can have with your computer on!"

Ahem. First, the most fun you can have with your computer on is to find a mood-enhancing screen-saver, turn off the other lights in the room, and do something amusing on the floor. Everybody already knows this.

Second, please inspect the screen in Figure 11-1. *That's* what you see when you sign on to GEnie. Think you can handle it? Got the blood-pressure medication ready? There's nothing particularly wrong with the opening screen, but it's hard to make a case that it's anything but the same-old by-the-numbers menu system available not just from CompuServe but from half the local computer bulletin boards in North America. To make it more insulting yet, my local access number is still 2400 bps, and my ID and password would embarrass a Martian.

```
CONNECT 2400
HHH
U#=XKY24249,SFKTRMBX

GEnie Logon at: 00:41 PDT on: 940518
Last Access at: 01:01 PDT on: 940317
        GEnie Announcements

  1. Uncle Yog's Storytime; coming soon to the..................SFRT1
  2. Author LYNN KERSTAN on blending humor & emotion in writing..ROMANCE
  3. The glory of the Gladiatorial Games, this weekend in........GEMSTONE
  4. KNITTING Machines are humming in...........................NEEDLE
  5. LAST NIGHT to register for CA$H and time tournament prizes..CHESS
  6. Deja vu - INTERNET MTS Transcript available from Menu on....GENIEUS
  7. Venez pratiquer votre francais au..........................CANADA
  8. Writing Astrological software 5/18 10pm - ASTROLOGY RT in...PROGRAMMING
  9. Refunding Premiums GREAT Gifts at a GREAT Price.............COLLECT
 10. Hug a KOALA May 17 --- Ride the EUROPEAN RAILS May 18.......TRAVEL
 11. The boss is on vacation - It's PARTY Time and it's FREE in..EAST
 12. Online Class on HOW TO MAKE ASCII ART, Sunday at 9pm EDT....FAMILY
```

Figure 11-1:
Wild fun,
thrills, and
chills.

And to belabor the point just a bit: When you follow the menu choices all the way down into the lists of available files, as shown in Figure 11-2, things aren't much different here from what you find elsewhere, either.

```
1159 NEWS090.ZIP          X NEWSLETTER   940515  19328   109   8
     Desc: ZIPped version of NEWSLTR.090
1158 NEWSLTR.090          X NEWSLETTER   940515  62592   105   8
     Desc: GEnie Online Newsletter, Issue #90!
1155 CYBRSIGN.TXT         X PROF.MARK    940510  50176   116   1
     Desc: Explains emoticons & abbreviations
1153 NEWUSER.TXT          X JEB          940506  25728   281   5
     Desc: A quick guide to GEnie for new users
1152 CHEAPER.GE           X BOMBADIL     940506  34944   259   5
     Desc: Guide to saving time & money online.
1151 GENIEUS.LIB          X PROF.MARK    940503  67584   119   3
     Desc: The GENIEus Software Library.
1149 INTERNET.MTS         X PROF.MARK    940502  51968   126   7
     Desc: The Internet Meet the SysOps RTC!
1148 NEWS089.ZIP          X NEWSLETTER   940430  17536   121   8
     Desc: ZIPped version of NEWSLTR.089
1147 NEWSLTR.089          X NEWSLETTER   940430  56448   106   8
     Desc: GEnie Online Newsletter, Issue #89!
1145 TCAROL.GIF           X T.CAROL      940427 184576   101  10
     Desc: A picture of me on my Motorcycle.
```

Figure 11-2:
GEnie files:
meat and
potatoes, no
radicchio.

Internet by Request

But bless its electric corporate heart — GEnie has done the One Big Thing all the other on-line services should have done: It has hired people to process your Internet requests. GEnie has provided a great service while offering the interim solution to the big Internet question, "What do we give them while we figure out what to do?"

You can use e-mail on CompuServe for Archie and FTP access, but this process is something you wouldn't do if you had a better alternative. Direct Archie and FTP is one better alternative. Even better than this alternative — especially if you're just starting out on the Net — is using someone with lots of experience to do your searching for you.

Help!

If you are a GEnie user and you're interested in an Internet topic or topics, you can send an e-mail message to the GE system operators of the Internet RoundTable (RoundTable is GEnie-speak for forum or conference). In the Mac front end, there's always a cute little mailbox icon you can click to do this; in the text-interface, mail is always available as an option.

The system operators do whatever Internet searching is required in Archie or fetch some files for you with FTP and send you the whole package. If you like, you can ask them to forward the search transcript so that you can see how the search was formulated. After you collect a dozen or so of these search transcripts to inspect, you'll see how to do the search for yourself.

GEnie people are really smart

You can send a message to the sysops (*system operators*) at GEnie. Even if your message contains typos, outright misspellings (horrors!), or fairly vague descriptions of what you want, you'll get something useful back. That's because people are pretty good at divining your intentions from a few remarks.

If you try this at the standard interface on a UNIX-based Internet server, however, you're likely to get error messages you can't even read. UNIX requires that you get your commands exactly right the first time, and it won't second-guess your intentions.

Placing an experienced Internet user between new users and the machines on the Net reduces the frustration level for everyone. Even a user with two weeks hands-on experience is smarter than the best interface that an artificial-intelligence design can produce. That's why GEnie uses trained searchers to find files for you. GEnie provides you with people who are the equivalent of reference librarians in a standard book-library—this experience will make things easier down the road when you do your own searches. This Internet-access program has been so successful thus far that GEnie is hiring full-time Internet reference specialists to assist the system operators.

A Solution For Internet Crowding

In 1993, about ten Internet books appeared in bookstores across the land. In aggregate, they probably sold nearly a million copies. Every one of the books tells you to try an Archie search at the same server at the University of Maryland. If 0.01 percent of the people who bought these books actually try this at any given time, the server won't be able to generate anything but the Internet equivalent of busy signals.

Channeling requests to sysops who can access the Internet at odd hours (GEnie pays them to do this) greatly relieves traffic problems. Instead of GEnie putting 100 newbies on the Net at 4:00 in the afternoon, the whole GEnie network generates managed bursts of access late at night. You make your requests any time you like (actually, this approach is thrifty with your own connect time as well), and GEnie processes the requests during low-traffic time.

The GEnie Internet RoundTable

Direct FTP and telnet, and presumably a special GEnie Gopher, will be available by early 1995. By that time, GEnie users who have been participating in the Internet RoundTable (see Figure 11-3) will be able to use these tools effectively because the users will have had on-line question-and-answer access to a talented group of systems people.

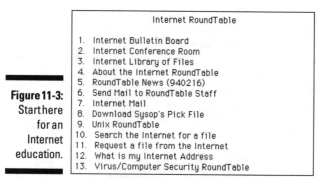

Figure 11-3: Start here for an Internet education.

```
                Internet RoundTable

    1.  Internet Bulletin Board
    2.  Internet Conference Room
    3.  Internet Library of Files
    4.  About the Internet RoundTable
    5.  RoundTable News (940216)
    6.  Send Mail to RoundTable Staff
    7.  Internet Mail
    8.  Download Sysop's Pick File
    9.  Unix RoundTable
    10. Search the Internet for a file
    11. Request a file from the Internet
    12. What is my Internet Address
    13. Virus/Computer Security RoundTable
```

GEnie is the only national on-line service that seems to have understood that there's a demand not just for Internet access but for something approximating training. Yes, yes, yes! I know that there are plenty of people who want full Internet access, and they want it right now. And once you get the hang of it, navigating the Internet isn't that hard. For a gentle introduction where you never see `ACCESS DENIED` flashing at you, this GEnie system has lots to recommend it.

E-Mail Basics

Like all other national services, you can send and receive Internet e-mail at GEnie. Using GEnie for e-mail is just a bit different from what you might expect.

Incoming

Tell your pals to send you mail at the following address:

```
yourname@genie.geis.com
```

The `geis` part is essential because General Electric manages more than one network. Sending a message to `genie.com` doesn't work.

Outgoing

In keeping with this last little delicately nuanced bit of weirdness, the mail you send has a funny address inside GEnie, too. To reach my old mailbox at another Internet host, for example, I would address the mail like so:

```
TO:chseiter@crl.com@INET#
```

That's right, we're talking about nearly the only scheme on earth with two @ symbols in the address. It works, though. Just follow the usual Internet address by @INET# and it will get to the right place on the Net.

GEnie Joins the Revolution

GEnie is working on a beautiful new Macintosh interface for the system, as shown in Figure 11-4. Now you don't have to crawl through endless numbered menus to get where you're going.

Figure 11-4
The magic
lamp
beckons.

In the new look, the standard-issue-geek's-delight sign-on screen is replaced with a list of options preceded by icons that look like open books (see Figure 11-5) because different sections of GEnie are cataloged as pages. The Internet RoundTable also has a new look, with neatly organized libraries (see Figure 11-6) and easy mail contact with the ever-helpful sysops.

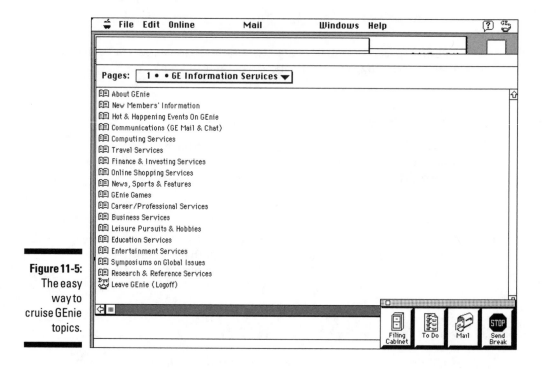

Figure 11-5:
The easy
way to
cruise GEnie
topics.

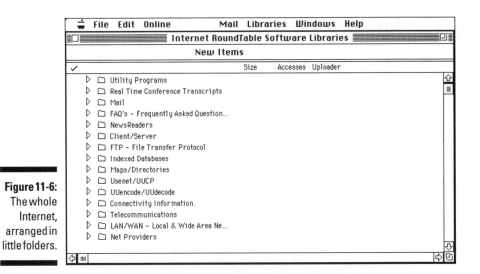

Figure 11-6:
The whole
Internet,
arranged in
little folders.

Finally, if you have any other problems, all you have to do in GEnie's new look is get the Help Window from the Windows menu and click your way to a state of clarity (Figure 11-7). This Help system is a pretty admirable piece of work.

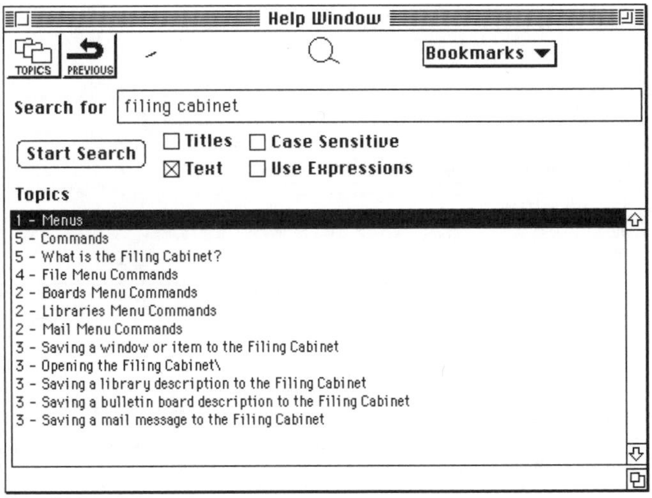

Figure 11-7:
The new
GEnie Help
system is
the best in
the on-line
world.

A Snapshot in Time

Fortunately, GEnie produced a working prerelease of its new Macintosh software in time for this book. The software is still rough in spots, but if GEnie can combine its program of providing sysop assistance for new Internet users with direct Internet access and this real-Mac front end, it will be the red-hot service its advertising describes by early 1995. As this was being written, GEnie was working to develop an icon-based access system to the full range of Internet features.

As Long As You're Here

GEnie has piled up an assortment of interesting reference and shopping services. One of the most impressive is the DIALOG service, a collection of professional databases on technical topics (Figure 11-8). DIALOG use invokes extra hourly charges beyond the monthly and hourly GEnie fees, but from astronomy to zoology it's the definitive reference. I found over the last few months, working for a consulting client on a patent in polymer surface treatment, that I can use DIALOG as a replacement for the chemical engineering libraries at Stanford and UC Berkeley. That's right — you guessed it — when I'm not writing computer books, I'm the kind of guy who knows how to have fun in a library. And now I can have all that fun at home!

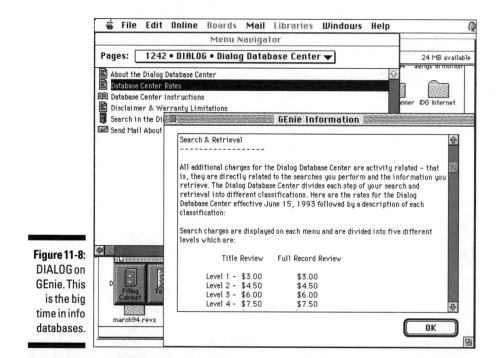

Figure 11-8: DIALOG on GEnie. This is the big time in info databases.

Another GEnie professional initiative is education. Figure 11-9 just hints at one of the things to come, which is the development of degree programs and other kinds of professional credentialling through on-line services. In the 1990s, not only are jobs disappearing and then appearing elsewhere at a terrifying rate, but your set of professional skills are being made obsolete almost monthly. There's going to be plenty of technical education flying around on the Net.

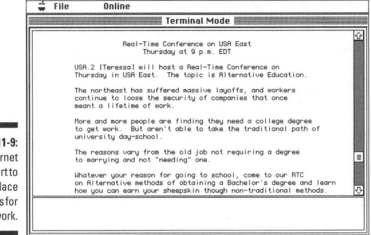

Figure 11-9:
The Internet
will start to
replace
schools for
coursework.

And once you get your information, collect your degree, and start bringing home the big bucks, GEnie will stand ready and able to help you lighten your pockets. The Mall on GEnie is a prototype for shopping services that will probably appear elsewhere on the Internet. Frankly, the main attraction of these services is quick ordering of products you already know. On-line book-stores, for example, tend to be very good, since they have better selection and prices than the local mall chain-bookstore. But it's hard to picture buying sporting goods or clothes from this sort of arrangement, since transfer of decent color pictures still takes too long even with a fast modem. Just wait and see (I probably shouldn't propose this) . . . some genius will figure a way to send you color pictures as a background activity when you're just looking at the screen trying to decode the menus.

Part IV

Do-It-Yourself
Internet

"WE'D LIKE TO TALK TO YOU BOYS ABOUT COMMERCIALIZING YOUR INTERNET FREEWARE APPLICATION."

In this part...

*I*f you're an adventurous spirit, you may want to strike out and get your own Internet connection, rather than use a national on-line service.

Frankly, a roll-your-own connection is harder to do, but this book still brings it within the reach of Dummies. I'll tell you all about the dazzling Mac software you can use to surf the Net.

Chapter 13, my personal favorite, is the only guide to SLIP connection for your Mac that gets down to the real what-next details of a direct-connect SLIP Internet account.

Chapter 12

Bulletin Boards — The Local Electronic Community

*A*nyone who can afford to leave a computer running all the time can operate a *bulletin board,* or its grander cousin, a *conferencing system.* Both terms really just mean a computer with incoming lines and a filing system for messages. A national on-line service like Delphi, for example, consists of big computers that carry hundreds of specialized message areas and thousands of files. A bulletin board may consist of a single Mac with only one or two incoming lines. But in both cases, you get to rummage around the files and see what's there, post messages, or join a discussion group.

The biggest urban bulletin boards can have tens of thousands of paying members and carry all the latest Mac files — some big boards are, in effect, mini-Delphis. Other smaller boards flourish by specialization. Specialty bulletin boards cater to people interested in steam locomotives, 18th-century antiques, phenomenally kinky sex, multiuser on-line games, chess, astronomy, and any other topic you can — or can't — imagine. The big boards are quite stable (the WELL in San Francisco was operating before most national services), whereas small ones require monthly reading of *Boardwatch Magazine* just to see who's still there and who's not.

In the past, bulletin boards rarely had Internet connections, but now it's becoming common. A board that is free (or charges a few dollars a month), has an Internet connection, and a local call for your modem is the cheapest connection you're likely to get. Unless, of course, you're a Stanford student, where your $20,000-per-year tuition includes absolutely *free* access to

---

Ten reasons to use bulletin boards

1. If you find a date, you both live in the same area code.

2. You can find cheap used Macs.

3. You're a hard-core nerd (EMS 301-924-3594 voice).

4. You're a Buddhist (Mt. Kailas 617-252-9988 modem).

5. You hunt elk (Vacation Source 800-868-7555 modem).

6. You hunt dragons (ONIX 215-879-6616 modem).

7. You're gay (Eye Contact 415-703-8200 modem).

8. You want to join Throbnet, Kinknet, and Wildnet (I'm not making this up! Blues Cafe 214-638-1186 modem).

9. All your credit cards are maxed out and Prodigy won't let you on.

10. You believe that the national on-line services are simply fronts for a giant market-research firm (I'm not sure that I don't believe this myself).

`sumex-aim.stanford.edu` (I vaguely remember some proverb about free lunches . . .). In this chapter, I give you a couple examples of bulletin board access to the Internet and then send you out looking for these local on-ramps to the information highway. All you need is a modem to dial the service and a willingness to use a text-based interface.

The WELL: It's Swell

Almost every big city has a bulletin board that's been a hangout for Macintosh fans for a decade now, and most of these boards are now Internet-ready. Some states have their own statewide boards: in Hawaii it's Hawaii FYI, in Montana it's Big Sky Telegraph, and in Michigan it's NovaLink.

Deluxe hand-holding

The San Francisco area's WELL (Internet name is `well.sf.ca.us`, voice phone 415-332-4335) is an excellent example of a community bulletin board. The name stands for Whole Earth 'Lectronic Link, as this bulletin board was founded by the crew of jolly futurist pirates who published the wildly successful "Whole Earth Catalog," a mild dose of counterculture during the 1980s. They took the profits from the catalog and used some of the money to start the bulletin board. With its foundation as a nonprofit, electronic-freedom pioneer, the WELL is similar to many other bulletin boards from a computing point of view, but it has a rather high-minded internal Net culture.

Figure 12-1 shows you what happens when the wireheads meet the hippies. The WELL is a UNIX system, but instead of leaving you with a one-character prompt, it gives you chatty little menus and live on-line help.

```
UNIX(r) System V Release 4.0 (well)

This is the WELL

Type    newuser    to sign up.
Type    trouble    if you are having trouble logging in.
Type    guest      to learn about the WELL.

login: chseiter
Password:

    May 17  Intermediate Tutorial (g wellcome ; s 93)           <== TOMORROW!
    May 20  WELL Office Party #92 (g news ; s 1541)             <== Friday
    Jul 23  Annual WELL Picnic (g news ; s 1515)

            Welcome to The WELLcome Conference!

Gotta question? Ask away over in topic 118: type    s 118 nor    then type    r
Introduce yourself in topic 119:               type    s 119 nor    then type    r
For immediate help from a real person:         type    helpers
For the WELLcome Conference menu:              type    wellcome
```

Figure 12-1: Wherever you go, there you are — WELL help covers it.

I don't know how they do it, but they have people around to answer your questions at 4:17 a.m. The whole system is as friendly as a Yorkshire terrier snoozing in your lap.

Real Internet, plus Help

But, you may ask, where's the Internet? It's all here, and for a text-based system, it's pretty spectacular. You type

```
g inet
```

and you're in the Internet conference. Then type

```
netmenu
```

and you see the choices shown in Figure 12-2. On the WELL, you don't really need to know these commands because you can ask for options or help at any point and the system gives you your choices.

```
OK (type a command or type  opt   for Options): netmenu

        T h e   I n t e r n e t   C o n f e r e n c e   M e n u

type  1  for Introductory Readings

type  2  for Rules and Regulations on the use of the Internet from the WELL

type  3  for Cheat-sheets on how to use Internet tools

type  4  for Information on Libraries online

type  5  for Information on FTP (File transfer protocol)

type  6  for Information on Internet Services

type  7  to look for an Internet site near you

type  8  for the Miscellaneous files
```

Figure 12-2:
Detailed
WELL
menus start
you on the
Internet.

Gopher on the Well

You get on-line cheat sheets for help with Archie, FTP, and telnet and also on-line versions of the standard Internet beginner's documents. Where this bulletin board really passes up the competition, however, is in its own Gopher, called, appropriately, wellgopher (see Figure 12-3). Because it's a real Gopher, this menu lets you automatically sail out into all the other computers on the Net, searching for the elusive wonder-file. And because it's the WELL, "Cyberpunk and Postmodern Culture" is one of the busiest topics.

Going down a more sedate wellgopher hole (Figure 12-4), you find yourself ready to scan the latest from the Advanced X-ray Astrophysics facility. (If this facility is advanced, is there a Beginner's X-ray Astrophysics site in a high school somewhere?) The wellgopher keeps telnetting to other Gophers until you're satisfied.

Fun and games

Some day, weary at last of advanced X-ray astrophysics, you may want to play an on-line game. The people at the WELL are so concerned for your happiness that they not only equip this bulletin board with plenty of interactive games, but they also include tip files (see Figure 12-5) so that you don't wander into a simulation as a "clueless newbie" and get killed off in 12 seconds. A bulletin board that defends you against your own cluelessness is a treasure indeed.

```
OK (type a command or type  opt  for Options): wellgopher
Welcome to the wonderful world of Gopher!
Press ? for Help, q to Quit
Root gopher server: gopher.well.sf.ca.us

  -->  1.  About this gopherspace (including a quick "How To" guide)/
       2.  See the latest additions to this gopherspace/
       3.  Search all menus on the WELLgopher <?>
       4.  Internet Outbound (*New!*)/
       5.  Art, Music, Film, Cultural works, etc/
       6.  Authors, Books, Periodicals, Zines (Factsheet Five lives here!)/
       7.  Business in Cyberspace: Commercial Ventures on the Matrix/
       8.  Communications and Media/
       9.  Community/
       10. Cyberpunk and Postmodern Culture/
       11. Environmental Issues and Ideas/
       12. Hacking/
       13. K-12 Education/
       14. The Matrix (information about the global networks)/
       15. The Military, its People, Policies, and Practices/
       16. Politics/
       17. Science/
       18. The WELL itself/
```

Figure 12-3: Do you feel lucky, cyberpunk?

```
        Internet Gopher Information Client 2.0 pl11

                  SCIENCE, MATH, STATISTICS

  1.  ASCinfo (Info. relating to Advanced XRay Astrophy. Facility) <TEL>

  2.  E-Math (Am. Math. Soc. bbs w/ software and reviews) <TEL>

  3.  Math Gopher (Math archives (software, teaching materials, other go../

  4.  Nuclear Data Center (National nuclear data) <TEL>

  5.  Particle Information (Lookup information on any particle!) <TEL>

  6.  Periodic Table (electronic periodic table of elements) <TEL>

 >7.  STIS (Science & Technology Information System) <TEL>

  8.  The Scientist (Biweekly paper targeted at science professionals)/
```

Figure 12-4: Serious information from around the globe.

```
People gather treasure, slay monsters (and each other), gain experience
points, and thereby become wizards, with powers that are useful in
playing the game. In a variety of MUD known as a Muse (Multi User
Simulation Environment), communication and education and worldbuilding
are the goal of the exercise, rather than gaining points in a game.

Some MUDs can be brutal. If other players can gain points by killing
off "clueless newbies" (which is what you will be until you learn the
ropes), you might find that the first action someone in a new world
takes is to slash at you with a virtual broadsword.

Other MUDs are entirely nonviolent. One good example is Cyberion City.
You can get there by telnetting (see topic #7 in the Internet
conference) to michael.ai.mit.edu, registering as guest, and connecting
as guest. If you decide that you want to get a character, follow the
instructions in the guest login screen.
```

Figure 12-5:
Tip files
keep your
cluelessness
from making
you lose
games too
quickly.

Power to the Public

The WELL is a private, nonprofit bulletin board that charges a monthly fee (basic fee is $12.50 a month). There are also private, for-profit bulletin boards, some of which justify their membership fees by providing harder-core stuff than the Internet, and some of which are very specialized and charge something just to make sure that you're really interested.

The Internet invades the library

Yet another type of bulletin board with Internet connection has appeared lately — the community information service. Typically, this service is organized by a library network, because once a library commits to the horrendous expense of replacing card catalogs with an on-line system with a big computer and terminals, the extra effort of joining the Net is negligible.

Library networks tend to have limited message systems and limited or no e-mail. After all, the library is supposed to serve up information for you, not run your errands. Figure 12-6 shows a typical sign-on screen from the local branch of a countywide library system. I can tell you with confidence that a community information service is coming to your town, if it's not there already, because the vendors have all the parts in place and are lobbying the librarians like crazy.

Moving out of the stacks

So there's the usual stuff you expect from a library, and then there's choice 13 on the menu in Figure 12-6, which is your gateway to the Internet. What the system does when you pick number 13 is fairly simple. A script behind the choice telnets you to a bigger computer — in this case, the main library at Sonoma State University (see Figure 12-7). Then *that* computer presents you with a menu that telnets you to other sites if necessary (refer to Figure 12-8).

Once you get out onto the Net, the choices keep expanding. The library system, you may have noticed, is really just a specialized Gopher in which all the other Gopher Internet sites happen to be libraries or on-line databases. Nonetheless, in the next few years, this system will be offering a large portion of the print material stored in traditional libraries.

```
16 JUNE 94              Healdsburg Library           10:45pm
                  PUBLIC ACCESS (402 , ttyd4p6)

                   Welcome to the online catalog.
             Please type the number and press the key labeled RETURN.

                   1. TITLE
                   2. AUTHOR
                   3. SUBJECT
                   4. MAIN WORDS IN TITLE
                   5. MAIN WORDS IN SUBJECT
                   6. SERIES
                   7. CONTENTS (Plays, short stories, etc.)
                   8. COMMUNITY RESOURCES
                   9. PERIODICAL INDEXES
                   10. Search Your Holds and Fines
                   11. Bulletin Board
                   12. Print Saved Bibliography
                   13. Other Searches (INTERNET)
                   14. Logoff
```

Figure 12-6: The library on the corner gets wired to the universe.

```
Connecting to ADMVAX.SONOMA.EDU on account OPAC -- PLEASE
WAIT
Password:
    SONOMA STATE UNIVERSITY      RUBEN SALAZAR LIBRARY      MERLIN SYSTEM

                        == MAIN MENU ==

    1    SSU Catalog -- Books, Media, Gov. Doc., Other Index/Full Text...

    2    SSU Library Information; Reserve Book Room; Tips on Using This System;
         Suggestion Box, etc...

    3    Indexes, Abstracts & Full-Text Databases--periodicals, encyclopedias,
         book reviews, company profiles, etc... (Password Required)

    4    Additional Libraries and Online Information Services...

    5    Quick Access to All Resources

    6    Exit
```

Figure 12-7: If the book you want is not at the local library, you can check the nearest college.

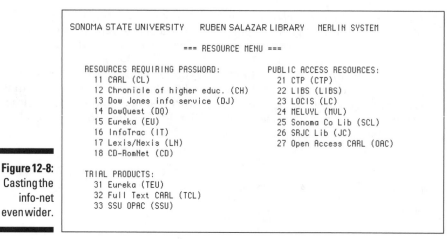

Figure 12-8:
Casting the
info-net
even wider.

The Internet in Your Backyard

People in my small town are often startled to discover that the Internet they've been reading about in the newspapers is the same Internet they can reach from terminals in the library. Our library system lets you dial it from home as well. It's worth checking in your town — if a system is in place, you can practice Internet navigating on the library system before you start shelling out $2 per hour on-line to get lost.

You should also make an effort to find local computer publications — you can usually find them in big-city newsracks. Not only do new private and public bulletin boards appear all the time, but lately, an amazing number of boards have decided to stop charging fees. An Internet-connected board with a decent system operator is as good an introduction to the Net as you're likely to find.

Chapter 13

Really Wired—Direct Connection

• •

In This Chapter

▶ Connecting yourself

▶ Using TCP and SLIP the easy way

▶ Fulfilling all your info needs with Fetch and Gopher

▶ Relating Mosaic to the future

• •

*1*f you have read this far, I'm assuming you haven't been completely seduced by the comforts of America Online or Delphi. Instead, you want to become a real, roll-your-own, big-time Internet "site." Now, instead of being just a user, you'll have your own number address (such as 121.113.8.214) and can even maintain files for other Internet users to access.

Now, here's a way to tell whether getting your own address is easy or not. Look up every book on the Internet you can find in your local library. (Remember, you're supposed to *buy* IDG books, but you're allowed to read the other ones for free if necessary.) Look up the section on MacTCP, if the book has one.

You will find that every last one of the authors says something like "Um, when you get to the part where you actually have to install the Internet connection, you better find a hotshot Mac guru to do it for you." Or "Find a net buddy." Or "Talk to your system administrator." That's not encouraging.

I'll tell you exactly how to get your own Internet connection. It's not exactly going to be summer beach reading, but it's no worse than learning to use a spreadsheet with *Excel For Dummies*, 2nd Edition. And while it may not be the good old Dummies song-and-dance exactly, it's the most detailed (and demystifying) explanation of SLIP connection you're going to see in print.

One of the reasons IDG selected TCP Connect II (see Chapter 7) was that Intercon's setup procedure is simpler than most. If you decide not to use TCP Connect II after the free trial period runs out (although, to tell you the truth, with the discount from InterCon it's a great deal) you will still have MacTCP and InterSLIP on your computer, and can then attempt to use other shareware (Fetch, TurboGopher, Mosaic) to get an Internet connection running. That's why we've included this chapter — you can still get on-line even if you don't take the InterCon offer.

Getting on the Internet

There are a few different ways to get an Internet account that lets you use Mac software. If you already have a Macintosh at a university that is directly connected to a network or you have a Mac on an office network, read the next chapter, not this one. This discussion is for individuals who are willing to find a service provider that offers SLIP accounts and who will be contacting the service with a modem. That's a *dial-up SLIP account*, in case your friends ask you. Back in Chapter 5, I told you that SLIP means *Serial Line Interface Protocol* without giving many technical details. Here come the details.

Step one: Collecting the tools

Don't take any of the following steps as your introduction to the Internet. Instead, take one of the free introductory offers from a national on-line service. In the five to ten hours of connect time you get free, you can not only orient yourself, but you can also get some software and files that you need.

Go to the Macintosh software archives on Pipeline and get your own copies of Fetch and TurboGopher. You might also want to collect the information files on MacTCP, too. Check to make sure you're running your modem at its highest speed also, since these files take a while to download.

If you ran the InterCon installer, you already have copies of MacTCP and InterSLIP in your System folder, but now you should check your configuration again. Note that MacTCP is to be included in System 7.5.

Step two: Call a SLIP provider

How do you find a SLIP account provider? The service runs ads that have the word *SLIP* in them. You can also look in Chapter 19 for services that say *SLIP* in the description. Alternatively, find *Boardwatch Magazine* or *Online Access* and leaf through the ads because new players appear in this game almost weekly. A local version (different cities produce different editions) of the tabloid computer monthly *Microtimes* is another good place to look because you can find it for free at newsstands in big cities.

Expect a setup fee and monthly fees between $15 and $25, but it's also typical not to have a per-hour charge. In the conversation about getting an account, ask for the customer-support number. Call the number and ask the person you reach at customer support if he or she is familiar with MacTCP and InterSLIP. Some services do ten Mac setups a day, and some can't be bothered. You want one that will bother. And get a fax number because you'll need it in a bit.

Step three: Setting up

After you get MacTCP, you put it in the Control Panels folder of your System folder. InterSLIP has a Control Panel too, called InterSLIP Control, and it goes in your System folder too. When you drag the icons for the MacTCP and InterSLIP Control panels to your System folder, the System itself will ask you if you want to put them inside the Control Panels folder.

Now take this book to a photocopier and make copies of Figures 13-1, 13-2, 13-3, and 13-4. I'm serious about this step. You should do the following tasks to save yourself and the customer support at the service untold agony:

1. **Fax these figures to customer support at the service.**

2. **Tell support to fill in the right numbers in the blank spaces.**

3. **Ask the support people to show you where to set the little slider for Subnet Mask setting in Figure 13-2.**

4. **Have the support people fax the whole set of figures back to you with all this information marked on the faxes.**

With this information, you'll be in great shape. I don't know why, but it's typical for Internet service providers to have their own forms, developed a few years ago, that are almost uniquely confusing. Insist that the service show you what to enter in these software screens. You're paying a setup charge to get a SLIP account, and any service worth having will be glad to consider this step as part of the setup.

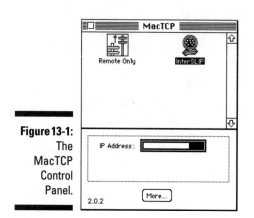

Figure 13-1:
The
MacTCP
Control
Panel.

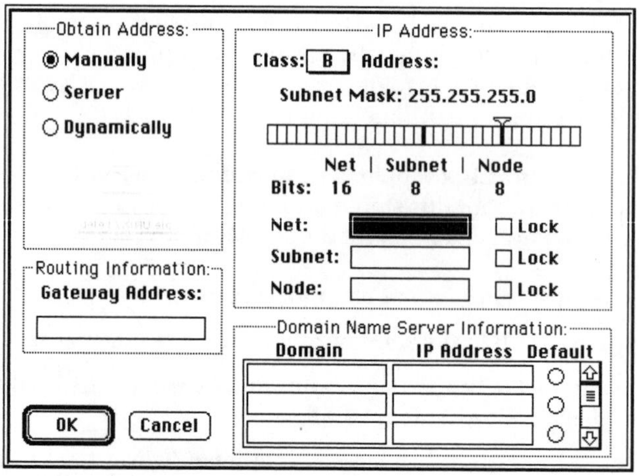

Figure 13-2:
MacTCP
Setup data
page.

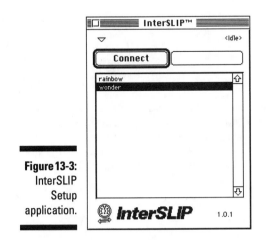

Figure 13-3:
InterSLIP
Setup
application.

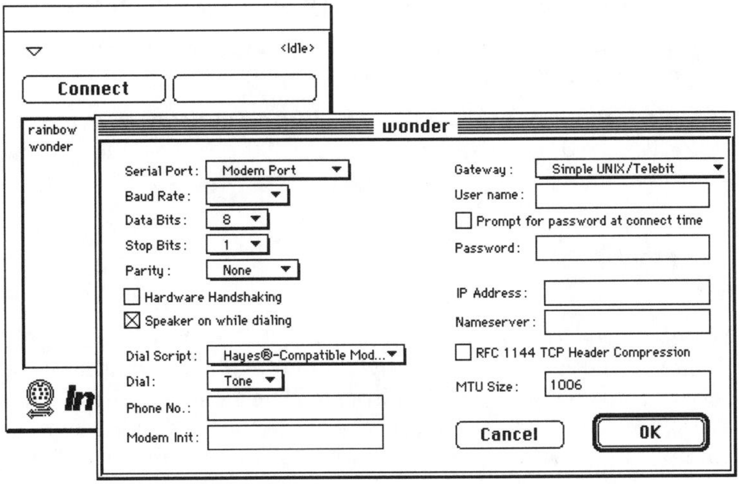

Figure 13-4:
InterSLIP
Setup data
page.

Countdown before Launch

I want to make sure you're all checked out before you press the InterSLIP Connect button. Watch for the following points.

MacTCP

1. **Find Control Panels under the Apple menu and select it to open it.**

2. **Find the MacTCP icon and double-click on it.** If your screen doesn't show an InterSLIP icon like the one in Figure 13-1, you haven't put the InterSLIP parts (Control Panel and Extension) in the right places. Fix this problem now (get the InterSLIP Control Panel in the Control Panels folder and the InterSLIP Extension into the Extensions folder), and then come back and type the IP Address.

More MacTCP

1. **Double-click on the More button in the MacTCP window.**

2. **Fill in the information the service gave you for Figure 13-2.**

3. **Make sure that you have the Obtain Address radio button set properly according to the fax from your service.**

4. **Move the Subnet Mask slider to the position the service recommended.** Fill in the Domain Name Server data at the lower-right of the window. Pick the default.

SLIP

You may have downloaded a version of SLIP that shows nothing in the scrolling list area in the InterSLIP window yet. To enter the information about your SLIP service provider, just pick New from the File menu and fill in a name in the dialog box. When you're done, click back to the window in Figure 13-3, double-click on your new filename, and you get to a screen that looks like Figure 13-4.

And more SLIP

In the Gateway option on the wonder window, choose Simple UNIX/Telebit because you're not a direct connection. In the Dial Script option, choose Hayes and pick your modem's speed. Every other bit of information should be on the fax of Figure 13-4 that you receive from the support people.

Launch!

When you have filled in every last scrap of data provided to you, double-click on the InterSLIP Setup icon (in the InterSLIP folder) to get to an InterSLIP window like the one in Figure 13-3. Click on the Connect button, and InterSLIP makes your connection.

Watch the top of the window. You see the message change from Idle, to Dialing, to Signing In, to Connected. Sometimes you'll see it pop back to Idle.

It's a good idea to check the Speaker on while dialing box in Figure 13-4 so that you can hear whether your dial-up number is busy or whether (as often happens) there just isn't a line. If you have problems for more than two days, call customer support. You'd be amazed at how often the service itself has made setup mistakes that it needs to fix (your password is wrong, for example).

The Big Payoff

I know this has been a tiresome section, but hey, if you think this is tiresome, you ought to try figuring out TCP/IP setups from scratch. I couldn't think of any other way to give you enough information to make this connection work. It was a slow news day on rec.humor.funny when I wrote this, too.

Your reward for being patient is that if you get a dial-up SLIP connection, you can use Fetch, TurboGopher, and Mosaic. There are other amazing Mac programs, and now that you can use Fetch, you can find them all in a few days, but these three are worth mastering.

Fetch

You've seen the rest; now try the best. For FTP, at least, this is a reasonable statement about Fetch, the lovable mascot from Dartmouth. Fetch is the premiere Macintosh utility for Internet file retrieval.

When the message in the InterSLIP window says you're connected, double-click on the Fetch icon. The wonder-pooch leaps into action, and you see the equivalent of Figure 13-5. I've clicked the little black triangle next to Shortcuts in the Open Connection window, and this action lets me pick any of the top Mac sites.

As a good citizen, you should fill in an assortment of Mac software collection sites (see "The Part of Tens" in this book for ten good examples) in the short-cuts. You can, of course, just type any site in the world you may want to visit anyway. Fetch logs you onto the site, and you can look through the available files just as if you were connected directly to a big hard drive. When you see a file you like, click the file to highlight it and click Fetch's Get button.

TurboGopher

Unless you get a commercial product called SLIPper ($95, Sysnet Corp., 800-683-5515), you can only run one of these programs at a time. Quit Fetch and double-click on TurboGopher. If you're calling at a nonpeak time, you'll usually find yourself connected to the Gopher server faster than you were connected to your service provider. That's because TurboGopher works with one computer direct-connecting to another over a fast network, instead of a modem connect-ing to a computer.

Good old TurboGopher. This animal has saved me from certain doom many times. The diligent creature has links to all the other Gophers in the world, so if you're looking simply to explore, this is an excellent place to start.

All you do is open these folders as if they were folders on your own Macintosh, and you can highlight files and tell Gopher to download them. The difference between Fetch and TurboGopher is that TurboGopher lets you search for files by title rather than having to page through the files yourself.

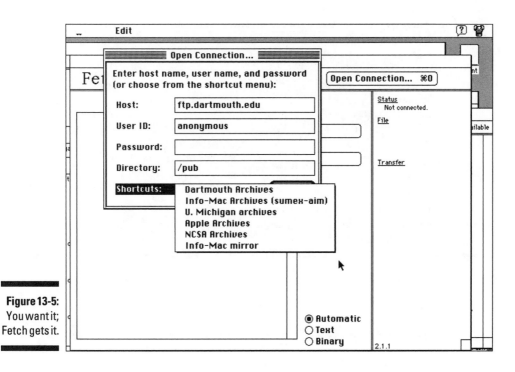

Figure 13-5:
You want it;
Fetch gets it.

Mosaic and its brethren

You already know about Mosaic from way back in Chapter 8. What I want to tell you here is to watch out for new versions, and new versions of other Web browsers. When you FTP to familiar sites, check the version numbers of the available types of browsers against your own.

Software advances in compression (and design advances in the balance of screen-structure-stored-on-your-computer vs. structure-sent-over-the-wire) will result in much faster Web browsers for SLIP modem connections. The Macintosh version (2.0) of Mosaic introduced in summer 1994 was a revolution in its day, but new versions that don't assume you have a fiber optic line to a supercomputer are going to revolutionize Mosaic itself for individuals.

What about e-mail?

A dial-up SLIP account can, in principle, be used for e-mail. In the software libraries of the national on-line services, you can find early versions of Eudora (now a commercial program) and LeeMail, a very nice shareware program.

A dial-up SLIP account has a problem in the way it gets to e-mail, however. You are now your own Internet address (a number). If you're not connected, your mailbox is not available. Some service providers have a mail-forwarding plan worked out, in which they take your mail on a big computer that is connected 24 hours each day and then notify you when you dial up with your SLIP connection. Other providers don't provide this service. The convenience of e-mail on a big system is one reason the national on-line services are so popular. I get mail at America Online and Delphi, and I have a SLIP account from CR Laboratories (see Chapter 19). This combination lets me pick the best way to accomplish any given on-line task.

Being Cool

A dial-up SLIP account will probably cost you more than an account at a national on-line service. But SLIP gives you direct access to some of the best Mac software available, so if you're serious about the Internet, it's worth the trouble and expense.

Alternatives to traditional SLIP that will let you run Mosaic over a shell account have recently started to appear. These alternatives assign a sort of "dynamic dummy" Internet numerical address when you sign on, so you don't have a four-part-number address of your own, and installation is simplified for the service provider.

One program called TIA (The Internet Adapter, from tia-sales@marketplace.com) has been accepted by some service providers, including CRL, although there are complaints about slowness compared to stock SLIP. Within a year, expect to see dial-up communications packages that can run a graphical Web browser with no special SLIP setup.

Chapter 14

Business Internet

....

In This Chapter

▶ An explosion of interest.

▶ Big business goes online with Mosaic.

▶ An Internet storefront for you?

▶ Hardware and software for business Internet.

....

Now You Don't See It, Now You Do

As late as March 1994, large parts of the Internet were a sort of electronic party for computer graduate students. I used to give Internet talks where business topics were handled in the question session at the end, and then I had to add a twenty-minute section on business, and now (late October 1994), I could put together a three-day seminar on Internet business. Whether there's gold out there or not, the Gold Rush is definitely happening.

A Mosaic of Business Pictures

To sell things on-line, you need to be able to show people pictures. That's why Mosaic, in several variations, has been the basis of most Internet business action. Perhaps the easiest way to follow developments is to fire up Mosaic, head to the What's New section of the NCSA Mosaic home page on the WWW, and just scroll down through the selections (Figure 14-1). There are nonprofits, such as the Library of Congress and universities, but you will also see platoons of businesses, typically signed up with one business network or other.

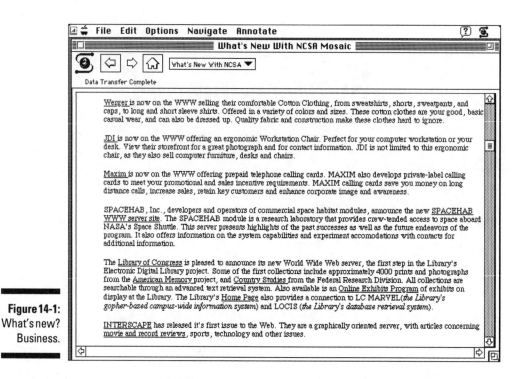

Figure 14-1:
What's new?
Business.

Lots of private organizations have sprung up to help you find your place on the World Wide Web. The Internet Business Center, for example (Figure 14-2) provides not just a way to sell your own services, but access to papers on marketing and commercial Internet statistics.

Another connection is the Internet Shopping Network (800-677-7467), which can provide you with a range of services. As Figure 14-3 shows, ISN has taken into account some of the problems of the full-graphics approach to the WWW — unless you have a connection that runs at 56 kbps or better, then you need, as an alternative, the patience of Mother Teresa.

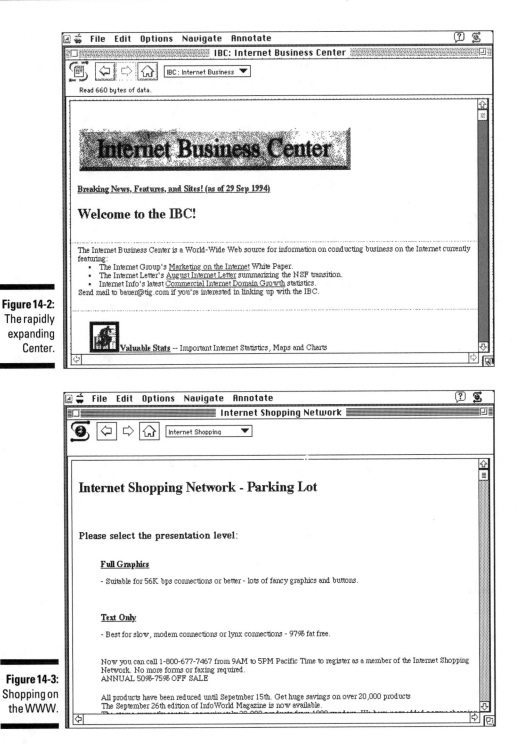

Figure 14-2:
The rapidly
expanding
Center.

Figure 14-3:
Shopping on
the WWW.

One of the areas you might want to visit is the Macintosh software area on ISN. Basically, every piece of Macintosh software is here, waiting only for your order, and it's here at a discount. I think this is probably one of the marketing areas on the Internet that actually works, because

1. **You already know the products.**

   You can read a review of Microsoft Excel 5, and if you're using version 4.1 you can decide if you would like to upgrade. The vendor doesn't have a big selling job to do.

2. **They're computer products.**

   If you find yourself looking at a Mosaic screen for Internet Shopping Network, you're in the first few percent of Internet pioneers and are likely the kind of person who does buy upgrades.

3. **Software purchasing is pretty straightforward.**

   There aren't different sizes or colors. An Internet shopping service can give you the same level of service as a paper catalog, only faster.

Figure 14-4:
Mac software on-line.

By the way, it's not just computer stuff out there on the Net. Specialized organizations are putting multipart catalogs and giant webs of directories together to service whole industries (see Figure 14-5). This Hollynet page is just a beginning — you can expect to see every industry and sub-industry have its own WWW information service by mid-1995, partly because the organizations driving commercialization are so helpful and ambitious and partly because developing HTML documents gets to be pretty easy once you have a modicum of practice.

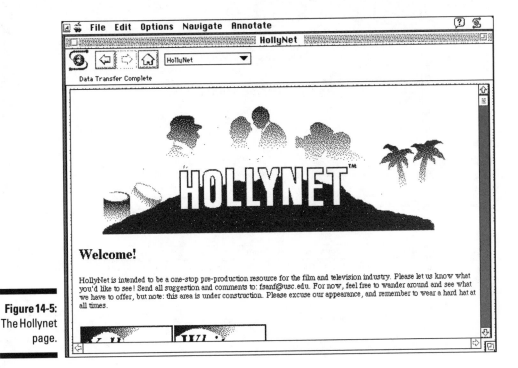

Figure 14-5:
The Hollynet
page.

Where Do You Fit In?

One place for you, if you have a modest array of product to sell, might be the WWW mall operated by Internet ShopKeeper (see Figure 14-6). The first such services were designed to put organizations like Pacific Bell and Amdahl Computers on the Internet; Internet Shopkeeper is pretty close to an ideal service for small businesses. One reason it's ideal is that the rates are survivably low (see Figure 14-7). Instead of a $2000 setup fee and a $500/month on-line charge, the setup fee is $5, and the rates are probably less than your phone bill.

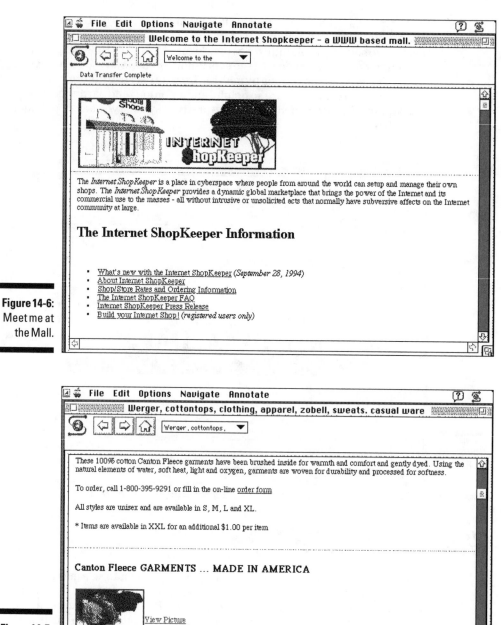

Figure 14-6:
Meet me at
the Mall.

Figure 14-7:
At last,
reasonable
"rents" for
online
stores.

What will your on-line shop look like? Here's an example, taken simply from the What's New page at NCSA. It's a sample catalog page (see Figure 14-8) from a clothing catalog, and on it you can see how simply the Mosaic small-graphics-plus-hyperlinks format adapts to Internet commerce. One of the links (shown in Figure 14-9) lets you see a bigger picture (the color, although we can't print it here, is as good as magazine graphics); another link calls up an order form on-screen (see Figure 14-10).

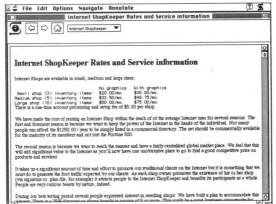

Figure 14-8:
A sample
catalog
page in
Mosaic.

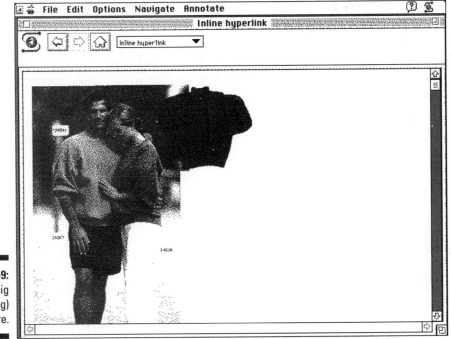

Figure 14-9:
The big
(catalog)
picture.

Getting Access in Organizations

So that's a chunk of Internet business news. Now all you need to know is how to get connected. If you are associated with any sort of large organization, you probably have a computer that's part of a network already. Everything we have said so far about Internet access strategies needs to be modified a bit for the workplace.

The difference between the single-user solutions for Internet access and solutions for networks is that on a network you'll have to get agreement from other people. So I'll look at the options available for network-user access to the Internet, but instead of running out and implementing them right away you'll have to speak to the Authorities first.

Thinking Positively about Administrators

Most of the time, an administrator is someone who tells you what you can't do. On a computer network, an administrator is an absolute necessity. If individual users run different versions of the *same* application, it's often enough to crash the whole network. If no one has been assigned the responsibility of watching out for viruses, the whole system will pick up a virus in no time. Besides this, there has to be some one around who simply knows what to do when there are problems. Even if you just buy a *three-user* license for the Macintosh database 4th Dimension, you'll have to name one of the three users the administrator.

If you have a computer account at a University, you're almost certainly in great shape for Internet access. Not only should there be great stacks of Internet reading material at your computer center, there are probably short classes on the Internet in general, and tutorials on Fetch, Mosaic, TurboGopher, and other Mac software. And you will have a direct connection instead of working through a bulletin board or cobbling together a SLIP link through an outside provider. The direct connection makes software like Mosaic really fly, making it the general solution for all Internet access.

Of course the people in schools have all this Internet stuff wired (pun only partially intended). They *invented* it. And universities tend to be heavy-duty Mac sites, so you're covered on that point too.

In business, things won't necessarily be that nice. You may have a Mac that's a minority member of a network crowded with PCs. You may have a system administrator whose hands are full just managing the upgrade to WordPerfect 3.0. You also may have company management that's concerned that one unhappy employee could blow a hundred company secrets out onto the whole Internet by e-mail in a fifteen-minute fit of temper. I'll give you some notes here on business Internet access; then it's up to you to call a meeting and present your case.

Internet Business Wish-List

This little catalog lists products ranging from the absurdly simple to the simply absurd. Give them a quick scan, and you should be able to talk a good line in the conference room.

Talking power

Apple has built all sorts of amazing communication tricks into PowerTalk in System 7 Pro. They all amount to the same thing: you can send a message to someone simply by dragging a document over to that person's icon on your screen (see Figure 14-2). The person can be anywhere on any network, as long as you have told PowerTalk how to connect. It's just amazing. You can drag a folder on the desktop from your hard drive to an e-mail box in Australia!

NetBits

This is just a little digression on terminology. If you have to discuss Mac Internet possibilities with the higher-ups at work, you don't want to sound like you don't know what you're talking about.

A *gateway* lets you connect two different kinds of network. Typical Macintosh networks run along rules specified by the AppleTalk standard, and the Internet uses, appropriately, Internet protocol (IP). You need software to translate messages designed for one network into messages that can be read properly by the other network. That's a gateway.

A *bridge* is typically hardware and software that connects two local networks of the same kind.

You might have two different AppleTalk networks in different parts of a building or in different departments. If you want the two networks to look like one big network, you have to buy a bridge, usually from the company that sold you the two networks.

A *router*, for Internet purposes, sends IP messages from one Internet network host to another. Most commercial routers also know how to translate messages coming from other kinds (non-IP) of networks. There are zillions of tricks involved in making routers efficient, and if you're reading this, it's somebody else's job to learn them.

StarNine Technologies (510-649-4949) is one of the first companies to take advantage of PowerTalk for Internet access. Mail*Link Internet for PowerTalk* is a "personal gateway" that allows System 7 Pro users to exchange messages with Internet mail users, if they're working on a network that uses the Internet's Simple Mail Transfer Protocol (SMTP). At $65 for a single user pack and $595 for a ten pack, Mail*Link Internet for PowerTalk* effectively makes the whole Internet part of your Macintosh desktop, at least for e-mail.

Being a better netter

For Internet connection, most networks simply need to be upgraded to support TCP/IP, the native language of the Internet. Shiva Corporation (800/458-3550), for example, now offers an upgrade to its LanRover software that lets corporate Macintosh users at remote sites dial into a company network (using AppleTalk or IP) and then get from the company network out to the Internet or national on-line services. Sitting in a motel in Sedona, Arizona, your Mac is just as connected as if you were back in the home office in mid-town Manhattan (Sedona's prettier; Manhattan has more places to do lunch). You can install the whole LanRover/E package for a bit more than $3,000 (you can see as I roll down the list I keep raising the ante), but then your whole company is as wired as it gets.

Buying it, big time

Network pioneer Cisco Systems (408-526-4000), for a mere $7,000 or so, will sell you a hardware-plus-software package that lets you hook up, from scratch, a few hundred computers to each other and to the Internet. Instructional CD-ROMs make this a do-it-yourself network approach (creating, perhaps, a market for *Internetworking Systems Management For Dummies*). Ya got a bunch of Macs using AppleTalk — hey, no problem! There's a CD-ROM for exactly this set-up. Go to it, Sparky!

This list of Internet business products is not intended to be comprehensive. It's meant to give you a starting point for discussions at the office, with some current information. If you're serious about internetworking hardware and software, your best bet is to follow network news in *Macworld* every month. The scene is changing every few weeks as new vendors try to stake out claims in the great Internet Gold Rush of '94.

Chapter 15

@ the Frontier:
The Future of the Internet

- -

In This Chapter

▶ Getting used to a brave new world

▶ Getting down to Internet business

▶ Dodging cops and robbers and Ph.D.s, oh my!

▶ Broadening your horizons with classes on the Net

- -

*T*he Internet is too new to have many traditions, but one tradition is free expression of opinion. In the spirit of this tradition, I will now treat you to a few pages of unfiltered speculation about what comes next in this huge, anarchic, nonsystem.

Whatever else can be said about the Internet, it certainly has a future. I don't know what its exact future will be — platoons of hucksters, idealists, bureaucrats, and others have visions of the Internet that may or may not materialize. Plenty of visions are more entertaining than those you read in the newspapers, too.

Wired

You owe it to yourself to read a science-fiction novel called *Snow Crash* by Neal Stephenson. I usually can't stand science fiction, but Stephenson happened to hypothesize a sort of Internet world in which most people's computers are a hundred times more powerful than a Macintosh Performa 475. Those computers will be here within a decade, so the speculation is a little closer to home than old-time classics like Ray Bradbury's *The Martian Chronicles.* I believe that you'll see faster computers; I don't believe that you'll see Martians.

In *Snow Crash,* people move around in their own interactive movie with other people on the Net. This capability has, to put it mildly, far-reaching social consequences. The book is also a cult favorite among early Internet enthusiasts, so you advance your hipness quotient by taking a look.

Growing like a Weed

When I agreed to do this book in 1994, the generally accepted figure was that about 12 million people had some sort of Internet access. As I finish the last chapters in late 1994, I've seen quotes from 25 to 50 million.

This inexactitude isn't really a problem, at least in terms of fundamental Internet structure. There are still plenty of addresses for one and all, at least. The big problem concerns access.

The Mac: A special Internet case

Access takes on a special meaning for Macintosh users because the Internet has just a handful of large, Mac file repositories. The Internet hosts at Stanford, Dartmouth, the University of Michigan, and the University of Illinois (through the National Center for Supercomputing Applications), together with Apple Computer itself, pretty much define the world of general-interest Mac files.

Mac archives will probably migrate to other Internet sites in the years to come, but these sites set the standards. If you take the number of UNIX users and divide it by the number of UNIX-archive Internet sites, you get a number in the thousands. If you divide the number of Mac users by the number of important Mac-archive sites, you get a number in the millions. Are you going to see ACCESS DENIED everywhere you turn, even as a result of (gulp!) this book?

A solution for the rest of us

Nope. You'll be just fine. Although there are only a few big sites and also just a few "mirror" sites with copies of the original archives, the national on-line services are de facto mirror sites for the most often accessed files. Getting files on astrophysics and Turkish linguistics will, of course, still require real Internet access. But studies of Internet traffic and traffic at CompuServe have shown that the on-line service can handle 98 percent of Internet file requests for Mac topics. That capability puts the users/archives quotient back to the same ratio that the UNIX people enjoy, *as long as you check for the files you want in the libraries of your own on-line service first!*

If you follow this simple rule, everything will be fine.

Is the Internet a Market?

Anytime enough people do the same thing, they constitute a market. Vastly more people in the United States, for example, use the Internet than play golf. (My editors didn't believe me, but it's true: Internet 35 million, golf 15-20 million. People in the Midwest chronically overestimate the percentage of golfers in the population.) Some Internet users may be underpaid graduate students, and others may be there because they want stuff for free, but in the eyes of the business community, a marketing opportunity has identified itself within the last year.

First, lots of businesses want to find a way to buy advertising space, which is currently prohibited. If you join a newsgroup like `rec.tennis`, you're an obvious target for electronic junk-mail offers.

Second, businesses want to find a way to use the communications network for their own organizations. Why should you install your own nationwide business network if you can scatter employees all over the country and connect them with Internet accounts? Who needs an office when you can put all your employees on Delphi?

The reason more businesses haven't done that is security. The thought of competitors reading your communications is unnerving. In real life, this stuff happens, too — cellular phones in Silicon Valley have been the source of all kinds of corporate leaks, through random and purposeful eavesdropping.

Locking it up

A company called Terisa Systems, a joint venture of RSA Data Security and Enterprise Integration Technologies, announced recently that it will sell software tools to help programmers design security systems into Internet telecommunications applications. This way, business e-mail would be absolutely private.

Ironically, RSA was a pioneer in the kind of encryption technology that the government is trying to impose on all telecommunications with the controversial Clipper chip (the Clipper chip lets you put messages into code that no one but the intended recipient and law enforcement agen-

cies can read). The biggest organization of Internet users, Computer Professionals for Social Responsibility, has issued a statement against the Clipper that includes 50,000 signatures (it looks like a Who's Who of the computer business).

In late-breaking news, a mathematician at AT&T reported a fundamental flaw in the Clipper plan, anyway. Historically, the Internet itself is nearly the only government-backed computer initiative that's been a major success. Maybe leaving well enough alone is an unanticipated but brilliant move.

Other Shady Business

Recent newspaper reports claim that police in large U.S. cities have taken to signing onto different local bulletin boards and Internet Relay Chat sessions in an attempt to identify pedophiles who want to lure 12-year-olds into motel rooms. You may confidently expect to read plenty of lurid stories in the months ahead, as police departments react to the need to present themselves as high-tech. Stories about other plans to entrap drug traffickers on the Internet are certain to be part of TV broadcasts soon. The accumulated weight of these stories will be used as a justification for more Internet regulation.

The first two or three of these stories reported in the San Francisco area are demonstrably false based on the evidence presented and appear to be wishful thinking dutifully relayed into print by gullible reporters (trust me, few newspaper reporters have a proper UNIX background). Because we live in a Spooky Monster society in which unspeakable peril lurks at every turn (at least on TV news), crime tales of the Internet are, unfortunately, going to be a big part of forthcoming publicity.

InterTerror

The following is your guide to the inevitable scary Internet stories of the next few years.

First, you need to know an interesting fact. In the early 1980s, the *Los Angeles Times* did a retrospective study of every Halloween-candy tampering incident it had reported in the previous ten years. Every story, *every one,* was found to be unverifiable. Researchers in criminology report that no incident has ever been verified nationally, either.

Honest, they don't occur. It's been thoroughly documented. The most typical case is that some kid's older brother tampers with the candy and claims they got it from mean Mr. Johnson, the PE teacher. The *LA Times*, the *New York Times*, and the two standard college textbooks on criminology all agree about the Halloween stuff. And no one ever dried a poodle in a microwave either.

Everybody knows that bad guys are out there doing these things every year. In fact, whether everybody knows it or not, it just doesn't happen, or at least it happens about 0.1% as much as people fear. Don't take my word for it — join an urban myth newsgroup and see for yourself.

Similarly, everybody knows that terrorists are everywhere these days, kept at bay only by expensive services that X-ray your underwear at every airport. The members of the Libyan hit squad who were said to be roaming the U.S. in the mid-1980s to assassinate President Reagan are now presumably using Internet Relay Chat or the newsgroup alt.kill.everyone to plan other fictitious capers. The historical record shows that various intelligence agencies do not hesitate to plant terror stories themselves. There are indeed some real terrorists in the world, but they won't be stopped by government security assaults on the Internet as long as there are still pay phones in New York.

The Internet and Education

Now some good news. No, really, I mean it. After all this talk about crowding and cops and Clipper chips, I'll tell you about the biggest single bright spot in the Internet's future: education.

Ten years ago, I was involved in a noble effort to provide college-credit classes over a network. It was great fun and a worthwhile service — I ran a statistics class, sending out lessons, correcting homework, and designing an on-line final exam.

The system design had one problem, however. With the 300-bps modems of 1985, the service lost about a nickel in connect charges on every homework assignment. In the classic business joke, I guess we made it up on volume!

These days, when half the students at large universities skip the lectures and buy class notes from professional note-taking services anyway, the fundamental idea of remote classes looks better than ever. With a 14.4-Kbps modem (that's 48 times faster than the old modems), you can even do so at a profit.

I bring excellent news to everyone who took a job right after high school, every lab technician who's supposed to take classes every few years to stay certified, every real-estate agent who wants to become a mortgage broker, and every middle-aged engineer who now needs a skill-set overhaul. Help is on the way! The same universities that make up the backbone of the Internet finally have found a convenient way to deliver their services to *you*. For anyone willing to crack the electronic books, great opportunities lie ahead.

Part V
The Part of Tens

In this part...

The Part of Tens, a patented Dummies feature, is a concentrated dose of Internet trivia, serious matters, and convenience.

I provide some alternate ways to find information so that as you and I use the Net, we can avoid colliding at peak times.

Chapter 16
Top Ten WWW Sites

*T*hese locations are good places to start roaming the World Wide Web. Actually, most WWW servers have some provision for jumping back out to one of the big sites, typically NCSA. Any Web browser, (not just Mosaic) will have an Open URL... command under the File menu. If you suddenly find yourself lost, bored, or irritable, just Open URL and type;

```
http://galaxy.einet.net
```

This will get you back to my favorite site, Galaxy, the home of MacWeb. Alternatively, you can try

```
http://www.ncsa.uiuc.edu
```

and you arrive at the Mother of All Home Pages, the original Mosaic site.

Here are some of my favorites. Please note that the Web is growing so rapidly that this is like naming a favorite bar in the Klondike during the Gold Rush. All these sites will show links to the newer sites as well, so you can always just check the What's New section of the home page on your server.

1. galaxy.einet.net

I don't know what the hardware setup looks like down at MCC in Texas, but I know that this site is always up and running 24 hours each day, with apparently three zillion never-busy incoming lines. This is a very rich site, with content ranging from the businesslike to the bizarre.

2. info.cern.ch

The pioneer WWW site in Switzerland is still the source for lots of unique material of scientific interest, and is a valuable reminder that, although America leads the world in Netheads per capita, the first W in WWW really does stand for World.

3. *www.cyfer.net*

This is a server devoted to non-profit organizations. Instant international connectivity is dramatically amplifying the capabilities of organizations such as Amnesty International and ecology-monitoring groups. Electronic daylight is now penetrating some formerly murky geopolitical swamps.

4. *www.commerce.net*

CommerceNet is an aggressively expanding business society based in Silicon Valley. As it happens, Silicon Valley was just waiting for something like this — Commercenet, after its first six months, was a bigger operation than the whole Web was in 1993.

5. *www.geo.net*

This is the new site name for www.global.net, a large mixed-bag resource. The subdivision www.geo.net:8210 has piles of catalogs, for example, while www.geo.net:8510/heart.html/ is an online job-search forum.

6. *web.cnam.fr*

These people would like to help you put your own business on the Web. Yes, they're in France (that's the .fr part of the address), but the show is staged in English anyway.

7. *www.cix.org*

The CIX acronym stands for Commerce Internet Exchange. It's the central clearinghouse for Internet business rules and regulations. Stop here to pick up background information on making your own business Net-aware.

8. www.ncsa.uiuc

The last bit stands for University of Illinois, Champaign-Urbana. Although it's one of my favorite places (the town, and for that matter the Web site) I'm convinced that this site's interest in supercomputing and Mosaic grew from the burning desire to produce something interesting from the flat, bare landscape of the cornfields.

9. tns-www.lcs.mit.edu

Check in here to find out how to make up your own host page — they've got a kit for you to use.

10. www.well.sf.ca.us

Take a look at the future of private computer organizations on the Web. This famous bulletin board has constructed an admirably idiosyncratic WWW site, and as a nonmember of the Well you can look at most of it.

Chapter 17
Top Ten Mac Software Sites

*M*ost of the sites listed in Table 17-1 are universities, so please try to tap in sometime after dinner or early in the morning. The directory given is where you can find the goodies.

In general, you should log in as anonymous and give your own Internet address as the password.

The Stanford site has practically everything worth having. But everyone knows this fact, so I marked three sites with an asterisk that are *mirrors,* or copies, of the Stanford collection. By the way, I included sites in different time zones, so you can access what you want without staying up round the clock.

Table 17-1	Ten Mac Software Sites	
Location	*Number*	*Directory*
mac.archive.umich.edu	141.211.32.2	/mac
sumex-aim.stanford.edu	36.44.0.6	/info-mac
ftp.apple.com	130.43.2.3	/dts
ftp.ncsa.uiuc.edu	141.142.20.50	/Mac (Mosaic)
ftp.funet.fi	128.214.6.100	/pub/mac
ftp.dartmouth.edu	129.170.16.54	/pub/mac (Dartmouth)
boombox.micro.umn.edu	128.101.95.95	/pub (gopher, more)
ftp.rrzn.uni-hannover.de (*)	130.75.2.2	/ftp1/mac [sumex]
ftp.ucs.ubc.ca (*)	137.82.27.62	/pub/mac/info-mac
shark.mel.dit.csiro.au (*)	144.110.16.11	/info-mac [sumex]

Chapter 18

Ten Communications Software Tips

Communications software is still full of bugs. The fact that shareware programs compete seriously with commercial applications indicates the unsettled state of things. If Apple had any sense of shame, it would have distributed a trouble-free communications program as part of System software long ago.

Anyway, give thanks to the clever people who write shareware. And be a good sport: Send them the modest registration fee if you use their software regularly.

Deflaking Your Modem

For a variety of reasons, communications software doesn't always reset your modem correctly when it starts up, and it doesn't always hang up properly at the end.

The solution: Keep your modem close enough to turn it off between sessions. Crude advice, I know, but sometimes it's the only way to get the darn thing to reset.

Sometimes the modem doesn't hang up. *If you're still connected, you're paying for it!* Make sure that you turn it off when you're done.

Deflaking Your Session Files, Part 1

Any good communications software keeps a *session log*, which is a record of all the stuff you saw on-screen while you were connected. Mastering your software's session log can save you untold grief. For example, there's nothing like watching a 10K text file roll past you on-screen and then finding that your software only logged the last page.

If you look under the File menu in your program, there will usually be a choice like Save Archive As... or Save Log File As... This choice lets you set the program to capture the entire session.

Deflaking Your Session Files, Part 2

As a Macintosh user, you are familiar with proportionally spaced fonts. Most of the computers running around the Internet, however, have never even heard of these lovely things. On UNIX computers, all the spacing considerations for laying out tables and lists assume that every character has the same width. When you capture a session file and open it with Geneva or Times as the font, all the tables and lists look ragged because the spacing has been changed by using a font in which *l* is narrower than *w*.

If you have a table of some sort in your session file, open the file in a word processor, select the table, and pick the Monaco font. Presto! All the text in the columns aligns properly.

Dealing with Weird Files

Stuff on the Internet comes in a baffling array of file formats. You may see `.zip`, `.z`, `.tar`, and all sorts of non-Mac creatures. You can collect a whole set of utilities for dealing with this situation (including HQXer, uuencode, and a half dozen others). Or, as soon as you have an account anywhere, you can download StuffIt Lite, which can turn the majority of these files into something you can recognize.

Upgrading Your Communications Software

StuffIt Lite can solve lots of file decoding problems. I also recommend downloading ZTerm if you are using the communications module in an integrated (Works-type) program.

Experiment with Downloads

Most communications programs support several download protocols, among them XMODEM, YMODEM, and Kermit. There are considerable differences in the actual download speed from one on-line service to the next, depending on the protocol you use. It's worth doing several experiments with small files to compare speeds.

Serious Money

CompuServe, Delphi, and GEnie have special interface applications that let you design searches off-line and set up e-mail message handling at high speed. My measurements with CompuServe Navigator, for example, show that the actual on-line time can be crunched down by a factor of ten!

These kinds of programs can type faster than you, and they don't sit there staring at the screen wondering what to do next: you can already have devised a plan, at no charge, off-line. If you take advantage of these timesaving applications, you can typically get all your on-line work done inside the "free" time allotment.

Modem Speed Optimism

Don't you just hate it when you sign on with your brand-new 14.4 Kbps modem, only to be told that the service is still running at 2400 bps? But don't despair, national on-line services and bulletin boards upgrade their hardware all the time, often without telling you. As a result, try a faster modem setting every week or so — it costs you only a few seconds of connect time and can save you gobs of time and money if it works.

If you set your communications software for 9600 and the service is running at only 2400, either your modem drops down to the slower speed or you get some nonsense characters and are forced to turn the modem off to disconnect.

File Name Creativity

Most communications software give you a generic name for session logs. If you do on-line Archie searches in a shell account or telnet to look through some directory, the software assigns every session the same name. The solution: For your sanity, come up with filenames that clearly indicate the content of your session logs. And you should usually include the date in the filename, too.

Don't get lazy when you are naming your on-line files. After you cruise the Net for a month, you'll have so much stuff that you'll never find anything if you don't label your files clearly.

For Hotshots Only

If you're a hard-core Mac hotshot who bought this book just for a quick over-view of Internet access, be sure to get the shareware program Modem Maker. You can use it to write modem scripts that can be used as small Internet telecommunications applications.

Chapter 19

Ten Internet Service Providers

*M*ost Internet service providers are scrambling to accommodate the dramatic increase in Internet demand. Meanwhile, conflicting factors affect access and cost. On the one hand, it's more efficient to run a service with 1,000 subscribers than 50, especially if the providers aren't fussy about handing out busy signals. On the other hand, increased demand gives the providers incentive to keep the rates up as long as they can. (It's like running the only restaurant at the edge of a gold rush town: the owners want to charge $5 for an egg, but at some point the miners start raising their own chickens.)

My guess is that within a year you'll be paying $12 a month for a SLIP account and even less for a shell account. And soon, no one will be able to impose a 9600 bps surcharge.

Now, the game is to find a local number from your service provider and avoid 800-number charges (or worse, long-distance rates). Check out any humble local computer publication or even the business section of your newspaper.

Note that some on-line services provide 800 numbers so that you can avoid long-distance phone charges from the phone company. The catch is that the service charges you extra (beyond your standard per-hour charge) for using the 800 number. It used to be common to see 800-charges of $5 to $10 per hour, but increased competition is now bringing these charges down.

a2i Communications

This service is very popular in the San Francisco Bay area (area codes 408 and 415). I recommend calling 408-293-8078 for current rate information and high-speed dial-up numbers. Internet address is `rahul.net`.

CR Laboratories Dialup Internet Access

This is one of the few organizations practiced enough to get you on-line as a Macintosh SLIP user. And you can access it cheaply across the country via more and more local numbers (CR Laboratories does shell accounts, too). Call 415-381-2800 and ask someone to fax their spiel. Internet address is `crl.com`.

Delphi

Practically every computer magazine has instructions detailing Delphi's free trial offer. If you can't find any, call 800-544-4005. Delphi, basically a shell account with extensive hand-holding, is an excellent value. Send e-mail to `walthowe@delphi.com`; Walt Howe runs the Internet section.

DIAL n' CERF USA

Shell or SLIP access anywhere in the U.S. through an 800 number. Call 800-876-2373 or send e-mail to `help@cerf.net`. Very helpful staff, too.

HookUp Communication Corporation

This Canadian service has shell or SLIP access with an 800 number and a reasonable price. Call 519-747-4110 or send a note to info@hookup.net for information.

InterAccess

InterAcess has local numbers covering the Chicago area, with shell and SLIP accounts. Usually, I try to recommend services with an 800 number, but I'm from Chicago and I feel that Cubs fans deserve special consideration in view of the burden they carry. Call 800-967-1580 or e-mail info@interaccess.com.

Millennium Online

This is a shell service with a network of local numbers. Call 800-736-0122 or e-mail mill.com.

Netcom Online Communication Services

Netcom has local numbers in most big cities, shell and SLIP accounts, and customer support that knows something about Macintoshes. Call 800-501-8649 or e-mail info@netcom.com.

NovaLink

This Boston-based shell service, which uses Sprint for national access, has laudably modest access fees. Call 800-274-2814 or send e-mail to info@novalink.com. (Have you noticed a pattern in some of these e-mail addresses?)

The World

Last time I looked, this service charged $5 a month. Lots of advanced thinkers hang out at this service. Call 617-739-0202 or send e-mail to office@world.std.com.

Institute for Global Communications

OK, OK, I know that this is item 11 in the list. I just feel compelled to plug this service, which handles the nonprofit organizations PeaceNet, EcoNet, ConflictNet, LaborNet, and HomeoNet. It mostly carries newsgroups for this assortment of causes; you can find a remarkable diversity of opinion represented here. Call 415-442-0220 or e-mail support@igc.apc.org.

Chapter 20
Ten Good Causes on the Internet

*T*he current Internet is probably the most remarkable swords-into-plowshares situation in history. In one decade, the Net turned from a service facility for defense contracts into a service attracting vast numbers of society's most altruistic souls.

I don't have any political ax to grind here — hey, I already listed the name of the Rush Limbaugh newsgroup. This top-ten list just recognizes the social activism slant embraced by many Net residents. Myself, I am not a member of any organized political party (that's an old Will Rogers joke).

isoc@isoc.org

The Internet Society itself is worth joining. Drop them a line and see what you can contribute.

ask@eff.org

The Electronic Frontier Foundation (EFF) was founded in July 1990 to ensure that the principles embodied in the Constitution and the Bill of Rights are protected as new communications technologies emerge. This effort will take plenty of work by us all. Help out, please.

lemming.uvm.edu

EcoMUSE is a "virtual community dedicated to environmental education, natural science, geography, multiculturalism, research, and communication." MUSE (for *multiuser simulation environment*) is an Internet technology applied here to a bit of ecological consciousness raising.

802-862-2030

Call this phone number for information on the Together Foundation and its ECOLINE service. The Together Foundation is putting together an international database of ecological and other data.

support@igc.apc.org

Five (that's right, *five*) noble endeavors reside at this Internet e-mail address. All carry extensive newsgroup coverage from all over the globe in their areas of interest.

ConflictNet

ConflictNet is a computer-based information and communication network dedicated to promoting the resolution of conflict through nonadversarial processes.

PeaceNet

PeaceNet serves peace and social justice advocates around the world in such areas as human rights, disarmament, and international relations.

EcoNet

EcoNet serves individuals and organizations working for environmental preservation and sustainability. Important issues covered include global warming, energy policy, rain forest preservation, legislative activities, water quality, toxics, and environmental education.

LaborNet

LaborNet serves groups, unions, and labor advocates interested in information sharing and collaboration with the intent of enhancing workers' rights and economic justice. (I suppose I should balance this entry with an e-mail address for RichGuyNet, but it doesn't exist yet.)

Women's Issues Conferences

`support@igc.apc.org` also carries about 20 conferences on women's issues, representing a remarkable variety of political opinion.

Your Name Here

If you've made it this far through the book, you know more about the Internet than 99 percent of the people in your immediate community. Go to your local library and ask about its Internet plans and need for Net volunteers; or offer to give a talk at a high school. You'll be amazed at the way the MTV generation takes to this Internet stuff.

Chapter 21

Ten Absolutely Free Access Sites

- -

In This Chapter

▶ Nyx

▶ Prairienet

▶ gorn

▶ m-net

▶ sdf

▶ Big Sky Telegraph

▶ O, Canada!

▶ O, Hio!

- -

*I*n this chapter, I provide tips on contacting no-charge Internet hosts. If you're lucky, you may live in a community where this free access service is already established. If you're not lucky, you may be soon because organizations that provide free access are making new sites spring up every month.

If you don't see a site you can access conveniently, call your local library. As libraries put their own catalogs on-line, they find that it's relatively simple to get on-line access to remote catalogs, and from there it's a short step to full Internet access. In addition, pick up a copy of *Computer Currents*, *MicroTimes*, or a similar tabloid at a newsstand and check the bulletin board directories, which are always located near the want ads (in the last few pages).

By the time you read this book, someone probably will have started an Internet access site in your area code, but it takes six months before the site turns up in national lists.

Some of the sites listed here don't offer every possible Internet feature. But they don't want $20 a month either, so they're a good place to begin learning about the Net. Most of them allow you to have a shell account, and you only need basic communications software like ZTerm or the communications module of a "Works" package.

The people who provide these services are wonderful folks; their hospitality is not to be abused. If you sign onto one of these services and use it, for example, to send a chain letter to 30 million people, I will be obliged to track you down like a dog and smash your modem. Remember, my henchmen are everywhere.

Our motto: Be nice.

I selected these ten sites (out of about 40 or so) because I like them.

Nyx

Nyx is a site in Denver, Colorado, maintained by the University of Denver. The dial-up number is 303-871-3324, and the Internet address is `nyx.cs.du.edu`. Its volunteer staff accepts donations if you are moved to offer them.

Prairienet

Prairienet, which is free to Illinois residents, has pretty much the whole range of Internet services. Dial up 217-255-9000 and log in as "visitor." Internet address is `@uiuc.edu`. To ask for details, call 217-244-1962.

gorn

An interesting bulletin board in Santa Cruz, California. Dial-up number is 408-458-2289; Internet address is `gorn.echo.com`. Log in as "gorn," and you will be asked a few questions.

m-net

A reliable contact operated by a nonprofit organization, m-net accepts donations. Dial-up number is 313-996-4644; Internet address is `m-met.ann-arbor.mi.us`.

sdf

sdf is a bulletin board in Dallas, Texas, supported by user contributions. Dial-up number is 214-436-3281; Internet address is `sdf.lonestar.org`.

Big Sky Telegraph

I don't know what's going on in Montana, but it certainly is an Internet hot spot. Log in as "bbs" at the dial-up number 406-683-7680. For some reason, the Internet address is usually listed as `192.231.192.1`.

O, Canada!

The National Capital free Internet site (`freenet.carleton.ca`) lets you log in as "guest" at the dial-up number 613-780-3733. Out on the West Coast, the Victoria free net (`freenet.victoria.bc.ca`) is at the dial-up number 604-595-2300.

I also should point out that Saskatoon is a major center of free Internet activity. I included these sites in an attempt to shame U.S. locations into catching up with the Canadians.

O, Hio!

Cleveland has one of the largest free nets in the country. Somehow, when talking about free access, everywhere else seems to be ahead of New York or Los Angeles, which simply may not be as aggressive commercially. Dial-up number is 216-368-3888; Internet address is `freenet-in-a.cwru.edu`.

Part VI
Appendixes

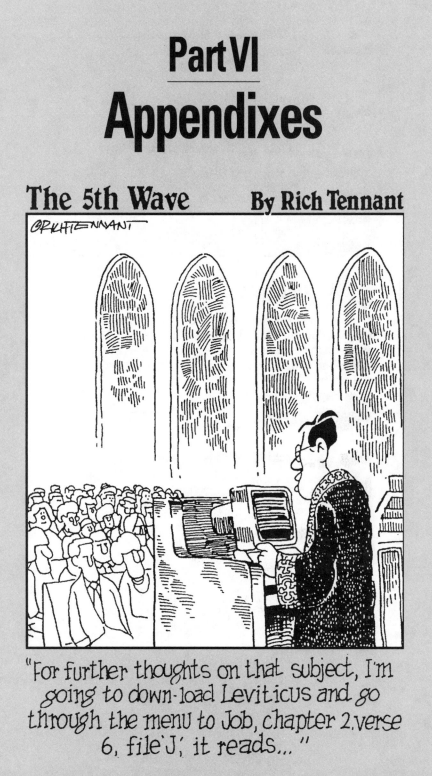

The 5th Wave   By Rich Tennant

"For further thoughts on that subject, I'm going to down-load Leviticus and go through the menu to Job, chapter 2, verse 6, file 'J', it reads..."

In this part...

*L*ots of information about the Internet is contained in Net documents and lists of various sorts. This part gives you the essentials you need to find interesting topics on the Net, and a few other tips to help you become a fine upstanding Internet citizen.

Appendix A

The Pedestrian's Guide to Internet Addresses

● ●

*I*nternet addressing can be confusing because it wasn't designed for you: it was designed for computers.

That explains everything.

I Want Oot, Find Me a Route!

After you get an account with an Internet service provider, you dial up the service, using your Mac and modem. At this point, you're connected to a network.

Now suppose that you want to use the telnet command to connect to another computer. For example, say that you want to visit the WELL in San Francisco as a guest. So you type

```
telnet well.sf.ca.us
```

to start the process.

Your network now calls another network—the main Internet high-speed network sponsored by the National Science Foundation.

Networks have relatively slow ports to the outside of modems (for your purposes, a *port* is just a phone number you can use) but faster connections inside the network. You may think that your 9600 bps modem is fast, but it's a poky little critter compared to real network-connection hardware. Networks call each other through a *router*, or a special hardware box that can connect networks that use the same plan for addresses and for message size. Technically, your messages are broken into little chunks called *packets*; the networks need to agree on the size of the packets.

You may think that you're calling up `well.sf.ca.us`. The machines involved, however, don't know a WELL from a bucket. The computer on the network won't tell you this, but inside the computer everything is a number. In the process of connecting to the WELL, both networks agree that the WELL is called

```
198.93.4.10
```

Strictly speaking, it's not even that user-friendly. The computers at either end of the transaction see a 32-digit *binary* number (0s and 1s).

The *real* Internet addresses, therefore, are numbers. But individuals can pick Internet addresses like

```
goofball@fishnet.org
```

and

```
starman@hollywood.ca.us
```

The routing system has translated the *Domain Names* (`fishnet` and `hollywood`) and the *Top-Level Domain Names* (`org` and `us`) into numbers. And it gets the numbers from a listing of Internet-assigned domain names, which are guaranteed to be unique.

When you issue a telnet command, the routing system gets the number of the site you're trying to reach; finding a file or a person at that site is up to you. When you send e-mail, the network at the other end calls up a table of *usernames* on that Net to determine that `goofball` is, in fact, Xenophon T. Biggles, cruelly nicknamed "goofball" in early childhood by playmates unable to pronounce the name of the great Athenian general.

What Domain Names Mean

You can usually count on the Top-Level Domain Name to be a type of group or else a country name. Country names are usually easy to guess, but some are a bit harder, like those little oval stickers you sometimes see on cars (*Hint:* the Germans don't call their country Germany, for example — it's Deutschland).

Here are some common Top-Level Domain names for groups:

.com	businesses
.edu	schools
.gov	government
.mil	military
.net	networks
.org	nonprofits

These are Top-Level Domain Names for countries you're likely to encounter:

.an	Australia
.au	Austria
.ca	Canada
.ch	Switzerland
.de	Germany
.fi	Finland
.it	Italy
.jp	Japan
.nz	New Zealand
.uk	United Kingdom
.us	United States

If you want to get the name for Brunei or other exotic climes (OK — you're dying of curiosity — Brunei is .bn), send a message to

```
isoc@isoc.org
```

the Internet Society itself.

Appendix B
Your Internet Phone Book

* *

1 wish I could tell you that this was going to be easy. Well, I could tell you, but you would find out anyway and send me nasty letters at *Macworld*.

You can make up a text file of Internet names and addresses, and then just cut and paste them into the To: part of messages. You'll have your very own Internet phone book, and once you get the entries right in the first place, you won't make any typos (a truly dreaded Internet problem). This works not only if you have a service with a cool interface like America Online, but even if you're just using primitive terminal software on a shell account on a UNIX network somewhere.

That's the good news. The bad news is that after years of explosive growth, it is very difficult to track down names and Internet addresses. In this appendix, I tell you some resources to use, but you're on your own after that. Good luck!

Just Say What?

If you're talking to someone whom you think you may want to reach someday by e-mail, ask that person for an Internet address on the spot. Maybe you won't need it for months, but months from now you probably won't be able to get it. Also, at least for the next few years, before Internet numbers are assigned at birth, asking for an e-mail address will make you look cool.

I know that this plan sounds simple, but it's the most reliable.

Da Phone, Boss, Da Phone!

Many organizations provide lists of e-mail addresses; simply ask the receptionist at the other end of the phone. Take it from me, the boss's nephew who's answering the phone for the summer has more intelligence than the cleverest UNIX network utility. And if he doesn't know what you need to know, he can almost always find someone who does, if necessary.

(In case you couldn't tell, I just delivered a searing indictment of the pitiful lack of organization in modern on-line communications. Welcome to the information supersidewalk.)

IDG to the Rescue — Again

This fine organization recently published *The 1994 Internet White Pages* by Seth Godin and James McBride (don't worry, this book will be updated every year). This carefully edited 800-page, fine-print download is as accurate as humanly possible. In other words, the addresses are good for

- ✔ People who are willing to sit still for a few years at the same job
- ✔ People who want their address known

While perusing this magnificent collection, you will find that computer-school gypsies (you know the ones: they spent three months at Carnegie Mellon before taking a temporary job at Thinking Machines before enrolling at Berkeley) are typically represented under multiple goofy names at several sites.

Meanwhile, the footloose and, similarly, the secretive (hey, I *know* Henry Kissinger has an e-mail address, but will he tell us?) are badly represented. Nonetheless, this hefty tome costs a tiny fraction of a cent for each good address, so it's a bargain.

Secret Agent X.500

Many Internet sites have on-line directory services called X.500. If you know practically enough to guess the address anyway, try the command

```
person tim langly, apple, us
```

on your Internet host directories (lots of commercial shell service providers have X.500). If this method doesn't work, please notice that if you have the person's name and organization, you can track down the address with a phone call anyway.

Netfind: Just What the Name Implies

I have had pretty good luck with netfind. Telnet to

```
bruno.cs.colorado.edu
```

(Do this during off-peak hours, please.) Then log in as "netfind"—with no password. Follow the subsequent menu, in which you provide almost but not quite as much information as you need to search an X.500 directory.

The search procedure is quite easy to follow, and good old bruno delivers the goods more often than anything else I've tried.

Appendix C

Netiquette, or Playing Nicely Together

. . . .

*A*s the Internet expanded, it gradually shed its role as an on-line gentlemen's club whose members were university researchers. Old hands felt obliged, however, to post some of the informal rules of conduct that they had developed over the years.

Back when there were only a few million people on the Net, these considerations were simply good manners, like not leaving chewing gum on a subway seat. Now that there are 30 million Net denizens, these "rules" take on new importance, like signs that make sure that you drive on the right side of the freeway.

In essence, this thing ain't gonna work any more unless we all behave like proper little ladies and gentlemen.

Here are four simple rules. Please take them seriously as friendly advice.

Watch Your :) and : (

Probably 90 percent of the content of face-to-face messages lies in expression and tone (this is even more true in Japan, which is why Internet e-mail is not so popular there). When you send e-mail, all these little clues to meaning we have developed over the centuries are absent. My advice is: if you're saying anything that might be taken two ways, throw in a smile (see the following list). And look over your mail carefully before you send it.

The Keyboard Symbol	What It Says
:)	smile
;)	wink
: *	kiss
: (	things are not OK
: >	fiendish grin

Download FAQs First and Read Them Off-Line

Every newsgroup has a file of FAQs (*f*requently *a*sked *q*uestions). You will be amazed (and I cast no aspersions on your originality) how often the things you want to know about rhododendrons or seismology are the *same things everyone else* wants to know. Don't bother the poor newsgroup moderators with questions that they've answered a hundred times.

In addition, you should read at your leisure the guide to local customs, a file usually called `etiquette.txt`.

Don't Send E-Mail to Thousands of People at Once

After you use the Internet for a while, you will figure out how to post e-mail to platoons of potential victims automatically. I didn't tell you how to do so, though. And for a good reason. I don't want you to. Neither does anyone else.

Think about the Simplest Way to Get What You Want

When all the national on-line services support telnet, which I predict will happen soon, you will be able to telnet to Finland (and elsewhere around the globe) to fetch chess games (and whatnot). Or you can find the same stuff on your own service.

If you want to get DNA sequence data from the molecular biology archives at Indiana University, please do so. Just don't bother the Hoosiers for calculator DAs, OK?

Appendix D

alt.newsgroups

• •

*T*he alt newsgroups arose as a way to distinguish popular topics from the original core topics (physics, math, computer science, and other serious matters) in the Usenet universe. They loom large in the mythology of the Internet because they're where the fun is, among other things.

This list is a severely edited version of a list posted regularly to a newsgroup called `news.lists`, which you can join from any Internet provider that offers Usenet newsgroups. The list is maintained by a volunteer named David C. Lawrence (Internet address `tale@uunet.uu.net`), who is thus the person to notify when groups are created or disappear. It's another example of the remarkable way the Internet operates — the list is a key piece of information about the Internet, and it's not under the control of an organization or business.

If you want the full version of the list, you should download it yourself — just look for it in the Internet-files library of any national on-line service. The complete list has topics and descriptions that are too X-rated for this little fun-for-the-whole-family book, and there's also an amazing amount of repetition — very similar topics often appear in three or four separate newsgroups. The groups identified as "moderated" here have someone who edits out the worst flames or the most inappropriate postings. The rest are just the absolute, raw, unedited transcript of all the messages contributed to the newsgroup.

Social Issues

This list is about one-fourth of the social-issue groups on Usenet. Different types of activist communities staked out their turf fairly early in Internet history.

`alt.abuse.recovery`	Helping victims of abuse to recover.
`alt.activism`	Activities for activists.
`alt.activism.d`	A place to discuss issues in `alt.activism`.
`alt.activism.death-penalty`	For people opposed to capital punishment.

(continued)

(continued)

`alt.adoption`	For those involved with or contemplating adoption.
`alt.child-support`	Raising children in a split family.
`alt.censorship`	Discussion about restricting speech/press.
`alt.current-events.bosnia`	The strife of Bosnia-Herzegovina.
`alt.current-events.clinton.whitewater`	The Clinton Whitewater scandal.
`alt.current-events.russia`	Current happenings in Russia.
`alt.current-events.usa`	What's new in the United States.
`alt.dads-rights`	Rights of fathers. (Moderated)
`alt.discrimination`	Quotas, affirmative action, bigotry, persecution.
`alt.education.disabled`	Education for people with physical/mental disabilities.
`alt.education.distance`	Learning from teachers who are far away.
`alt.feminism`	Like `soc.feminism`, only different.
`alt.fraternity.sorority`	Discussions of fraternity/sorority life and issues.
`alt.individualism`	Philosophies where individual rights are paramount.
`alt.missing-kids`	Locating missing children.
`alt.parents-teens`	Parent-teenager relationships.
`alt.politics.greens`	Green-party politics and activities worldwide.
`alt.politics.usa.constitution`	U.S. Constitutional politics.
`alt.recovery`	For people in recovery programs (for example, AA, ACA, GA).
`alt.recovery.codependency`	Mutually destructive relationships.
`alt.sexual.abuse.recovery`	Helping others deal with traumatic experiences.
`alt.support`	Dealing with emotional situations and experiences.
`alt.support.cancer`	Emotional aid for people with cancer.
`alt.support.depression`	Depression and mood disorders.

alt.support.divorce	Discussion of marital breakups.
alt.support.step-parents	Helping people with their stepparents.
alt.support.stuttering	Support for people who stutter.
alt.war	Not just collateral damage.

At the Extremes

These groups contain plenty of interesting speculative material.

alt.alien.visitors	Space Aliens on Earth! Abduction! Gov't Cover-up!
alt.conspiracy	Be paranoid — they're out to get you.
alt.out-of-body	Out-of-body experiences.
alt.paranet.skeptic	"I don't believe they turned you into a newt."
alt.paranet.ufo	"Heck, I guess naming it 'UFO' identifies it."
alt.paranormal	Phenomena that are not scientifically explicable.
alt.sci.physics.new-theories	Scientific theories you won't find in journals.

Computer Stuff

Please note that these are discussion groups, rather than sources of software. You can, however, get plenty of advice if you want it.

alt.bbs.internet	BBSs that are hooked up to the Internet.
alt.best.of.internet	It was a time of sorrow, it was a time of joy.
alt.gopher	Discussion of the gopher information service.
alt.irc.questions	How-to questions for IRC (International Relay Chat).
alt.lang.basic	The language that would not die.
alt.online-service	Large commercial on-line services, and the Internet.
alt.online-service.america-online	Discussions and questions about America Online.

(continued)

(continued)

`alt.online-service.compuserve`	Discussions and questions about CompuServe.
`alt.online-service.delphi`	Discussions and questions about Delphi.
`alt.online-service.freenet`	Public FreeNet systems.
`alt.online-service.prodigy`	The Prodigy system.
`alt.sources.mac`	Source file newsgroup for the Apple Macintosh computers.

Critters

I expect that as more dog and cat owners get on the Internet, there will be postings of upcoming shows and the like. It's pretty hard to believe there's a skunks group and not at least one for Persian cat fanciers.

`alt.animals.badgers`	Badgers (meles meles and others).
`alt.animals.dolphins`	Flipper, Darwin, and all their friends.
`alt.animals.foxes`	Everything you ever wanted to know about vulpines.
`alt.aquaria`	The aquarium and related as a hobby.
`alt.fan.lemurs`	Little critters with BIG eyes.
`alt.pets.rabbits`	Coneys abound.
`alt.skunks`	Enthusiasts of skunks and other mustelidae.
`alt.wolves`	Discussing wolves and wolf-mix dogs.

Games

There are more groups actually playing games on the Internet than discussing them.

`alt.anagrams`	Playing with words.
`alt.games.mtrek`	Multi-Trek, a multiuser Star Trek-like game.
`alt.games.netrek.paradise`	Discussion of the paradise version of netrek.
`alt.games.video.classic`	Video games from before the mid-1980s.

`alt.sega.genesis`	Another addiction.
`alt.super.nes`	Like `rec.games.video.nintendo`, only different.

Sports

I'm only listing a few of the groups for professional sports teams. Your favorite team is almost certainly listed, in the same format as these, as `alt.sports.<sports>.<team-name>`.

`alt.archery`	Robin Hood had the right idea.
`alt.caving`	Spelunking.
`alt.fishing`	Like `rec.outdoors.fishing`, only different.
`alt.skate-board`	Discussion of all aspects of skateboarding.
`alt.sport.bowling`	In the gutter again.
`alt.sport.darts`	Look what you've done to the wall!
`alt.sport.falconry`	The taking of live game by using a trained raptor.
`alt.sport.jet-ski`	Discussion of personal watercraft.
`alt.sport.officiating`	Problems related to officiating athletic contests.
`alt.sport.pool`	Knock your balls into your pockets for fun.
`alt.sport.racquetball`	All aspects of indoor racquetball and related sports.
`alt.sport.squash`	With the proper technique, vegetables can go very fast.
`alt.sports.baseball.chicago-cubs`	Chicago Cubs major league baseball.
`alt.sports.basketball.nba.la-lakers`	Los Angeles Lakers NBA basketball.
`alt.sports.college.ivy-league`	Ivy League athletics.
`alt.sports.football.mn-vikings`	Minnesota Vikings football.
`alt.sports.football.pro.gb-packers`	Green Bay Packers NFL football.

(continued)

(continued)

`alt.sports.hockey.nhl.tor-mapleleafs`	Toronto Maple Leafs NHL hockey.
`alt.surfing`	Riding the ocean waves.

Fan Clubs

This listing represents roughly eight percent of the fan-club material on the lists. These were selected for no other reason than personal eccentricity.

`alt.books.anne-rice`	The vampire stuff.
`alt.elvis.king`	You've heard of this guy.
`alt.fan.blues-brothers`	Jake and Elwood ride again!
`alt.fan.disney.afternoon`	Disney Afternoon characters and shows.
`alt.fan.hofstadter`	Douglas Hofstadter, Godel, Escher, Bach and others.
`alt.fan.howard-stern`	Fans of the abrasive radio and TV personality.
`alt.fan.jimmy-buffett`	A white sports coat and a pink crustacean.
`alt.fan.laurie.anderson`	Will it be a music concert or a lecture this time?
`alt.fan.letterman`	One of the top ten reasons to get the alt groups.
`alt.fan.noam-chomsky`	Noam Chomsky's writings and opinions.
`alt.fan.oingo-boingo`	Have you ever played Ping-Pong in Pago Pago?
`alt.fan.penn-n-teller`	The magicians Penn and Teller.
`alt.fan.rush-limbaugh`	Just what it says.
`alt.fan.u2`	The Irish rock band U2.
`alt.fan.wodehouse`	Discussion of the works of humor author P.G. Wodehouse.
`alt.fan.woody-allen`	The diminutive director.
`alt.music.peter-gabriel`	Discussion of the music of Peter Gabriel.
`alt.ql.creative`	The "Quantum Leap" TV show.
`alt.tv.barney`	He's everywhere. Now appearing in several alt groups.

The Arts, More or Less

This list uses a fairly elastic definition of art.

alt.artcom	Artistic community, arts and communication.
alt.arts.ballet	All aspects of ballet and modern dance as performing art.
alt.binaries.pictures.cartoons	Images from animated cartoons.
alt.binaries.pictures.fine-art.d	Discussion of the fine-art binaries. (Moderated)
alt.binaries.pictures.fine-art.digitized	Art from conventional media. (Moderated)
alt.binaries.pictures.fine-art.graphics	Art created on computers. (Moderated)
alt.books.reviews	"If you want to know how it turns out, read it!"
alt.folklore.urban	Urban legends, a la Jan Harold Brunvand.
alt.guitar	Strumming and picking.
alt.magic	For discussion about stage magic.
alt.music.a-cappella	Like rec.music.a-cappella, only different.
alt.music.alternative	For groups having two or less platinum-selling albums.
alt.music.blues-traveler	For "All fellow travelers."
alt.music.progressive	Yes, Marillion, Asia, King Crimson, and so on.
alt.music.synthpop	Depeche Mode, Erasure, Pet Shop Boys, and much more!
alt.music.techno	Bring on the bass!
alt.music.world	Discussion of music from around the world.
alt.prose	Postings of original writings, fictional and otherwise.
alt.tv.mst3k	The finest cultural newsgroup on earth (author's opinion)!
alt.zines	Small magazines, mostly noncommercial.

Religion

This area is full of many lively discussions. It's sometimes strange to think of comments on ancient manuscripts flying back and forth on high-speed, fiber-optic links.

`alt.christnet`	Gathering place for Christian ministers and users.
`alt.christnet.bible`	Bible discussion and research.
`alt.christnet.philosophy`	Philosophical implications of Christianity.
`alt.christnet.theology`	The distinctives of God of Christian theology.
`alt.hindu`	The Hindu religion. (Moderated)
`alt.messianic`	Messianic traditions.
`alt.philosophy.zen`	Zen for everyone.
`alt.religion.christian`	Unmoderated forum for discussing Christianity.
`alt.religion.gnostic`	History and philosophies of the gnostic sects.
`alt.religion.islam`	Discussion of Islamic faith and society.

Funny Business

Humor is a giant newsgroup topic. If you're the only person in Nonesuch, Wyoming, who thinks Dave Barry is funny, you can find pals on the Net. In Usenet humor newsgroups like `alt.humor.best-of-usenet`, off-color jokes are typically encoded in a simple substitution cipher, so if you go to the trouble of decoding it, you don't have much business complaining about your sensibilities being assaulted.

`alt.comedy.british`	Discussion of British comedy in a variety of media.
`alt.comedy.british.blackadder`	The Black Adder programme.
`alt.comedy.firesgn-thtre`	Firesign Theatre—in all its flaming glory.
`alt.comedy.standup`	Discussion of stand-up comedy and comedians.
`alt.fan.dave_barry`	Electronic fan club for humorist Dave Barry.
`alt.fan.monty-python`	Electronic fan club for those wacky Brits.
`alt.fan.mst3k`	A forum of incisive cultural comment.
`alt.humor.best-of-usenet`	What the moderator thinks is funniest. (Moderated)

ClariNet — The News Source

● ●

*T*he alt newsgroups are fun, and the sci newsgroups are high-powered. But newcomers to the Internet are justified in wondering where they can find all the information that's relevant to the average hardworking citizen.

The answer is all that stuff — more than a megabyte a day — is on ClariNet. ClariNet is a commercial newsgroup service provider that collects news from all over, principally from wire services, such as UPI and Reuters. The news then is sorted into appropriate groups so that you don't drown in the sheer amount of text available.

ClariNet is a service with fees, so your Internet provider may or may not have secured access (but national on-line services now typically have a ClariNet connection). In this appendix, I list the newsgroups so that you can see what's available. If you're a serious news demon, you'll want to get the following:

- ✔ clari.news.flash
- ✔ clari.news.bulletin
- ✔ clari.news.urgent

This will put you about an hour ahead of television news and about eight hours ahead of the newspapers. Also look in the list for the designation "top" in different categories, such as sports or business.

I think the real value of ClariNet, however, is providing news that is not frequently reported by the mainstream press. During the O.J. Simpson pretrial hearings, for example, you may have thought that whole continents had ceased to exist and that the national research community had disbanded. They were still on ClariNet, though. So you can use ClariNet as a way to insulate yourself a bit from the pack journalism of the major networks and newspapers. There's also a reasonable amount of humor, including clari.feature.dave_barry and "Dilbert," the only good comic strip left (IMHO).

Anyway, look over the list in Table E-1 and use features like America Online's Newsgroup Expert Add to create your own tailored information service.

Table E-1   Guide to ClariNet Newsgroups

ClariNet Newsgroup	*Description*
clari.biz.briefs	Business newsbriefs.
clari.biz.commodity	Commodity news and price reports.
clari.biz.courts	Lawsuits and business-related legal matters.
clari.biz.earnings	Businesses' earnings, profits, losses.
clari.biz.economy	Economic news and indicators.
clari.biz.economy.world	Non-U.S. economy stories.
clari.biz.features	Business feature stories.
clari.biz.finance	Finance, currency, corporate finance.
clari.biz.finance.earnings	Earnings & dividend reports.
clari.biz.finance.personal	Personal investing & finance.
clari.biz.finance.services	Banks and financial industries.
clari.biz.industry.agriculture	Agriculture, fishing, forestry.
clari.biz.industry.automotive	The car and truck industry.
clari.biz.industry.aviation	Airlines and airports.
clari.biz.industry.banking	Banks and S&Ls.
clari.biz.industry.broadcasting	The television and radio industry.
clari.biz.industry.construction	The construction industry.
clari.biz.industry.dry_goods	Consumer goods, clothing, furniture.
clari.biz.industry.energy	Oil, gas, coal, alternatives.
clari.biz.industry.food	Food processing, markets, restaurants.
clari.biz.industry.health	The health care business.
clari.biz.industry.insurance	The insurance industry.
clari.biz.industry.manufacturing	Heavy industry.
clari.biz.industry.mining	Mining for metals, minerals.

ClariNet Newsgroup	Description
clari.biz.industry.print_media	Newspapers, publishers, magazines.
clari.biz.industry.real_estate	Housing and real estate.
clari.biz.industry.retail	Retail stores and shops.
clari.biz.industry.services	Consulting, brokerages, services.
clari.biz.industry.tourism	The tourism and hotel industry.
clari.biz.industry.transportation	Trains, buses, transit, shipping.
clari.biz.invest	News for investors.
clari.biz.labor	Strikes, unions, and labor relations.
clari.biz.market	General stock market news.
clari.biz.market.amex	American Stock Exchange reports & news.
clari.biz.market.commodities	Commodity reports.
clari.biz.market.dow	Dow Jones NYSE reports.
clari.biz.market.misc	Bonds, money market funds, and so on.
clari.biz.market.news	News affecting financial markets.
clari.biz.market.ny	NYSE reports.
clari.biz.market.otc	NASDAQ reports.
clari.biz.market.report	General market reports, S&P, and so on.
clari.biz.market.report.asia	Asian market reports.
clari.biz.market.report.europe	European market reports.
clari.biz.market.report.top	Overview of the markets.
clari.biz.market.report.usa	U.S. market reports.
clari.biz.market.report.usa.nyse	NYSE reports.
clari.biz.mergers	Mergers and acquisitions.
clari.biz.misc	Other business news.
clari.biz.products	Important new products and services.

(continued)

Table E-1 (continued)

ClariNet Newsgroup	Description
clari.biz.review	Daily review of business news.
clari.biz.top	Top business news.
clari.biz.urgent	Breaking business news.
clari.biz.world_trade	GATT, free trade, trade disputes.
clari.canada.biz	Canadian business summaries.
clari.canada.features	Alamanac, Ottawa Special, Arts.
clari.canada.general	Short Canadian news stories.
clari.canada.gov	Government-related news (all levels).
clari.canada.law	Crimes, courts, and the law.
clari.canada.newscast	Regular newscast for Canadians.
clari.canada.politics	Political and election items.
clari.canada.trouble	Mishaps, accidents, and serious problems.
clari.feature.dave_barry	Columns of humorist Dave Barry.
clari.feature.dilbert	The comic strip "Dilbert" (MIME/uuencoded GIF).
clari.feature.mike_royko	Chicago opinion columnist Mike Royko.
clari.feature.miss_manners	Judith Martin's humorous etiquette advice.
clari.living	Fashion, leisure, lifestyle.
clari.living.animals	Human interest stories about animals.
clari.living.arts	News of the arts.
clari.living.bizarre	Unusual or funny news stories.
clari.living.books	News about books and authors.
clari.living.celebrities	Famous people in the news.

ClariNet Newsgroup	Description
clari.living.consumer	Consumer issues and products.
clari.living.entertainment	Entertainment news.
clari.living.goodnews	Stories of success and survival.
clari.living.history	News and human interest about history.
clari.living.history.today	Today in history feature.
clari.living.human_interest	General human interest stories.
clari.living.movies	News of film and movies.
clari.living.music	News of the music scene.
clari.living.tv	News of TV programs and events.
clari.local.alabama	News of Alabama.
clari.local.alaska	News of Alaska.
clari.local.alberta.briefs	Local news briefs.
clari.local.arizona	Local news.
clari.local.arizona.briefs	Local news briefs.
clari.local.arkansas	News of Arkansas.
clari.local.bc.briefs	Local news briefs.
clari.local.california	Local news.
clari.local.california.briefs	Local news briefs.
clari.local.chicago	Local news.
clari.local.chicago.briefs	Local news briefs.
clari.local.colorado	News of Colorado.
clari.local.connecticut	News of Connecticut.
clari.local.delaware	News of Delaware.
clari.local.florida	Local news.
clari.local.florida.briefs	Local news briefs.
clari.local.georgia	Local news.
clari.local.georgia.briefs	Local news briefs.
clari.local.hawaii	News of Hawaii.
clari.local.headlines	Various local headline summaries.

(continued)

Table E-1 *(continued)*

ClariNet Newsgroup	Description
clari.local.idaho	News of Idaho.
clari.local.illinois	Local news.
clari.local.illinois.briefs	Local news briefs.
clari.local.indiana	Local news.
clari.local.indiana.briefs	Local news briefs.
clari.local.iowa	Local news.
clari.local.iowa.briefs	Local news briefs.
clari.local.kansas	News of Kansas.
clari.local.kentucky	News of Kentucky.
clari.local.los_angeles	Local news.
clari.local.los_angeles.briefs	Local news briefs.
clari.local.louisiana	Local news.
clari.local.maine	News of Maine.
clari.local.manitoba.briefs	Local news briefs.
clari.local.maritimes.briefs	Local news briefs.
clari.local.maryland	Local news.
clari.local.maryland.briefs	Local news briefs.
clari.local.massachusetts	Local news.
clari.local.massachusetts.briefs	Local news briefs.
clari.local.michigan	Local news.
clari.local.michigan.briefs	Local news briefs.
clari.local.minnesota	Local news.
clari.local.minnesota.briefs	Local news briefs.
clari.local.mississippi	News of Mississippi.
clari.local.missouri	Local news.
clari.local.missouri.briefs	Local news briefs.
clari.local.montana	News of Montana.
clari.local.nebraska	Local news.
clari.local.nebraska.briefs	Local news briefs.

ClariNet Newsgroup	Description
clari.local.nevada	News of Nevada.
clari.local.new_england	Local news.
clari.local.new_hampshire	Local news.
clari.local.new_jersey	Local news.
clari.local.new_jersey.briefs	Local news briefs.
clari.local.new_mexico	News of New Mexico.
clari.local.new_york	Local news.
clari.local.new_york.briefs	Local news briefs.
clari.local.north_carolina	News of North Carolina.
clari.local.north_dakota	News of North Dakota.
clari.local.nyc	Local news (New York City).
clari.local.nyc.briefs	Local news briefs.
clari.local.ohio	Local news.
clari.local.ohio.briefs	Local news briefs.
clari.local.oklahoma	News of Oklahoma.
clari.local.ontario.briefs	Local news briefs.
clari.local.oregon	Local news.
clari.local.oregon.briefs	Local news briefs.
clari.local.pennsylvania	Local news.
clari.local.pennsylvania.briefs	Local news briefs.
clari.local.rhode_island	News of Rhode Island.
clari.local.saskatchewan.briefs	Local news briefs.
clari.local.sfbay	Stories datelined San Francisco Bay Area.
clari.local.south_carolina	News of South Carolina.
clari.local.south_dakota	News of South Dakota.
clari.local.tennessee	News of Tennessee.
clari.local.texas	Local news.
clari.local.texas.briefs	Local news briefs.
clari.local.utah	Local news.
clari.local.utah.briefs	Local news briefs.

(continued)

Table E-1 *(continued)*

ClariNet Newsgroup	Description
clari.local.vermont	News of Vermont.
clari.local.virginia+dc	Local news.
clari.local.virginia+dc.briefs	Local newsbriefs.
clari.local.washington	Local news.
clari.local.washington.briefs	Local newsbriefs.
clari.local.west_virginia	News of West Virginia.
clari.local.wisconsin	Local news.
clari.local.wisconsin.briefs	Local newsbriefs.
clari.local.wyoming	News of Wyoming.
clari.matrix_news	Monthly journal on the Internet.
clari.nb.apple	Newsbytes Apple/Macintosh news.
clari.nb.business	Newsbytes business & industry news.
clari.nb.general	Newsbytes general computer news.
clari.nb.govt	Newsbytes legal and government computer news.
clari.nb.ibm	Newsbytes IBM PC World coverage.
clari.nb.review	Newsbytes new product reviews.
clari.nb.summary	Daily summary of Newsbytes news.
clari.nb.telecom	Newsbytes telecom & on-line industry news.
clari.nb.top	Newsbytes top stories (cross-posted).
clari.nb.trends	Newsbytes new developments & trends.
clari.nb.unix	Newsbytes UNIX news.
clari.net.admin	Announcements for news admins at ClariNet sites.

ClariNet Newsgroup	Description
clari.net.announce	Announcements for all ClariNet readers.
clari.net.answers	Monthly postings for ClariNet readers.
clari.net.info	Occasional announcements for readers.
clari.net.newusers	On-line info about ClariNet.
clari.net.products	New ClariNet products.
clari.net.talk	Discussion of ClariNet — not moderated.
clari.net.talk.admin	Discussion of adminstrative topics — not moderated
clari.net.talk.news	Discussion of events in the news — not moderated
clari.news.aging	News of senior citizens and aging.
clari.news.alcohol	Drunk driving, alcoholism.
clari.news.almanac	Daily almanac — quotes, this date in history, and so on.
clari.news.arts	Stage, drama, & other fine arts.
clari.news.aviation	Aviation industry and mishaps.
clari.news.blacks	Black news.
clari.news.books	Books & publishing.
clari.news.briefs	Regular news summaries.
clari.news.bulletin	Major breaking stories of the week.
clari.news.canada	News related to Canada.
clari.news.cast	Regular U.S. news summary.
clari.news.censorship	Censorship, government control of media.
clari.news.children	Stories related to children and parenting.
clari.news.civil_rights	Freedom, civil rights, human rights.

(continued)

Table E-1 *(continued)*

ClariNet Newsgroup	Description
clari.news.conflict	War, conflict, peace talks.
clari.news.consumer	Consumer news, car reviews, and so on.
clari.news.corruption	Corruption in government.
clari.news.crime.abductions	Kidnappings, hostage-taking.
clari.news.crime.abuse	Spouse and child abuse.
clari.news.crime.issue	The social issue of crime.
clari.news.crime.juvenile	Crimes by children and teenagers.
clari.news.crime.misc	Other crimes.
clari.news.crime.murders	Murders and shootings.
clari.news.crime.organized	Organized crime.
clari.news.crime.sex	Sex crimes, child pornography.
clari.news.crime.top	Well-known crimes.
clari.news.crime.white_collar	Insider trading, fraud, embezzlement.
clari.news.demonstration	Demonstrations around the world.
clari.news.disaster	Major problems, accidents, & natural disasters.
clari.news.drugs	Drug abuse and social policy.
clari.news.economy	General economic news.
clari.news.education	Primary and secondary education.
clari.news.education.higher	Colleges and universities.
clari.news.election	News regarding U.S. and international elections.
clari.news.entertain	Entertainment industry news & features.
clari.news.ethnicity	Ethnicity issues.
clari.news.europe	News related to Europe.
clari.news.family	Families, adoption, marriage.

ClariNet Newsgroup	Description
clari.news.features	Unclassified feature stories.
clari.news.fighting	Clashes around the world.
clari.news.flash	Ultra-important once-a-year news flashes.
clari.news.gays	Homosexuality and gay rights.
clari.news.goodnews	Stories of success and survival.
clari.news.gov	General government-related stories.
clari.news.gov.agency	Government agencies, FBI, and so on.
clari.news.gov.budget	Budgets at all levels.
clari.news.gov.corrupt	Government corruption, kickbacks, and so on.
clari.news.gov.international	International government-related stories.
clari.news.gov.officials	Government officials & their problems.
clari.news.gov.state	State government stories of national importance.
clari.news.gov.taxes	Tax laws, trials, and so on.
clari.news.gov.usa	U.S. government news. (high volume).
clari.news.group	Special-interest groups.
clari.news.group.blacks	News of interest to black people.
clari.news.group.gays	Homosexuality and gay rights.
clari.news.group.jews	Jews & Jewish interests.
clari.news.group.women	Women's issues and abortion.
clari.news.guns	Gun control and other gun news.
clari.news.headlines	Hourly list of the top U.S./world headlines.
clari.news.hot.east_europe	News from Eastern Europe.
clari.news.hot.laquake	News on the L.A. earthquake.

(continued)

Table E-1 *(continued)*

ClariNet Newsgroup	*Description*
clari.news.hot.somalia	News from Somalia.
clari.news.hot.ussr	News from the Soviet Union.
clari.news.immigration	Refugees, immigration, migration.
clari.news.interest	Human interest stories.
clari.news.interest.animals	Animals in the news.
clari.news.interest.history	Human interest & history in the making.
clari.news.interest.people	Famous people in the news.
clari.news.interest.people.column	Daily "people" column — tidbits on celebs.
clari.news.interest.quirks	Unusual or funny news stories.
clari.news.issues	Stories not covered elsewhere.
clari.news.issues.civil_rights	Freedom, racism, civil rights issues.
clari.news.issues.conflict	Conflict between groups around the world.
clari.news.issues.family	Family, child abuse, and so on.
clari.news.jews	Jewish news.
clari.news.labor	Unions, strikes.
clari.news.labor.layoff	Layoffs in the news.
clari.news.labor.strike	Strikes.
clari.news.law	General group for law-related issues.
clari.news.law.civil	Civil trials & litigation.
clari.news.law.crime	Major crimes.
clari.news.law.crime.sex	Sex crimes and trials.
clari.news.law.crime.trial	Trials for criminal actions.
clari.news.law.crime.violent	Violent crime & criminals.
clari.news.law.drugs	Drug-related crimes & drug stories.
clari.news.law.investigation	Investigation of crimes.

ClariNet Newsgroup	Description
`clari.news.law.police`	Police & law enforcement.
`clari.news.law.prison`	Prisons, prisoners, & escapes.
`clari.news.law.profession`	Lawyers, judges, and so on.
`clari.news.law.supreme`	U.S. Supreme Court rulings & news.
`clari.news.lifestyle`	Fashion, leisure, and so on.
`clari.news.military`	Military equipment, people, & issues.
`clari.news.movies`	Reviews, news, and stories on movie stars.
`clari.news.music`	Reviews and issues concerning music & musicians.
`clari.news.politics`	Politicians & politics.
`clari.news.politics.people`	Politicians & political personalities.
`clari.news.poverty`	Poverty, homelessness, hunger.
`clari.news.punishment`	Prison conditions, torture, death penalty.
`clari.news.religion`	Religion, religious leaders, televangelists.
`clari.news.reproduction`	Abortion, contraception, fertility.
`clari.news.review`	Daily news review.
`clari.news.sex`	Sexual issues, sex-related political stories.
`clari.news.smoking`	Smoking and tobacco issues.
`clari.news.terrorism`	Terrorist actions & related news around the world.
`clari.news.top`	Top U.S. news stories.
`clari.news.top.world`	Top international news stories.
`clari.news.trends`	Surveys and trends.
`clari.news.trouble`	Less major accidents, problems, & mishaps.
`clari.news.tv`	TV news, reviews, & stars.

(continued)

Table E-1 *(continued)*

ClariNet Newsgroup	*Description*
`clari.news.urgent`	Major breaking stories of the day.
`clari.news.usa.gov.financial`	U.S. financial policy.
`clari.news.usa.gov.foreign_policy`	U.S. foreign policy.
`clari.news.usa.gov.misc`	Miscellaneous U.S. domestic policy.
`clari.news.usa.gov.personalities`	Personalities and private lives.
`clari.news.usa.gov.politics`	Party politics and electioneering.
`clari.news.usa.gov.state+local`	State and local governments.
`clari.news.usa.gov.white_house`	Presidential news.
`clari.news.usa.law`	Legal news and U.S. lawsuits.
`clari.news.usa.law.supreme`	The U.S. Supreme Court.
`clari.news.usa.military`	News of the U.S. military.
`clari.news.weather`	Weather and temperature reports.
`clari.news.women`	Women's issues: sexism, harassment.
`clari.sfbay.briefs`	Twice-daily news roundups for SF Bay Area.
`clari.sfbay.entertain`	Reviews and entertainment news for SF Bay Area.
`clari.sfbay.fire`	Stories from the fire depts. of the SF Bay.
`clari.sfbay.general`	Main stories for SF Bay Area.
`clari.sfbay.misc`	Shorter general items for SF Bay Area.
`clari.sfbay.police`	Stories from the police depts. of the SF Bay.
`clari.sfbay.roads`	Reports from Caltrans and the CHP.
`clari.sfbay.short`	Very short items for SF Bay Area.

ClariNet Newsgroup	Description
clari.sfbay.weather	SF Bay and California weather reports.
clari.sports.baseball	Baseball scores, stories, stats.
clari.sports.baseball.games	Baseball games and box scores.
clari.sports.basketball	Basketball coverage.
clari.sports.basketball.college	College basketball coverage.
clari.sports.briefs	General sports scoreboard.
clari.sports.features	Sports feature stories.
clari.sports.football	Pro football coverage.
clari.sports.football.college	College football coverage.
clari.sports.football.games	Coverage of individual pro games.
clari.sports.golf	Golf coverage.
clari.sports.hockey	NHL coverage.
clari.sports.misc	Other sports, plus general sports news.
clari.sports.motor	Racing, motor sports.
clari.sports.olympic	The Olympic Games.
clari.sports.review	Daily review of sports.
clari.sports.tennis	Tennis news & scores.
clari.sports.top	Top sports news.
clari.tw.aerospace	Aerospace industry and companies.
clari.tw.biotechnology	Biotechnology news.
clari.tw.computers	Computer industry, applications, and developments.
clari.tw.defense	Defense industry issues.
clari.tw.education	Stories involving universities & colleges.
clari.tw.electronics	Electronics makers and sellers.
clari.tw.environment	Environmental news, hazardous waste, forests.

(continued)

Table E-1 *(continued)*

ClariNet Newsgroup	Description
clari.tw.health	Disease, medicine, health care, sick celebs.
clari.tw.health.aids	AIDS stories, research, political issues.
clari.tw.misc	General technical industry stories.
clari.tw.new_media	On-line services, multimedia, the Internet.
clari.tw.nuclear	Nuclear power & waste.
clari.tw.science	General science stories.
clari.tw.space	NASA, astronomy, & spaceflight.
clari.tw.stocks	Regular reports on computer & technology stock prices.
clari.tw.telecom	Phones, satellites, media, & general telecom.
clari.tw.top	Top technical stories.
clari.world.africa	Translated reports from Africa.
clari.world.africa.south_africa	News from South Africa.
clari.world.americas	News on the Americas.
clari.world.americas.canada	General Canadian news.
clari.world.americas.canada.business	Canadian business news.
clari.world.americas.canada.review	Daily review of Canadian news.
clari.world.americas.caribbean	News of the Caribbean island nations.
clari.world.americas.central	News of Central America.
clari.world.americas.mexico	News of Mexico.
clari.world.americas.south	News of South America.
clari.world.asia	News from Asia and the Pacific Rim.
clari.world.asia.central	Ex-Soviet republics in Central Asia.

ClariNet Newsgroup	Description
clari.world.asia.china	News of China.
clari.world.asia.hong_kong	News of Hong Kong.
clari.world.asia.india	News of India.
clari.world.asia.japan	News of Japan.
clari.world.asia.koreas	News of North and South Korea.
clari.world.asia.south	News of South Asia (Pakistan, Bangladesh, and so on).
clari.world.asia.southeast	News of Vietnam, Cambodia, Laos, Thailand.
clari.world.asia.taiwan	News of the Republic of China (Taiwan).
clari.world.briefs	World events.
clari.world.europe.alpine	Austria, Switzerland, Liechtenstein.
clari.world.europe.balkans	Former Yugoslavia, Romania, Bulgaria.
clari.world.europe.benelux	Belgium, the Netherlands, Luxembourg.
clari.world.europe.central	Poland, Czech Rep., Slovakia, Hungary.
clari.world.europe.eastern	Translated reports from Eastern Europe.
clari.world.europe.france	News of France and Monaco.
clari.world.europe.germany	News of Germany.
clari.world.europe.greece	News of Greece.
clari.world.europe.iberia	Spain, Portugal, Andorra.
clari.world.europe.ireland	News of the Republic of Ireland.
clari.world.europe.italy	News of Italy and San Marino.
clari.world.europe.northern	Scandinavia, Finland, Iceland.
clari.world.europe.russia	News of Russia.
clari.world.europe.uk	News of the United Kingdom.

(continued)

Table E-1 *(continued)*

ClariNet Newsgroup	Description
clari.world.europe.union	News about the European Union.
clari.world.europe.western	Stories on western Europe.
clari.world.mideast	News from the Middle East.
clari.world.mideast.arabia	News of the Arabian Peninsula.
clari.world.mideast.iran	News of Iran.
clari.world.mideast.iraq	News of Iraq.
clari.world.mideast.israel	News of Israel and occupied lands.
clari.world.mideast.turkey	News of Turkey.
clari.world.oceania	News of Oceania.
clari.world.oceania.australia	News of Australia.
clari.world.organizations	The UN and other organizations.
clari.world.top	Top news from around the world.

Appendix F
A New Kind of Service

●●

*A*ctually, there's not just one kind of new service but several. All the traditional modes of using the Internet are changing, making it easier to use but more demanding on the people doing the programming. Since you're an end-user buying this book, this is good news for you. I'll tell you about some Internet news in this appendix — all late-breaking stuff at the end of 1994.

Netscape

Look I had to say a lot about Mosaic in this book because Mosaic is the most famous Web browser. But in daily life, I use Mac Web instead — that's why it's included in the software set — because it's really fast. There are new Web browsers appearing every month. Mosaic is not the last word in this business.

If you prefer a more lush Web environment, just go to the Mosaic Communications home page at

```
www.mcom.com
```

and you can download a copy of Netscape. This is the new product of Mosaic Communications (see Figures F-1, F-2), the people who wrote Mosaic in the first place back at the University of Illinois. This product Author:incorporates the orginal design team's ideas on how Mosaic might be improved, so it's got lots of nice touches.

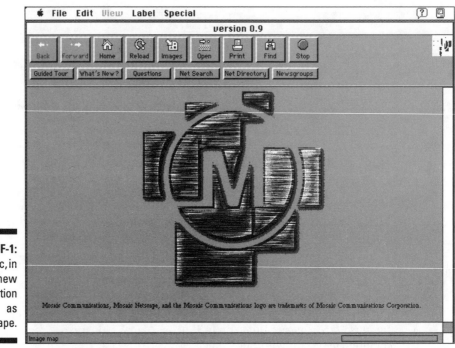

Figure F-1:
Mosaic, in
its new
incarnation
as
Netscape.

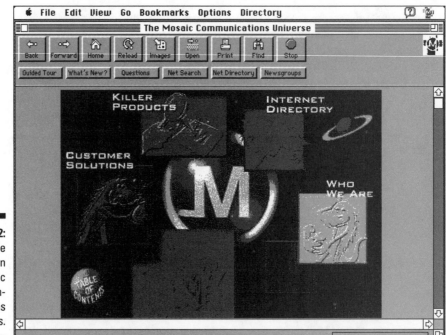

Figure F-2:
A clickable
introduction
to Mosaic
Com-
munications
Services.

The principle difference between Netscape and Mosaic is that Netscape has added some services (notably newsgroups) that were missing in the original product, and that Netscape makes better use of buttons and the rest of the Mac interface. Also, Netscape has a dragon (called Mozilla) (see Figure F-3) and a better-organized collection of points of interest (see Figure F-4).

Figure F-3: The dragon Mozilla on the Netscape welcome page. You're a long way from the old text-based Web at this point...

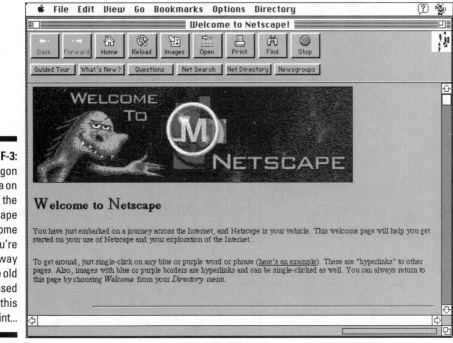

Getting around inside Netscape is simple. Either you use the directory (see Figure F-5) (just click the Net Directory button) or, if you already have a set of favorite WWW pages, pick Open Location.. from the File menu.

Because the team behind Netscape knows that you're looking for a good time on the Net, you can cut directly to a well-maintained Best Of (see Figure F-6) directory that has all sorts of amusing and valuable material.

And as a well-bahaved browser, Netscape has no trouble with the other sites you might want to visit, and it continues to offer you some nice extra button services.

Figure F-4:
Including
What's New
from as
early as
mid-1994, for
Web
archaeol-
ogists!

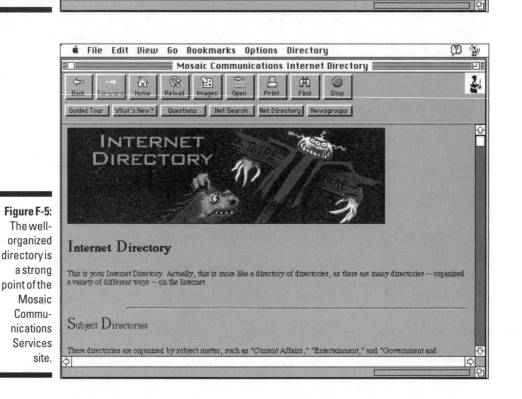

Figure F-5:
The well-
organized
directory is
a strong
point of the
Mosaic
Commu-
nications
Services
site.

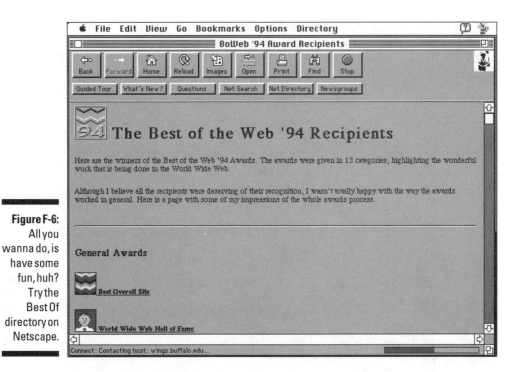

Figure F-6:
All you
wanna do, is
have some
fun, huh?
Try the
Best Of
directory on
Netscape.

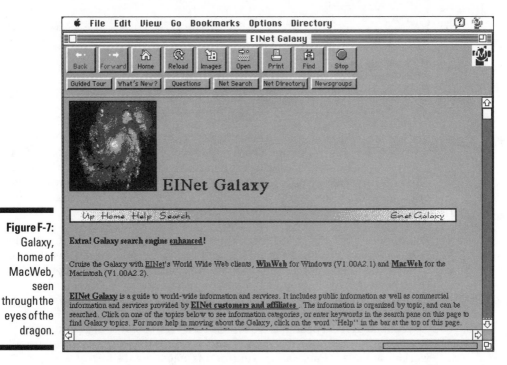

Figure F-7:
Galaxy,
home of
MacWeb,
seen
through the
eyes of the
dragon.

If you bought this book in IDG's Starter Kit bundle, you should already have a printed copy of Internet White pages. Unless you have a free Internet connection, I would recommend browsing for addresses on paper first and then searching the on-line White Pages (see Figure F-8). I calculated that at the $2/hr charge from my SLIP provider, using Netscape White Pages, cost me about $40 in November 1994. And things won't get better as the Net grows!

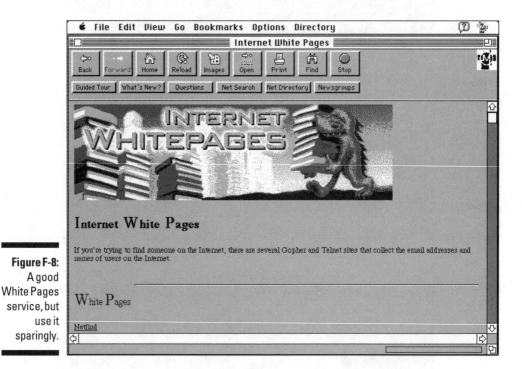

Figure F-8:
A good
White Pages
service, but
use it
sparingly.

The Netscape Directory menu (see Figure F-9) gives you a good idea of the orientation of Mosaic Communications. Right on the menu (see Figure F-10) is an item for "What's Cool," and they're not kidding. The stuff really is cool. If you're interested in WWW because of all the hype you may have seen in *Wired* magazine or elsewhere, going directly to this item will save you some effort. There's a time to surf, and there's a time for Norwergian Cruise Lines to Barbados.

For example, the Grafica Obscura link (see Figure F-11) from What's Cool is the best collection of computer graphics tips I've ever encountered. Tons of useful material, updated more frequently than book publishers can do it, pours down the pipe to you. By the way, as long as you're here, you should see the awful amount of labor involved in doing anything that looks good on the Web — pick View Source (see Figure F-12) under the Edit menu for a glimpse of the Stone-Age commands that produce the screen. New Web tools are appearing constantly, so you can hope that someday you could have your own page without working as hard as Paul Haeberli did for this magnificent effort.

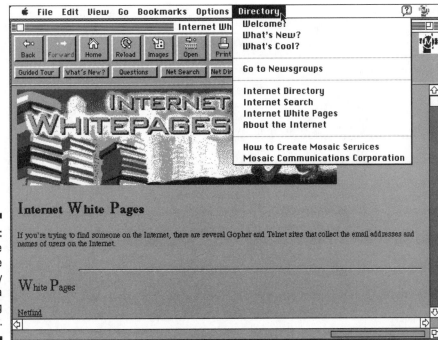

Figure F-11:
A fabulous
collection of
tips. Cool
indeed.

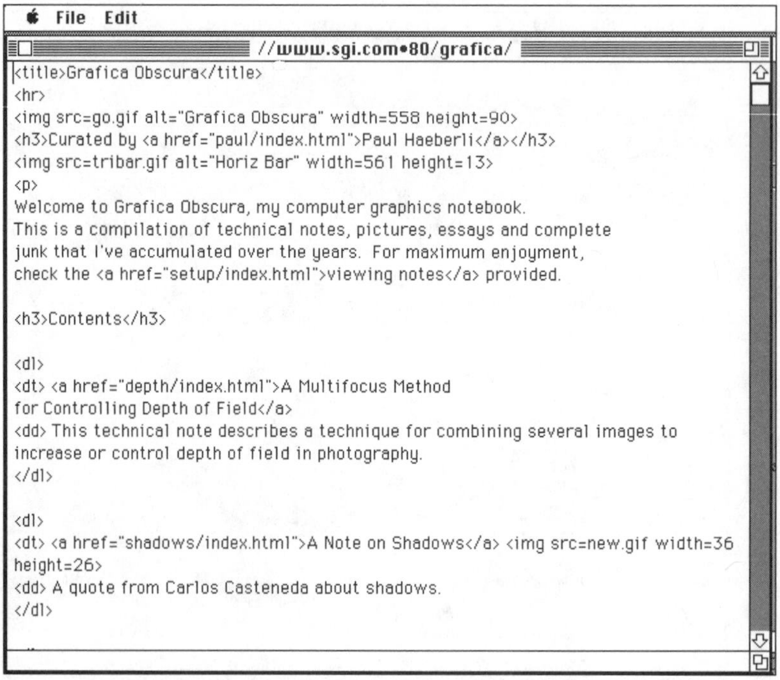

Figure F-12:
Down in the
engine
room of the
Web —
the nasty
little
hypertext
mark-up
commands.

New Newsgroup Services

Although I'm not covering CompuServe and Prodigy in this book, mainly because they have been passed up recently by America Online, and also because they're not in the same class with Pipeline as Internet providers, they nonetheless are slowly getting up to speed.

Here's the latest word on newsgroups:

CompuServe

On CompuServe you can now select USENET from the starting menu when you sign on the service. The USENET interface gives you a basic repertoire of access actions (see Figure F-13).

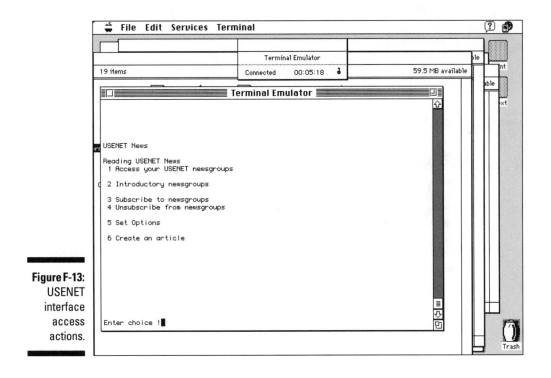

Figure F-13:
USENET
interface
access
actions.

The newsreader actions (see Figure F-14) in the CompuServe menu are simple choices that cover most of the same commands available in the old-time UNIX newsreader *nn* (sorry, no way to kill whole newsgroup threads or topics though). Because the internal organization of newsgroups is all based on these older readers, presenting this kind of simple menu works pretty well.

When you select the option Subscribe to newsgroups at the starting USENET screen, you get the set of choices in Figure F-15. Following by-the-numbers menu, CompuServe takes you into the newsgroup threads with the options in the last figure.

```
USENET News

Choices
 1 REPLY
 2 REPLY with Quotation
 3 MAIL
 4 CREATE an article
 5 CANCEL article

 6 REREAD this article
 7 HOLD this article
 8 NEXT article
 9 NEXT THREAD
10 PARENT article

11 CLEAR articles in this newsgroup
12 IGNORE
13 DOWNLOAD this article


Enter choice !
```

Figure F-14:
Newsreader actions in the CompuServe menu.

Prodify

A graphical, menu-driven interface greatly simplifies adding and removing newsgroups from your personal list. Even Prodigy (see Figure F-16), a service with the gravest trepidation about the Internet and its nasty newsgroups, has finally added a point-and-click newsgroup interface in its latest software version. Prodigy makes you promise that you're an adult before you can sign on, but it offers the whole list of newsgroups. This is progress indeed.

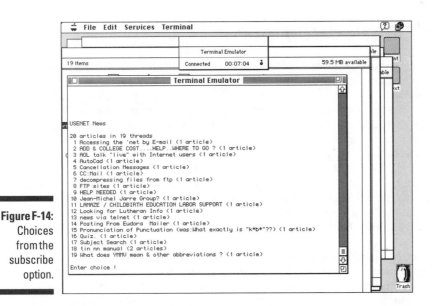

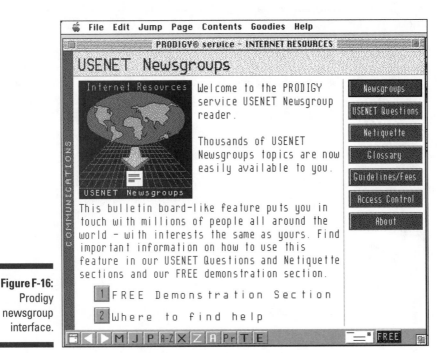

A New Connection Type: TIA

Lately, there's a new type of Internet access in the form of a software fix-up that lets a standard UNIX shell account impersonate a SLIP account. It's called The Internet Adapter (TIA) (for more information, send e-mail to the company at `tia-sales@marketplace.com`), it's starting to revolutionize activities at traditional Internet shell account providers, and at least one national on-line service is investigating using a modified version of TIA to provide real Mosaic on what's basically just an e-mail system.

I would have included a TIA section in this book, but the first wave of users have reported so many heart-breaking installation problems with the first Mac version that I'm going to let the programmers cook it a bit longer and add some oregano and cheese before I do a chapter on it in a Dummies book.

And if it's possible to program something like TIA, it's possible to make all the graphical software of any type run over a standard dial-up connection. It's basically a gross defect of System software that you should have to know anything personally about TCP or SLIP to run a program like Mosaic — you don't have to know about matrix inversion or how the NuBus works to run Photoshop, for example.

What keeps programmers employed is making software accessible to more people, and that's just what's happening on the Internet, with new solutions to connections problems occuring every month.

Glossary

These are terms you are likely to encounter while roaming the Net or planning your next adventure.

a2i

A major Internet service provider. See Chapter 19.

account

There are two main kinds of Internet access for civilians: shell accounts and SLIP accounts. In a shell account, you usually dial up a computer with your modem and then navigate with UNIX commands. With a SLIP account (see SLIP), you are a real Internet site yourself, so you can use special Mac software for graphical-interface access.

address

A person's Internet address is the line with the @, as in chseiter@aol.com. From the Internet's point of view, an address is a set of four numbers, such as 132.34.115.31. The numbers correspond to a name that you can remember, such as zapp.com or simple.net. Check Appendix A for more on addresses.

alt

The newsgroups with the highest entertainment value are all in the unofficial alternative newsgroup hierarchy, and their names start with alt. Look in Appendix D for examples.

Anarchie

Anarchie is a Macintosh shareware program that performs Archie searches. It's very good, and every national on-line service has it in Mac software libraries.

anonymous FTP

Anonymous FTP is a procedure for logging into computers that maintain file archives that are accessible to anyone. You use *anonymous* as your user name and your e-mail address as your password.

AppleLink

Apple's own on-line service, soon to be merged into eWorld.

AppleTalk

Apple's own set of hardware and software for managing local-area networks. It's a slow protocol, best for smaller networks.

Archie

Archie is the basic Internet system for finding files. An Archie server is a computer that has lists of available archived files all over the Internet.

archive

An archive is a collection of files. At a site that maintains archives, someone is responsible for updating files and checking the archive for viruses.

ARPA

The Advanced Research Projects Agency, the government agency that funded ARPANET, a precursor to the Internet.

ARPANET

The ARPANET was the basis for networking research in the 1970s. The ARPANET has essentially disappeared into the Internet.

ASCII

ASCII stands for *American Standard Code for Information Interchange*, a definition that associates each character with a number from 0 to 255. An ASCII file is a text file of characters.

backbone

A high-speed set of network connections. On the Internet, this usually means the NSFNET, a government-funded set of links between large computer sites.

BBS

Shorthand for *bulletin board system*. A BBS can be an old Mac II in a garage or a gigantic system with 10,000 users.

Big Sky Telegraph

A public-access Internet service, located in Montana. One of the best of its kind.

binary file

A file of 0s and 1s, which can represent pictures and sound, as well as text.

binhex

A file transmission fix-up. Most mail programs can only handle ASCII, so a binhex utility program converts binary programs to ASCII so that people can mail you a binary file. At the receiving end, you have to decode the file back to binary with the programs BinHex (4.0 or 5.0), HQXer, or uudecode.

BITNET

A large network that passes material back and forth to the Internet. See Chapter 2.

biz

A newsgroup where you find discussions that have to do with (gasp!) money. Generally, you're not supposed to use other newsgroups for commercial purposes.

bounce

When you send a piece of e-mail and it comes back as undeliverable, it is said to have "bounced," much like an uncashable check.

bridge

A bridge is a set of hardware and software that lets two different networks appear to be a single larger network to people connecting from outside the system.

bug

A software programming or design problem. Unfortunately, bugs are plentiful in communications software.

chat

If you send messages to an electronic mailbox, that's e-mail. If you're sending messages back and forth to someone in real time, that's chat. See IRC.

ClariNet

ClariNet is a special newsgroup system that provides first-rate, commercially important news and charges a fee. Some Internet service providers carry it; some don't.

ClarisWorks

ClarisWorks is an integrated software package with a communications module that's better than some but not particularly useful in a world where you can get older versions of ZTerm for free.

com

This is the top-level domain name that identifies businesses.

communications software

The software that controls your modem and dials out to other networks. Mac examples are ZTerm, Microphone, White Knight, and the communications modules of Microsoft Works and ClarisWorks.

comp

The term comp in the middle of a newsgroup name means that the discussions will be computer-oriented. I'm sorry to report that the majority of these groups are oriented towards UNIX or PCs, not Macintoshes.

Computer Currents

A tabloid-format computer magazine that turns up on newspaper racks in big cities. A good source of local bulletin board numbers.

country code

A top-level domain name that identifies a site by country: well.sf.ca.us, for example, has the country code us because San Francisco is physically, if not emotionally, part of the United States.

.cpt

The file extension .cpt at the end of a filename means that the file was compressed with Compact Pro. You can expand it either with that program or with one of the StuffIt series from Aladdin Software.

CR Laboratories

A shell and SLIP account provider in Larkspur, California, with local dial-up numbers all over the United States. They're *my* SLIP provider, and they know how to set up MacTCP and InterSLIP for you.

cyberspace

This somewhat overworked term first appeared in the science fiction novel *Neuromancer,* by William Gibson. It refers to the digital world represented by all computers and their interaction.

dial-up

A dial-up connection is one that works only while you're connected by phone. The other type of connection is direct, where you're wired to a network and are connected all the time.

Dial 'n' cerf

A national Internet access provider (see Chapter 19).

DIALOG

A huge information service, managed by Lockheed, with lots of technical databases.

DNS

The domain name system, used to convert Internet names to their corresponding Internet numbers.

domain

An Internet site address has two parts, the domain and the top-level domain name. For America Online — aol.com — aol is the domain name and com is the top-level part. The domain roughly corresponds to the name of a particular network.

DOS

The original operating system that Microsoft cooked up (actually, Microsoft bought it in a one-sided deal) for IBM PCs. Don't bother looking in DOS file collections.

dotted quad

Every now and then you'll hear an old-time Internet hipster refer to the four numbers of an Internet address as a "dotted quad."

Electronic Frontier Foundation (EFF)

This organization is something like the conscience of the Internet, as opposed to its administration. Go look for the EFF area on your Internet service provider.

elm

This is considered a "good" UNIX e-mail utility, meaning that as a Mac user you've probably never seen anything as cryptic or difficult.

e-mail

Electronic mail. It's a message you compose on your computer to be received on someone else's computer, although some services let your message be delivered as a fax or (this sounds weird, but it's true) *an actual piece of paper!*

edu

Usually this is the Internet address identifier for a university. The universities of the United States are the reason the Internet is the vast wonderland it is today.

Ethernet

An Ethernet network is a very common, much faster alternative to Apple's original built-in networking stuff. Newer Macs for business now have Ethernet capability as part of the system.

Eudora

A Macintosh program for handling e-mail. The first versions were shareware, but now it's a commercial program from QualComm software.

FAQ

*F*requently *a*sked *q*uestion. Trust me, your questions will be just like anyone else's. When you sign up with an Internet service provider — and before you make any contributions to newsgroups — read the FAQ files that are prominently displayed in menus. This saves you embarrassment and saves everyone else from your three-millionth-time newbie questions.

Fetch

A truly wonderful Macintosh FTP program from Dartmouth, available from all Internet service providers.

file transfer protocol

See FTP.

finger

On UNIX-based Internet systems, finger is a utility that lets you get a profile of a user (including the user's real name).

firewall

You may wonder how other computers you can reach by telnet keep you out of private areas. Networks have *firewalls* in different places to block access to unauthorized users.

flame

A flame is the sort of extreme opinion that the sender probably wouldn't have the nerve to deliver in person. Although some Internet old-timers seem to generate four flames a day, I think that as a matter of decorum you should never flame (it's a verb or a noun) anyone ever, no matter what.

freenet

There are about 30 or 40 freenets around the United States. These are networks that don't charge you a monthly or per-hour fee. Cool, huh? Your local librarian is likely to have the phone numbers.

freeware

Freeware is software that is offered by its author for no charge. This is different from shareware (see shareware). There's some amazingly good freeware on the Net.

FTP

FTP stands for *file transfer protocol.* On the Internet, it usually refers to a UNIX-system utility program that lets you collect files from archives at other sites (see Chapter 5).

FTP-by-mail

FTP-by-mail, explained in Chapters 7 and 8, is a way to use e-mail to get files sent to you automatically from FTP sites, even if your own Internet service provider doesn't have FTP implemented.

gateway

A gateway is hardware that lets messages be sent between two different kinds of networks. You need a gateway, for example, to communicate at network speeds between a Macintosh AppleTalk-based network and a UNIX-based network.

Graphic Interchange Format (GIF)

GIF stands for graphics interchange format — you see it as a file extension on picture files as `flower.gif`. GIF files are very common on the Internet, and most sites offer a shareware program called GIFwatcher to read them. Adobe Photoshop and other large image-handling programs also can work with GIF files.

gnu

Every time you look in a big archive, you see gnu folders. The Free Software Foundation has developed gnu as a sort of UNIX-clone operating system, complete with C-language compiler and lots of utilities, that it distributes for free, as a matter of principle.

Gopher

A Gopher is a file search-and-retrieval system that's usually the right basic Internet tool for finding the file you want. For the Macintosh, there's TurboGopher.

gopherspace

Gopherspace is a cutesy name for the total of all the gophers in the world and the information in them.

gov

Gov is the top-level name, or zone, for any type of government organization.

host

Most kinds of Internet access using a modem will have you dialing a host computer, which is a big computer with its own Internet address.

.hqx

When you see this as a file extension, it means that the file is in binhex (see binhex) format. You have to decode it to get the original file, and the easiest way to decode it is with HQXer.

HQXer

As you can guess from the name, this shareware utility processes files into and out of .hqx format. It's available in the libraries of every Internet service provider.

hypertext

Hypertext is a set of text files in which individual words link one file to the next.

HyTelnet

This program can be used to manage telnet functions, but it can also be used off-line as a comprehensive directory of telnet sites.

information superhighway

No one knows what this means, including me, so I thought I'd put it in the glossary. Internet fans think it means the Internet, cable TV companies think it's what will happen when cable fibers carry data, and phone companies think it's what will happen when they can force you to buy computers from them. The Internet fans are closest.

Internet protocol (IP)

A set of definitions that govern transmission of individual packets of information on the Internet.

Internet Society

A bunch of good people who discuss policies and make recommendations about Internet management.

InterNIC

The name stands for *Inter*net *N*etwork *I*nformation *C*enter. The word *InterNIC* turns up on the menus of many Internet service providers, and it's a good place to look for the history and future of the Net.

InterSLIP

A freeware program from Intercon that works with MacTCP to give your Mac a SLIP connection.

IRC

IRC stands for *I*nternet *R*elay *C*hat, an on-line forum of almost unimaginable liveliness that's offered by real Internet providers, such as Delphi.

jpeg

A compressed file format for images.

Jughead

Because there was a program called Archie and another called Veronica, someone decided that Jughead would be a good name for a Gopher searching tool.

Kermit

A slow but reliable file transfer protocol named, in fact, after the frog on "The Muppet Show."

LISTSERV

LISTSERV programs manage mailing lists by sending messages automatically to everyone on a given list.

log in

Log in and log on are different terms for making contact with a remote computer. They're used interchangeably.

lurking

In Internet jargon you are said to be lurking if you join a discussion group and just read other people's messages. Oh, well, better a lurker than a flamer.

Mac Binary

A special format for storing Macintosh binary files on other computers.

MacTCP

Apple's program (a Control Panel, actually) that you need to use a SLIP account. MacTCP translates your files and messages into Internet-compatible chunks of information.

MacSLIP

An alternative to InterSLIP.

MacWAIS

An excellent shareware program for WAIS, the *w*ide *a*rea *i*nformation *s*erver.

mail server

A mail server is a program on a host computer that saves your mail for you until you make a dial-up connection and have a chance to download your mail and read it.

Matrix

Lots of early Net visionaries use the term Matrix to denote the total of all connected computers in the world. It used to be used as a cool name for the Internet plus everything else.

Metaverse

A graphical version, more or less, of the Internet, but with a better plot. This electronic structure is the basis of Neal Stephenson's science fiction masterpiece *Snow Crash*.

MicroTimes

A tabloid-format computer magazine that turns up on newspaper racks in big cities. A good source of local bulletin board numbers.

mil

The top-level domain name of military sites on the Internet. Just about all U.S. military sites are Internet sites.

MIME

This acronym stands for *M*ultipurpose *I*nternet *M*ail *E*xtension, an Internet standard that lets you add sound and images to e-mail. It's not widely implemented yet, but it will be.

mirror

A mirror site is an archive that keeps a copy of the files in another site.

misc

Newsgroups that don't fit under any other recognizable category get put into `misc`.

modem

The device that lets your computer make telephone calls to other computers.

moderated

A moderated newsgroup has someone who filters out the really pointless or offensive material, leaving only moderately pointless or offensive messages.

Mosaic

Mosaic is the original freeware program for access to the World Wide Web hypertext system. Commercial versions of Mosaic will appear soon.

MUD

*M*ulti-*U*ser *D*ungeons are on-line fantasy games that can have dozens of players.

Multi-User Simulated Environment (MUSE)

A *M*ulti-*U*ser *S*imulated *E*nvironments is a sort of highbrow MUD. A multiplayer version of the Mac game SimCity would be a MUSE.

NCSA

*N*ational *C*enter for *S*upercomputing *A*pplications, managed by the University of Illinois, is the home of Mosaic, along with lots of big computers.

Netcom

A large national Internet service provider, and a big FTP server.

network

Any set of computers that can communicate directly with each other constitutes a network.

newbie

A faintly derogatory term for users in their first months on the Internet, employed freely by people who have been on the system one week longer.

newsgroup

A collection of people and messages on a particular topic of interest.

node

The term *node* in Internet context means a central computer that's part of an Internet-connected network. Sometimes used interchangeably with site or host.

NovaLink

A big-time Internet service provider. Look in Chapter 19 for the phone number.

NSFNET

The *N*ational *S*cience *F*oundation *Net* is a principal Internet traffic carrier.

packet

A block of information, complete with addresses for destination and source, traveling over the Internet.

page

The basic unit of the World Wide Web information service is the page. Pages are linked by hypertext references to other pages.

password

OK, you know what a password is. Just try to think of a nonobvious password (usually, it shouldn't be a real word from a dictionary, much less your nickname) to save yourself potential grief.

PDIAL

The PDIAL list, available on every Internet service, is a regularly updated registry of public Internet access providers.

ping

An Internet program that is used to determine if a site is still active.

poker

OK, you may be wondering why I keep putting definitions next to their acronyms. Years ago at Caltech, I asked a French postdoc in my research group if he wanted to join the lunchtime graduate student poker game. He looked puzzled (he was just learning vernacular English, although he could write better than we could). I wrote the word "poker" on a blackboard, he looked at it, frowned, and looked it up in a bilingual dictionary, where the entry read (I'm not kidding)

poker (n.) *poker*

The light bulb went off, he said "Ah, poker!", sat down, and cleaned us out.

point of presence

A local phone number for high-speed access maintained by an Internet provider.

POP

Post Office Protocol is an e-mail protocol used for downloading mail from a mail server.

PPP

Point to Point Protocol is an alternative to SLIP for dial-up full Internet access. You would use MacPPP instead of InterSLIP or MacSLIP for this kind of connection. Your Internet service provider's system administrator will tell you which to use.

protocol

A protocol is a definition that controls communication on a network.

rec

Newsgroups for recreational purposes are signaled with rec. There's plenty of overlap between rec and alt, in practice.

RFC/RFD

Requests For Comment and *Requests For Discussion* are study-group documents with an important role in settling general Internet questions about design and use.

rlogin

An alternative to telnet, rlogin is a UNIX command for connecting to remote computers.

router

A router is a gateway (see gateway) between two networks that use Internet protocol.

sci

Serious research newsgroups in science and mathematics belong to this newsgroup hierarchy.

.sea

This file extension stands for *self-extracting archive*. If you double-click on a .sea file, it usually turns itself into a folder containing an application and some documentation files.

server

A computer that stores files as a central resource for other computers, called clients, that can connect to the server to get files for themselves.

shareware

Shareware is software you can download free to test. If you like it and use it, you are obliged as a matter of honor to send the requested payment to the author.

.sit

Files compressed with StuffIt from Aladdin Software show this file extension. You can expand them with UnStuffIt, available from all the national on-line services and most bulletin boards.

SLIP

Serial Line Internet Protocol lets you become a dial-up Internet site. You also need MacTCP to make a SLIP connection with a Macintosh. SLIP is an alternative to PPP.

SMTP

The *Simple Mail Transport Protocol* is the e-mail protocol standard for the Internet.

soc

The soc newsgroups on social issues overlap many of the alt social issue newsgroups.

.tar

This file extension indicates files compressed with a special UNIX program. You can expand them with StuffIt Deluxe.

TCP/IP

The whole system, *Transport Control Protocol* and *Internet Protocol*, makes up a standard guideline for network hardware and software design.

telnet

The core of all Internet services is the UNIX utility telnet, a program that lets users connected to one host dial up a different Internet host.

terminal

In the old days, a terminal could only receive and send characters to the real computer at the other end of the wires. A terminal program lets your sophisticated Macintosh mimic this primitive arrangement.

thread

A series of connected messages in a newsgroup.

TurboGopher

A brilliant Macintosh Gopher program for searching all the files of the Internet. As freeware, TurboGopher is available everywhere in the libraries of on-line services.

UNIX

The operating system that runs the Internet. Developed over many years, it's capable of meeting any networking challenge and is very thrifty with computing resources. The downside consequence of these virtues is that UNIX is hard for beginners to use.

Usenet

The network, linked at different points to the Internet, that supports all the newsgroups.

uuencode

Uuencode is a program that turns binary files into ASCII files so that you can send them through e-mail. Uudecode takes the files back to binary. Mac shareware utilities for this function are available in most libraries.

Veronica

Veronica is a program that searches for files over all available Gopher servers, making it the program to use whenever it's available. Higher-level searches are preferable to direct use of Archie.

VT-100/102

These are two very common terminals and, hence, two very common terminal-software options. As a first guess, pick vt100 as the terminal setting when you dial up almost any service using standard communications software.

WAIS

Wide area information servers are text databases with a superior search method that looks inside the text rather than just looking at document titles.

WELL

A very popular Bay Area bulletin board with full Internet access. About half the computer journalists on earth seem to hang out on this service.

Windows

An attempt to stick a Macintosh-like face on the ugly reality of DOS.

WWW

World Wide Web is an Internet service consisting of hypertext-linked documents. When we all have faster Macs and faster connections, WWW will probably be the best kind of Internet facility because it's so easy for beginners to operate.

whois

A command available on some Internet services to find the real name of a user based on the user's screen name.

X, Y, and ZMODEM

XMODEM is a 15-year-old file transfer protocol; YMODEM is newer; and ZMODEM is the fastest and best.

.z

Another type of UNIX-system compressed file extension, also expandable with UnStuffIt.

zip

The most common compressed-file format for PCs. Unless it's a text file, you probably won't be able to do anything with a .zip file on a Mac even if you expand it, so don't bother unless there's a compelling reason to put yourself through the trouble.

ZTerm

The favorite communications software for many Mac users. It's reliable and fast for downloading large files from bulletin boards.

Index

Notes

Notes

Notes

Notes

Notes

Internet Society

Application for Individual Membership

❑ Please enroll me as an individual member of the Internet Society. I understand that membership, in addition to fostering the evolution of the Internet and its use, entitles me to receive the quarterly Internet Society News, reduced fees for attendance at Internet Society conferences and other benefits. Membership will extend for 12 months from the month of application receipt. I am applying for:

❑ Individual membership at $35.00

❑ Student individual membership at $25.00

Name: _____

Postal Address: _____

_____

_____

Internet Email address: _____

Fax (optional): _____ Telephone (optional): _____

Payment Information

Payment of annual dues may be made by check, money order, credit card or wire transfer.
    ❑ Payment is included with this application   ❑ Please bill me

For credit card payments

❑ VISA   ❑ MasterCard   ❑ AMEX   ❑ Diner's Club   ❑ Carte Blanche

Card Number: _____

Name on Card (please print): _____

Expiration Date: _____

Signature: _____

Send wire transfers to:

Riggs Bank of Virginia   Bank ABA number: 056001260
8315 Lee Highway   Account number: Internet Society 148 387 10
Fairfax VA 22031
USA

Please telephone toll-free or send by post, fax or email to:

Email: <membership@isoc.org>
Fax: +1 703 648 9887
Tel: +1 703 648 9888
Tel: 800 468 9507 (USA only)

Internet Society
12020 Sunrise Valley Dr, suite 270
Reston VA 22091
USA

For office use only	
Enrollment:	_____
Receipt:	_____
Date:	_____
By:	_____
Check #:	_____

MicroPhone ™ Pro for Macintosh

The World's No. 1 Communications Software — from Software Ventures — *Now available for $89.95!*

MicroPhone™ Pro for Macintosh is, simply, the most powerful and comprehensive communications program available. With a complete suite of TCP/IP tools for easy Internet connectivity, a powerful scripting language and graphical interfaces for information services, MicroPhone will take you where you want to go with point-and-click Macintosh ease. We're so convinced that you'll love our product that we're prepared to let users of other communications software packages try us out for a special price. Send this coupon with proof of ownership of a competing Macintosh product — a photocopy of your master disks will do — and we'll upgrade you to MicroPhone Pro for $89.95. *That's a savings of at least $100!*

Just complete the enclosed coupon and mail to the address below. California residents add 8.25% state sales tax. US customers: $5 shipping. Canadian customers: $20 shipping (includes 7% GST); payment in US dollars, please. One product per coupon. Offer expires December 31, 1995.

How to Place Your Order
Mail this ENTIRE form with your payment to: Software Ventures, Attn: MicroPhone Pro MFD Upgrade, 2907 Claremont Ave., Berkeley, CA 94705. For faster service, use our (510) 601-1088 fax number.

Customer Information *(print clearly, please no P.O. boxes)*

Name _____ Company _____

Address _____

City _____ State/Province _____ Zip/Postal Code_____

Phone (   ) _____ Fax (   ) _____

Payment Information *(no purchase orders or CODs)*

☐ Check enclosed *(payable to Software Ventures)*
☐ Bill my credit card   ☐ Visa ☐ MasterCard

Credit Card Number _____/_____/_____/_____ Exp. Date _____

Signature_____ Cardholder Name _____

GEnie
The most fun you can have with your computer on.

No other online service has more cool stuff to do or more cool people to do it with than GEnie. Join dozens of awesome special interest RoundTables on everything from scuba diving to Microsoft to food and wine, download over 200,000 files, access daily stock quotes, talk to all those smart guys on the Internet, play the most incredible multi-player games, and so much more you won't believe your eyeballs.

And GEnie has it all at a standard connect rate of just $3.00 an hour.[1] That's one of the lowest rates of all the major online services! Plus, because you're a reader of *The Internet For Macs For Dummies*, you get an even cooler deal[2]. If you sign up before December 31, 1995, we'll waive your first monthly subscription fee (an $8.95 value) and include ten additional hours of standard connect time (another $30.00 in savings). That's fourteen free hours during your first month — *a $38.95 value!*

You can take advantage of this incredible offer immediately — just follow these simple steps:

1. Set your communications software for half-duplex (local echo) at 300, 1200, or 2400 baud. Recommended communications parameters 8 data bits, no parity and 1 stop bit.
2. Dial toll-free in the U.S. at 1-800-638-8369 (or in Canada at 1-800-387-8330). Upon connection, type **HHH** (please note: every time you use GEnie, you need to enter the HHH upon connection).
3. At the U#= prompt, type **JOINGENIE** and press <Return>.
4. At the offer code prompt, enter GDF225 to get this special offer.
5. Have a major credit card ready. In the U.S., you may also use your checking account number. (There is a $2.00 monthly fee for all checking accounts.) In Canada, VISA and MasterCard only.

Or, if you need more information, contact GEnie Client Services at 1-800-638-9636 from 9am to midnight, Monday through Friday, and from noon to 8pm Saturday and Sunday (all times are Eastern).

[1] U.S. prices. Standard connect time is non-prime time: 6pm to 8am local time, Mon. - Fri., all day Sat. and Sun., and selected holidays.
[2] Offer available in the United States and Canada only.
[3] The offer for ten additional hours applies to standard hourly connect charges only and must be used by the end of the billing period for your first month. Please call 1-800-638-9636 for more information on pricing and billing policies.

Effective date as of 7/1/93. Prices subject to change without notice. Offer limited to new subscribers only and one per customer.

Online Users... Save 50% Today!

You save 50% off the newsstand price right now when you sign up for a subscription to **Online Access** magazine, the first magazine to bring you complete coverage of the online world.

Every issue of **Online Access** brings you the best, the fastest, the smartest and the most economical ways to grab the thousands of opportunities that are available to you online.

If you want information about:
- The Internet
- Investment Services
- Major Online Services
- E-mail
- Information Databases
- Bulletin Board Services
- Wireless Communication
- Anything and everything that you need to do online...

Online Access magazine is your one stop choice.

Subscribe today and sign up for a one year, 10 issue subscription for only $24.75*, a savings of 50% off the newsstand price! Simply fill out the information below and send it in today.

Your subscription is risk-free...if you're not completely satisfied with **Online Access**, you may cancel at any time and receive a refund of any unmailed copies.

EXPLORE the INTERNET
——— FREE! ———

DELPHI is the only major online service to offer you full access to the Internet. And now you can explore this incredible resource with no risk. You get 5 hours of evening and weekend access to try it out for free!

Use electronic mail to exchange messages with over 20 million people throughout the world. Download programs and files using "**FTP**" and connect in real-time to other networks using "**Telnet**." Meet people from around the world with "**Internet Relay Chat**" and check out "**Usenet News**," the world's largest bulletin board with over 10,000 topics.

If you're not familiar with these terms, don't worry; DELPHI has expert **online assistants** and a large collection of help files, books, and other resources to help you get started. After the free trial you can choose from two low-cost membership plans. With rates as low as $1 per hour, no other online service offers so much for so little.

Put the world at your fingertips.

Join the world's largest international network of people with personal computers. Whether it's computer support, communications, entertainment, or continually updated information, you'll find services that meet your needs.

Your introductory membership will include one month of free basic services plus a $15 usage credit for extended and premium CompuServe services.

To get connected, complete and mail the card below. Or call **1-800-524-3388** and ask for Representative 370.

CompuServe®

☐YES!

Send me my FREE CompuServe Introductory Membership including a $15 usage credit and CompuServe basic services membership free for one month.

Name:_____

Address:_____

City:_____State:_____ZIP:_____

Phone:_____

Clip and mail this form to: CompuServe
P.O. Box 20212
Dept. 370
Columbus, OH 43220

Title	Author	ISBN	Price

INTERNET / COMMUNICATIONS / NETWORKING

Title	Author	ISBN	Price
CompuServe For Dummies™	by Wallace Wang	1-56884-181-7	$19.95 USA/$26.95 Canada
Modems For Dummies™, 2nd Edition	by Tina Rathbone	1-56884-223-6	$19.99 USA/$26.99 Canada
Modems For Dummies™	by Tina Rathbone	1-56884-001-2	$19.95 USA/$26.95 Canada
MORE Internet For Dummies™	by John R. Levine & Margaret Levine Young	1-56884-164-7	$19.95 USA/$26.95 Canada
NetWare For Dummies™	by Ed Tittel & Deni Connor	1-56884-003-9	$19.95 USA/$26.95 Canada
Networking For Dummies™	by Doug Lowe	1-56884-079-9	$19.95 USA/$26.95 Canada
ProComm Plus 2 For Windows For Dummies™	by Wallace Wang	1-56884-219-8	$19.99 USA/$26.99 Canada
The Internet For Dummies™, 2nd Edition	by John R. Levine & Carol Baroudi	1-56884-222-8	$19.99 USA/$26.99 Canada
The Internet For Macs For Dummies™	by Charles Seiter	1-56884-184-1	$19.95 USA/$26.95 Canada

MACINTOSH

Title	Author	ISBN	Price
Macs For Dummies®	by David Pogue	1-56884-173-6	$19.95 USA/$26.95 Canada
Macintosh System 7.5 For Dummies™	by Bob LeVitus	1-56884-197-3	$19.95 USA/$26.95 Canada
MORE Macs For Dummies™	by David Pogue	1-56884-087-X	$19.95 USA/$26.95 Canada
PageMaker 5 For Macs For Dummies™	by Galen Gruman	1-56884-178-7	$19.95 USA/$26.95 Canada
QuarkXPress 3.3 For Dummies™	by Galen Gruman & Barbara Assadi	1-56884-217-1	$19.99 USA/$26.99 Canada
Upgrading and Fixing Macs For Dummies™	by Kearney Rietmann & Frank Higgins	1-56884-189-2	$19.95 USA/$26.95 Canada

MULTIMEDIA

Title	Author	ISBN	Price
Multimedia & CD-ROMs For Dummies™, Interactive Multimedia Value Pack	by Andy Rathbone	1-56884-225-2	$29.95 USA/$39.95 Canada
Multimedia & CD-ROMs For Dummies™	by Andy Rathbone	1-56884-089-6	$19.95 USA/$26.95 Canada

OPERATING SYSTEMS / DOS

Title	Author	ISBN	Price
MORE DOS For Dummies™	by Dan Gookin	1-56884-046-2	$19.95 USA/$26.95 Canada
S.O.S. For DOS™	by Katherine Murray	1-56884-043-8	$12.95 USA/$16.95 Canada
OS/2 For Dummies™	by Andy Rathbone	1-878058-76-2	$19.95 USA/$26.95 Canada

UNIX

Title	Author	ISBN	Price
UNIX For Dummies™	by John R. Levine & Margaret Levine Young	1-878058-58-4	$19.95 USA/$26.95 Canada

WINDOWS

Title	Author	ISBN	Price
S.O.S. For Windows™	by Katherine Murray	1-56884-045-4	$12.95 USA/$16.95 Canada
MORE Windows 3.1 For Dummies™, 3rd Edition	by Andy Rathbone	1-56884-240-6	$19.99 USA/$26.99 Canada

PCs / HARDWARE

Title	Author	ISBN	Price
Illustrated Computer Dictionary For Dummies™	by Dan Gookin, Wally Wang, & Chris Van Buren	1-56884-004-7	$12.95 USA/$16.95 Canada
Upgrading and Fixing PCs For Dummies™	by Andy Rathbone	1-56884-002-0	$19.95 USA/$26.95 Canada

PRESENTATION / AUTOCAD

Title	Author	ISBN	Price
AutoCAD For Dummies™	by Bud Smith	1-56884-191-4	$19.95 USA/$26.95 Canada
PowerPoint 4 For Windows For Dummies™	by Doug Lowe	1-56884-161-2	$16.95 USA/$22.95 Canada

PROGRAMMING

Title	Author	ISBN	Price
Borland C++ For Dummies™	by Michael Hyman	1-56884-162-0	$19.95 USA/$26.95 Canada
"Borland's New Language Product" For Dummies™	by Neil Rubenking	1-56884-200-7	$19.95 USA/$26.95 Canada
C For Dummies™	by Dan Gookin	1-878058-78-9	$19.95 USA/$26.95 Canada
C++ For Dummies™	by Stephen R. Davis	1-56884-163-9	$19.95 USA/$26.95 Canada
Mac Programming For Dummies™	by Dan Parks Sydow	1-56884-173-6	$19.95 USA/$26.95 Canada
QBasic Programming For Dummies™	by Douglas Hergert	1-56884-093-4	$19.95 USA/$26.95 Canada
Visual Basic "X" For Dummies™, 2nd Edition	by Wallace Wang	1-56884-230-9	$19.99 USA/$26.99 Canada
Visual Basic 3 For Dummies™	by Wallace Wang	1-56884-076-4	$19.95 USA/$26.95 Canada

SPREADSHEET

Title	Author	ISBN	Price
1-2-3 For Dummies™	by Greg Harvey	1-878058-60-6	$16.95 USA/$21.95 Canada
1-2-3 For Windows 5 For Dummies™, 2nd Edition	by John Walkenbach	1-56884-216-3	$16.95 USA/$21.95 Canada
1-2-3 For Windows For Dummies™	by John Walkenbach	1-56884-052-7	$16.95 USA/$21.95 Canada
Excel 5 For Macs For Dummies™	by Greg Harvey	1-56884-186-8	$19.95 USA/$26.95 Canada
Excel For Dummies™, 2nd Edition	by Greg Harvey	1-56884-050-0	$16.95 USA/$21.95 Canada
MORE Excel 5 For Windows For Dummies™	by Greg Harvey	1-56884-207-4	$19.95 USA/$26.95 Canada
Quattro Pro 6 For Windows For Dummies™	by John Walkenbach	1-56884-174-4	$19.95 USA/$26.95 Canada
Quattro Pro For DOS For Dummies™	by John Walkenbach	1-56884-023-3	$16.95 USA/$21.95 Canada

UTILITIES / VCRs & CAMCORDERS

Title	Author	ISBN	Price
Norton Utilities 8 For Dummies™	by Beth Slick	1-56884-166-3	$19.95 USA/$26.95 Canada
VCRs & Camcorders For Dummies™	by Andy Rathbone & Gordon McComb	1-56884-229-5	$14.99 USA/$20.99 Canada

WORD PROCESSING

Title	Author	ISBN	Price
Ami Pro For Dummies™	by Jim Meade	1-56884-049-7	$19.95 USA/$26.95 Canada
MORE Word For Windows 6 For Dummies™	by Doug Lowe	1-56884-165-5	$19.95 USA/$26.95 Canada
MORE WordPerfect 6 For Windows For Dummies™	by Margaret Levine Young & David C. Kay	1-56884-206-6	$19.95 USA/$26.95 Canada
MORE WordPerfect 6 For DOS For Dummies™	by Wallace Wang, edited by Dan Gookin	1-56884-047-0	$19.95 USA/$26.95 Canada
S.O.S. For WordPerfect™	by Katherine Murray	1-56884-053-5	$12.95 USA/$16.95 Canada
Word 6 For Macs For Dummies™	by Dan Gookin	1-56884-190-6	$19.95 USA/$26.95 Canada
Word For Windows 6 For Dummies™	by Dan Gookin	1-56884-075-6	$16.95 USA/$21.95 Canada
Word For Windows For Dummies™	by Dan Gookin	1-878058-86-X	$16.95 USA/$21.95 Canada
WordPerfect 6 For Dummies™	by Dan Gookin	1-878058-77-0	$16.95 USA/$21.95 Canada
WordPerfect For Dummies™	by Dan Gookin	1-878058-52-5	$16.95 USA/$21.95 Canada
WordPerfect For Windows For Dummies™	by Margaret Levine Young & David C. Kay	1-56884-032-2	$16.95 USA/$21.95 Canada

Fun, Fast, & Cheap!

CorelDRAW! 5 For Dummies™ Quick Reference
by Raymond E. Werner

ISBN: 1-56884-952-4
$9.99 USA/$12.99 Canada

Windows "X" For Dummies™ Quick Reference, 3rd Edition
by Greg Harvey

ISBN: 1-56884-964-8
$9.99 USA/$12.99 Canada

Word For Windows 6 For Dummies™ Quick Reference
by George Lynch

ISBN: 1-56884-095-0
$8.95 USA/$12.95 Canada

WordPerfect For DOS For Dummies™ Quick Reference
by Greg Harvey

ISBN: 1-56884-009-8
$8.95 USA/$11.95 Canada

Title	Author	ISBN	Price
DATABASE			
Access 2 For Dummies™ Quick Reference	by Stuart A. Stuple	1-56884-167-1	$8.95 USA/$11.95 Canada
dBASE 5 For DOS For Dummies™ Quick Reference	by Barry Sosinsky	1-56884-954-0	$9.99 USA/$12.99 Canada
dBASE 5 For Windows For Dummies™ Quick Reference	by Stuart J. Stuple	1-56884-953-2	$9.99 USA/$12.99 Canada
Paradox 5 For Windows For Dummies™ Quick Reference	by Scott Palmer	1-56884-960-5	$9.99 USA/$12.99 Canada
DESKTOP PUBLISHING / ILLUSTRATION/GRAPHICS			
Harvard Graphics 3 For Windows For Dummies™ Quick Reference	by Raymond E. Werner	1-56884-962-1	$9.99 USA/$12.99 Canada
FINANCE / PERSONAL FINANCE			
Quicken 4 For Windows For Dummies™ Quick Reference	by Stephen L. Nelson	1-56884-950-8	$9.95 USA/$12.95 Canada
GROUPWARE / INTEGRATED			
Microsoft Office 4 For Windows For Dummies™ Quick Reference	by Doug Lowe	1-56884-958-3	$9.99 USA/$12.99 Canada
Microsoft Works For Windows 3 For Dummies™ Quick Reference	by Michael Partington	1-56884-959-1	$9.99 USA/$12.99 Canada
INTERNET / COMMUNICATIONS / NETWORKING			
The Internet For Dummies™ Quick Reference	by John R. Levine	1-56884-168-X	$8.95 USA/$11.95 Canada
MACINTOSH			
Macintosh System 7.5 For Dummies™ Quick Reference	by Stuart J. Stuple	1-56884-956-7	$9.99 USA/$12.99 Canada
OPERATING SYSTEMS / DOS			
DOS For Dummies® Quick Reference	by Greg Harvey	1-56884-007-1	$8.95 USA/$11.95 Canada
UNIX			
UNIX For Dummies™ Quick Reference	by Margaret Levine Young & John R. Levine	1-56884-094-2	$8.95 USA/$11.95 Canada
WINDOWS			
Windows 3.1 For Dummies™ Quick Reference, 2nd Edition	by Greg Harvey	1-56884-951-6	$8.95 USA/$11.95 Canada
PRESENTATION / AUTOCAD			
AutoCAD For Dummies™ Quick Reference	by Bud Smith	1-56884-198-1	$9.95 USA/$12.95 Canada
SPREADSHEET			
1-2-3 For Dummies™ Quick Reference	by John Walkenbach	1-56884-027-6	$8.95 USA/$11.95 Canada
1-2-3 For Windows 5 For Dummies™ Quick Reference	by John Walkenbach	1-56884-957-5	$9.95 USA/$12.95 Canada
Excel For Windows For Dummies™ Quick Reference, 2nd Edition	by John Walkenbach	1-56884-096-9	$8.95 USA/$11.95 Canada
Quattro Pro 6 For Windows For Dummies™ Quick Reference	by Stuart A. Stuple	1-56884-172-8	$9.95 USA/$12.95 Canada
WORD PROCESSING			
Word For Windows 6 For Dummies™ Quick Reference	by George Lynch	1-56884-095-0	$8.95 USA/$11.95 Canada
WordPerfect For Windows For Dummies™ Quick Reference	by Greg Harvey	1-56884-039-X	$8.95 USA/$11.95 Canada

11/11/94

Order Center: **(800) 762-2974** *(8 a.m.–6 p.m., CST, weekdays)*

IDG BOOKS

Quantity	ISBN	Title	Price	Total

Shipping & Handling Charges

	Description	First book	Each additional book	Total
Domestic	Normal	$4.50	$1.50	$
	Two Day Air	$8.50	$2.50	$
	Overnight	$18.00	$3.00	$
International	Surface	$8.00	$8.00	$
	Airmail	$16.00	$16.00	$
	DHL Air	$17.00	$17.00	$

*For large quantities call for shipping & handling charges.
**Prices are subject to change without notice.

Ship to:

Name _____

Company _____

Address _____

City/State/Zip _____

Daytime Phone _____

Payment: ☐ Check to IDG Books (US Funds Only)

☐ Visa ☐ Mastercard ☐ American Express

Card # _____ Expires _____

Signature _____

Subtotal _____

CA residents add
applicable sales tax _____

IN, MA and MD
residents add
5% sales tax _____

IL residents add
6.25% sales tax _____

RI residents add
7% sales tax _____

TX residents add
8.25% sales tax _____

Shipping _____

Total _____

Please send this order form to:

IDG Books Worldwide
7260 Shadeland Station, Suite 100
Indianapolis, IN 46256

Allow up to 3 weeks for delivery.
Thank you!

IDG Books Worldwide License Agreement

Alternate Disk Format Available.

The enclosed disks are in 3 1/2" 1.44MB, high-density format. If you have a different size drive, or a low-density drive, and you cannot arrange to transfer the data to the disk size you need, you may write for more information on available formats to the following address: IDG Books Disk Fulfillment Department, Attn: *The Internet For Macs For Dummies Starter Kit,* IDG Books Worldwide, 3250 N. Post Rd., Ste. 140, Indianapolis, IN 46226, or call 800-762-2974. Please specify the size of disk you need, and please allow 3 to 4 weeks for delivery.

Installation Instructions for
The Internet For Macs For Dummies Starter Kit

Before you install the contents of the companion disks, please read the License Agreement on the preceding page. The companion disks contain software that is described in Part II of this book.

Disk Contents at a Glance

- Pipeline 1.05
- TCP Connect II Extended
        (includes FTP, Gopher, USENET)
- InterSLIP
- MacTCP
- MacWeb 1.00

Step 1: Installing onto Your Hard Drive

All the software on these disks is offered in the form of self-extracting archives (the file name on the floppy ends in ".sea" That means that you double-click on the appropriate icon on the floppy and you'll see a dialog box asking you where you want the software to be installed.

1. **Insert Internet for Macs For Dummies (IMD) Starter Kit Disk 1.**

    This disk contains software for Pipeline and for MacWeb.

2. **Double-click the Pipeline file icon.**

3. **Select the hard disk folder (you may have to make yourself a new folder) where you want to install Pipeline.**

4. **Click Install.**

5. **Do the same for the MacWeb file, which you probably want to install in its own folder.**

6. **Eject Disk 1 and insert Disk 2.**

    When you double-click the Installer icon for the TCP software, it will install a number of files in the correct locations in your System folder.

Step 2: Using the Software

Using Pipeline is straightforward. Follow the instructions in Chapter 6 (make sure your modem is dialing the Pipeline on-line access phone number **212-267-8606**). You can sign on in free-trial mode as "guest", in which case you only have a limited amount of time per sign-on, or you can register as a new Pipeline user.

IDG has included Pipeline software because, frankly, Pipeline is very cost-effective real Internet access. Call Pipeline voice access at **212-267-3636** (think of explaining the meaning of "voice access" to someone ten years ago!)

As was explained in Chapter 7, you need to take advantage of a service-provider agreement offered here (see the last pages of this book) or find your own local SLIP service provider to use TCP Connect II or MacWeb.

When you start TCP Connect, the software asks you for an authorization code. You get this code by calling:

800-468-7266

Or, if it's busy and you're impatient, call 703-709-5500

It's only fair to tell you that SLIP connection is a bit trickier than Pipeline, and that you can expect to be talking to customer support at your SLIP service provider more than once, to make sure that you have entered all the right information in your MacTCP and InterSLIP setup windows.

IDG BOOKS WORLDWIDE REGISTRATION CARD

Title of this book: THE INTERNET FOR MACS FOR DUMMIES STARTER KIT

My overall rating of this book: ❑ Very good [1] ❑ Good [2] ❑ Satisfactory [3] ❑ Fair [4] ❑ Poor [5]

How I first heard about this book:

❑ Found in bookstore; name: [6] _____

❑ Advertisement: [8] _____

❑ Word of mouth; heard about book from friend, co-worker, etc.: [10]

❑ Book review: [7] _____

❑ Catalog: [9] _____

❑ Other: [11] _____

What I liked most about this book:

_____
_____
_____

What I would change, add, delete, etc., in future editions of this book:

_____
_____
_____

Other comments:

_____

Number of computer books I purchase in a year: ❑ 1 [12] ❑ 2-5 [13] ❑ 6-10 [14] ❑ More than 10 [15]

I would characterize my computer skills as: ❑ Beginner [16] ❑ Intermediate [17] ❑ Advanced [18] ❑ Professional [19]

I use ❑ DOS [20] ❑ Windows [21] ❑ OS/2 [22] ❑ Unix [23] ❑ Macintosh [24] ❑ Other: [25] _____
(please specify)

I would be interested in new books on the following subjects:
(please check all that apply, and use the spaces provided to identify specific software)

❑ Word processing: [26] _____

❑ Data bases: [28] _____

❑ File Utilities: [30] _____

❑ Networking: [32] _____

❑ Other: [34] _____

❑ Spreadsheets: [27] _____

❑ Desktop publishing: [29] _____

❑ Money management: [31] _____

❑ Programming languages: [33] _____

I use a PC at (please check all that apply): ❑ home [35] ❑ work [36] ❑ school [37] ❑ other: [38] _____

The disks I prefer to use are ❑ 5.25 [39] ❑ 3.5 [40] ❑ other: [41] _____

I have a CD ROM: ❑ yes [42] ❑ no [43]

I plan to buy or upgrade computer hardware this year: ❑ yes [44] ❑ no [45]

I plan to buy or upgrade computer software this year: ❑ yes [46] ❑ no [47]

Name: _____ Business title: [48] _____ Type of Business: [49] _____

Address (❑ home [50] ❑ work [51]/Company name: _____)

Street/Suite# _____

City [52]/State [53]/Zipcode [54]: _____ Country [55] _____

❑ **I liked this book!** You may quote me by name in future
IDG Books Worldwide promotional materials.

My daytime phone number is _____

IDG BOOKS

THE WORLD OF
COMPUTER
KNOWLEDGE

_Am. 800-433-7300_

☐ **YES!**
Please keep me informed about IDG's World of Computer Knowledge.
Send me the latest IDG Books catalog.